THE EARLY HISTORY OF DATA NETWORKS

Gerard J. Holzmann

Computing Science Research Center
AT&T Bell Laboratories
Murray Hill, New Jersey, U.S.A.

Björn Pehrson

Department of TeleInformatics
Royal Institute of Technology
Stockholm, Sweden

WILEY-INTERSCIENCE
A JOHN WILEY & SONS, INC., PUBLICATION

The Early History of Data Networks / Gerard J. Holzmann.
    p.   cm.
    Includes bibliographical references (p. 273) and index.
    ISBN 0-8186-6782-6
    1. Telegraph--History. I. Pehrson, Björn. II. Title.
TK5115.H67 1994   94-31429
384.1'09--dc20   CIP

A NOTE TO THE READER
This book has been electronically reproduced from
digital information stored at John Wiley & Sons, Inc.
We are pleased that the use of this new technology
will enable us to keep works of enduring scholarly
value in print as long as there is a reasonable demand
for them. The content of this book is identical to
previous printings.

Catherine Harris / Acquisitions editor
Lynne Bush / Copy editor
Alexander Torres / Cover design

10 9 8 7 6 5 4 3   ISBN 0-8186-6782-6

IEEE Computer Society Press   IEEE Computer Society   IEEE Computer Society
Publications Office   European Office   Ooshima Building
10662 Los Vaqueros Circle   13 Avenue de l'Aquilon   2-19-1 Minami-Aoyama
Los Alamitos, CA 90720–1264   B-1200 Brussels, Belgium   Minato-Ku, Tokyo 107, Japan
Phone: (714) 821-8380   Phone: 32-2-770-2198   Phone: 81-3-408-3118
Fax: (714) 761-1784   Fax: 32-2-770-8505   Fax: 81-3-408-3553

Contents

Appendices

"The capitals of distant nations might be united by chains of posts, and, the settling of those disputes which at present take up months or years might then be accomplished in as many hours.
An establishment of telegraphs might then be made like that of the post; and instead of being an expence, it would produce a revenue."

Encyclopaedia Britannica, 1797, in the first entry on the telegraph.

Preface

It is hard to imagine what daily life must have been like two centuries ago, without radios, movies, telephones, or electricity. Marconi, Edison, Bell and Maxwell had not yet been born, and neither had their parents. The streets in the larger cities were lit by candles. In New York, for example, a city ordinance had been in effect since 1697:[1]

> ... that the lights be hung out in the darke time of the moon within this citty, and for the use of the inhabitants; and that every 7th house doe hang out a lanthorn and a candle in it.

Mail was delivered by stagecoach in the United States, and by merchant vessels and mounted couriers throughout most of Europe. This system operated quite efficiently, also by today's standards. A letter or newspaper took only a few days to travel from London to Stockholm, and to get a piece of mail delivered within one of the larger cities took just hours. It was not unusual to extend a dinner invitation by regular mail in the morning, and to receive the response well in time to make the final preparations for that day.

An eyewitness described the dress code in 1789, when George Washington was sworn in as the first president of the United States, as follows:[2]

> There stood Washington, invested with a suit of dark silk velvet, of the old cut, steel-hilted small-sword by his side, hair in a bag and full powdered, in black silk hose, and shoes with silver buckles, as he took the oath of office.

This was the time of chamber music, of horse-drawn carriages, the time of Mozart, Haydn, and Beethoven, of Gauss and Fourier, and the time of James Watt, Claude Chappe, and Abraham Edelcrantz.

James Watt's work is well known. His improved steam engine designs gave a decisive push to the industrial revolution. The names of Chappe

---

1. The notes to the preface start at p. 245.

and Edelcrantz, however, are not nearly as well known, even though they had an equally revolutionary impact on society. In the eighteenth century they managed to develop the world's first nationwide data communications networks.

Let us go back to September 1794. Imagine Abraham Niclas Edelcrantz, a Swedish nobleman and scholar, in his library in the center of Stockholm, say in front of a nice big fireplace. He is reading *Gentleman's Magazine*.[3] The September 1794 issue of this journal contained a report on a new French contraption that caught Edelcrantz's attention. This is, in part, what Edelcrantz read:[4]

> . . . a method to acquaint people at a great distance, and in very little time, with whatever one pleased. This method is as follows: let persons be placed in several stations, at such distances from each other, that, by the help of a telescope, a man in one station may see a signal made by the next before him; he immediately repeats this signal, which is again repeated through all the intermediate stations. This, with considerable improvements, has been adopted by the French, and denominated a Telegraphe; and, from the utility of the invention, we doubt not but it will be soon introduced in this country.

The invention was attributed to Claude Chappe.

> The machines are the invention of Citizen Chappe, and were constructed before his own eyes; he directs their establishment at Paris.

The letter in *Gentleman's Magazine* described the telegraph that Chappe had developed for the construction of an optical telegraph line connecting Lille to Paris, over a distance of roughly 230 km (143 miles). The line was, by any standard, the first of its kind, and news of its construction was spreading quickly through Europe.

Edelcrantz began experimenting with his own optical telegraph designs the month that the article was published.[5] Two months later he was able to demonstrate a first working version. Edelcrantz's first design still looked much like Chappe's, with articulated arms and flaps. Edelcrantz would later, after many experiments, switch to a shutter telegraph design that is similar to one of the first designs that Chappe had used in 1791 and 1792 and abandoned. There is no indication that Edelcrantz knew about these earlier experiments of Claude Chappe at this time.[6] Why Chappe rejected the shutter principle and replaced it with semaphore arms, and Edelcrantz rejected the semaphore arms and replaced it with shutters is a mystery. Both designs were quite successful, and received much following.

For almost half a century, optical telegraphs became part of the landscape in Europe. They can be spotted in the background of many paintings from this period. They are also mentioned, at least in passing, in several novels and poems.[7] Victor Hugo (1802–1885), for instance, wrote a long poem called *Le Télégraphe*. The Swedish poet Elias Sehlstedt dedicated a collection of poems to the optical telegraph, titled *Telegrafen—Poetisk Kalender för 1858*. The telegraphs also feature prominently in Stendhal's *Lucien*

Leuwen, which was first published in 1842.[8] The following passage appears in *The Count of Monte Cristo*, published in 1844:[9]

> "Thank you," said Monte Cristo, "and now, please allow me to take leave of you. I'm about to go see something which has often made me thoughtful for hours on end."
>
> "What is it?"
>
> "A telegraph. I was almost ashamed to say it, but now you know."
>
> "A telegraph ?" repeated Madame de Villefort.
>
> "Yes, that's right. I've often seen those black shining arms rising from the top of a hill or at the end of a road, and it has never been without emotion for me, for I've always thought of those strange signs cleaving the air for three hundred leagues to carry thoughts of one man sitting at his desk to another man sitting at his desk at the other end of the line. It has always made me think of genii, sylphs or gnomes; in short, of occult powers, and that amuses me. Then one day I learned that the operator of each telegraph is only some poor devil employed for twelve hundred francs a year, constantly occupied in watching another telegraph four or five leagues away. I then became curious to see that living chrysalis at close quarters and watch the comedy he plays for the other chrysalis by pulling on his strings."
>
> "What telegraph are you going to visit ?" asked Villefort.
>
> "Which line would you advise me to study ?"
>
> "Why, the one that's the busiest now, I suppose."
>
> "That would be the line from Spain, wouldn't it ?"
>
> "Yes. But you'd better hurry; it will be dark in two hours and you won't be able to see anything."
>
> "Thank you," said Monte Cristo. "I'll tell you about my impressions when I see you Saturday."

Monte Cristo proceeds to bribe a telegraph operator to transmit a false message to Paris. How likely or unlikely this might have been will become clear in the following chapters.[10]

OVERVIEW

When optical telegraphs were superseded by electrical telegraphs, much of their history was forgotten. Today, at the bicentennial of the optical telegraphs, we would like to look back, and record the fascinating story of their discovery and use.

The first chapter gives an overview of the attempts made throughout history to come up with effective methods for long-distance communication. Apart from the more obvious courier and beacon systems, remarkably sophisticated devices were developed, in some cases more than two thousand years ago. In the second chapter we look at Claude Chappe's struggle to build a communications network in the late eighteenth century in France. The third chapter tells the story of Edelcrantz's attempts in Sweden to accomplish the same goal. Edelcrantz documented his design in a wonderful booklet called *Treatise on Telegraphs* that was first published in 1796. Almost immediately after its publication, the document

Distance Metrics

Unit	Feet	Meters
Swedish Mile	32,577	10,689
German Mile	25,000	7,620
French Mile	14,000	4,267
English (U.S.) Mile	5,280	1,609
League	15,840	4,827
Km	3,280	1,000
Fathom	6	1.83
Ell	1.948	0.594
Cubit	1.72	0.52

was translated into French and German, but for some reason, it was never translated into English. Chapter Four contains our translation, which gives a glimpse of the world of a serious eighteenth century scholar attacking a twentieth century problem. In Chapter Five we take a closer look at the developments in some of the other countries, both in Europe and elsewhere. In most countries similar optical telegraph lines were built, though not quite on the same scale as in Sweden and France. Chapter Six concludes the book with a comparison of Chappe's and Edelcrantz's system and a brief look at the contributions that they each made to the art of signaling.

Three appendices contain documents on Chappe's and Edelcrantz's designs. Appendix A reproduces three letters that appeared in late 1794 in *Gentleman's Magazine*, recording the first reactions to Chappe's experiments from earlier that year. Appendix B has the instructions and regulations for the French optical telegraphs. Appendix C gives the station instructions and a penal code for the Swedish design.

The words *telegraph*, *telescope*, and *semaphore*, used throughout this book, have a Greek origin, though they are not part of the original language. *Tele* means "at a distance," *graphos* means "writer" or "signaler," and *skopos* means "watcher" or "observer." *Sema* means "sign" or "symbol," and *phoros* means "bearer" or "carrier." Telescopes were invented in 1608 (see p. 31); the words telegraph and semaphore first entered the language in the late eighteenth century (p. 59), as a result of the experiments that we will describe.

The distance metrics in use today are considerably younger than many of the sources that we refer to in this book. In 1794 Swedish, French, German, and English miles all represented different lengths. Wherever possible, we use the metric system here, occasionally with the equivalent in U.S. (i.e., English) miles in parentheses. In all other cases, the distances are disambiguated with a country prefix. For reference, the relevant conversions are listed in the table of distance metrics shown above.

This book is the product of many years of enjoyable sleuthing into the history of communication systems. We have been helped by many wonderful people along the way, and it is a true pleasure to acknowledge them here. They include:

Stephane Baier, Jon Bentley, Bertil Båge, M. Blanloeil, Pierre Bosom, Jan Brans, Warren Burstein, André Butrica, Rosa Busquets, Lynne Bush, Patrice Carré, John Chaves, Lorinda Cherry, Gérard Contant, Dan Doernberg, Richard Drechsler, Maija Elo, Terje Ellefsen, Ari Epstein, Patrik Ernberg, Patrice Godefroid, Johan Goudsblom, Ron Hardin, Catherine Harris, Jay B. Haviser, Richard Q. Hofacker Jr., Lars Johannesson, M. Katz, Brian W. Kernighan, Srinivasan Keshav, Olga Lopez, Erik Ludwig, Jim Mais, M. Marchand, M. Douglas McIlroy, A. Beate Oestreicher, Helly Oestreicher, Nils Olander, Michel Ollivier, Judith A. Paone, Robert M. Papp, Craig Partridge, Rob Pike, Pilar Prieto, Marty Rabinowitz, Jim Reeds, Frank Reichert, Dennis M. Ritchie, C. van Romburgh, Johan Romstad (owner of the telegraph house in Furusund), Nelly Roussel, Carl-Erik Sundberg, Maureen Tate (Language Center New York), Teller, Chris Wagner, John Wait, Phil Winterbottom, Jan Zwijnenberg,

and of course the many dedicated researchers at the libraries, archives, and museums we visited in Amsterdam, Barcelona, Brûlon, Grenoble, La Flèche, London, Nantes, New York, Paris, Pleumeur Bodou, Sacramento, San Francisco, Stockholm, The Hague, and Uppsala.

Our objective has been to provide an account that is both accurate and readable. To convince ourselves of the accuracy, we checked and double-checked every fact, by going back to the original sources where available. Nonetheless, it is possible that we have missed important details. We would be grateful to any reader who can correct the story, or add to it.

It was our great privilege to present an early edition of this book to King Carl XVI Gustaf of Sweden on 22 June 1994, at the bicentennial celebration of the first experiments with optical telegraphs in Sweden.

gerard@research.bell-labs.com   *Gerard J. Holzmann*
bjorn@it.kth.se   *Björn Pehrson*

Chapter One
Torches and Beacons

The communication network that is available to us today allows anyone to talk instantly to almost anyone else on the globe, as long as both are near one of the approximately 500 million telephones connected to the network. It is tempting to think that the inventions that have made this possible were all made within the last century. The need for effective communication with a distant party, however, did not suddenly start in 1876 when the telephone was first patented.[1] That need must have been felt every bit as much by the Egyptian Pharaohs, and their workers, as it is by us today.

How It Began
It is quite amazing to see how people have dealt with the problems of long-distance communication throughout history. References to telegraphic systems can be found in almost every period from which written records survive. A fairly obvious method to communicate is, of course, to hire somebody to deliver a message as fast as possible. Famous is the story of Phidippides, the runner who, according to legend, in 490 B.C. ran the 36.2 km (22.5 miles) from Marathon to Athens to warn the Athenians of an approaching Persian army.[2] The Persians, after having been defeated in the battle of Marathon, were on their way to what they hoped would be an undefended city.

490 B.C.

The Greek historian Herodotus, who lived ca. 484–424 B.C., does describe an event like this in *The History*. But in his account, Phidippides did not run to Athens *after* the battle of Marathon was fought; he ran 240 km from Athens to Sparta *before* the battle started, to obtain the support of the Spartans. This is how Herodotus described it:[3]

1. The notes to this chapter start at p. 245.

First of all, when the generals were still within the city, they sent to Sparta a herald, one Phidippides, an Athenian, who was a day-long runner and a professional. . . . This Phidippides, being sent by the generals, and after, as he said Pan had appeared to him, arrived in the city of Sparta the day after he had left Athens. He came before the rulers and said: "Men of Lacedaemon, the Athenians beg you to help them; do not suffer a most ancient city in Greece to meet with slavery at the hands of the barbarians."

Herodotus then describes the battle itself, where the Athenians successfully defeated the Persian army without the help of the Spartans. He continued:[4]

With the rest of the fleet, the barbarians, backing water . . ., rounded Cape Sunium, because they wished to get to Athens before the Athenians could reach it. . . . They rounded Sunium, all right; but the Athenians, rushing with all speed to defend their city, reached it first, before the barbarians came, and encamped. . . . The barbarians anchored off Phalerum—for in those days that was the harbor of Athens—and, after riding at anchor there for a while, they sailed off, back to Asia.

There is no mention in Herodotus's account that Phidippides was the first to arrive back in Athens after the battle, and then died from strain, but it is possible.

It is not too surprising that references to runners or human messengers are plentiful throughout history. They were certainly common in the days of Herodotus. The first descriptions of ancient courier systems, however, date back still farther. A recent encyclopedia says:[5]

As early as the second millennium B.C. in Egypt and the first millennium in China, relay systems were developed using messengers on horseback and relay stations situated on major roads.

1928 B.C. In old records, references to messenger systems can indeed be found that date back almost 4,000 years to the Egyptian King Sesostris I, who reigned from 1971 to 1928 B.C.[6]

Messenger systems were also used in ancient Babylon. In his study of the history of intelligence-gathering methods, Francis Dvornik reported, for instance:[7]

We learn from an inscription that Hammurabi's messengers rode the long distance from Larsa to Babylon in two days, traveling, of course, both day and night.

1750 B.C. Hammurabi was king of Babylonia from 1792 to 1750 B.C.

By the thirteenth century B.C. messenger services must have been quite routine. Dvornik, for instance, refers to a log that was kept by an Egyptian guard during the reign of King Merneptah (the successor of King 1225 B.C. Ramses II), from 1237 to 1225 B.C.[8] In the fragment of the log that is preserved, we find a record of all special messengers that passed through a guard post at the Palestinian border with Syria. According to the log at

2

least once or twice a day a messenger would pass through with either military or diplomatic missives.

Originally, the messengers traveled the normal roads between the main cities of the ancient empires. Their safety, however, was by no means guaranteed.[9]

> We read in the Babylonian archives, found in Boghazhöi, complaints about attacks by Bedouins on royal couriers, and of the closing of Assyria to Babylonian messengers.

This crime problem led to a decision by the early Babylonian kings to place royal guards at regular distances along the roads. These guards were originally intended only for the protection of travelers, but their presence led quite naturally to a number of major improvements in the messenger system. The first was the establishment of a relay system, where a message was passed from guard station to guard station, each time carried by a new runner. The second decision was to equip the guard posts with fire beacons, so that simple alarm or warning signs could be passed quickly from one end of the road to the other, without the need for a human runner.

Unfortunately, it can no longer be determined precisely when these two crucial improvements were made, but they were probably in place by 650 B.C. One of the records reproduced in Luckenbill, for instance, describes the way in which the inauguration of King Shams-shum-ukin of Babylonia was celebrated around that time:[10]   650 B.C.

> Beechwood was kindled, torches lighted. Every bêru a beacon was set up.

The *bêru* was an Assyrian distance unit, corresponding to a two-hour journey. It can be assumed that the beacons referred to here were not quickly improvised for the occasion, but part of a permanent network of roads and guard posts. To support this assumption, Dvornik and Fries quote from a letter containing a magical chant, found in the library of King Ashurbanipal who ruled Assyria from 668 to 626 B.C. It reads, in part:[11]   626 B.C.

> Well, my witch, who art kindling fire every bêru and who art sending out thy messengers every two bêrus, I know thee and I will post watchmen in order to protect myself.

Both beacon signals and courier systems were quite familiar, at least to this writer. We can even speculate that the guard posts were placed at one bêru intervals, and that every other guard post served as a relay station for messengers; but, of course, this is only speculation.

The Biblical book of Jeremiah, from ca. 588 B.C., also contains a clear reference to the relay system:[12]   588 B.C.

> One post shall run to meet another, and one messenger to meet another, to shew the king of Babylon [Nebuchadnezzar] that his city is taken.

King Cyrus the Great, who lived from 599 to 530 B.C., and ruled Persia the

3

530 B.C. last nineteen years of his life, was credited with improvements of the courier system. Xenophon (430–355 B.C.), writing more than a century later, described it in *Cyropaedia*, his biography of Cyrus, as follows:[13]

> We have observed still another device of Cyrus' for coping with the magnitude of his empire; by means of this institution he would speedily discover the condition of affairs, no matter how far distant they might be from him: he experimented to find out how great a distance a horse could cover in a day when ridden hard, but so as not to break down, and then he erected post-stations at just such distances and equipped them with horses, and men to take care of them; at each one of the stations he had the proper official appointed to receive the letters that were delivered and to forward them on, to take in the exhausted horses and riders and send on fresh ones. They say, moreover, that sometimes this express does not stop all night, but the night-messengers succeed the day messengers in relays, and when this is the case, this express, some say, gets over the ground faster than the cranes.

The system lasted. In *The History*, Herodotus describes with admiration how the relay system functioned at the time that Xerxes ruled Persia, between 486 and 465 B.C.:[14]

> At the same time that he was doing these things, Xerxes sent to Persia to tell of the present calamity. Than this system of messengers there is nothing of mortal origin that is quicker. This is how the Persians arranged it: they saw that for as many days as the whole journey consists in, that many horses and men are stationed at intervals of a day's journey, one horse and one man assigned to each day. And him neither snow nor rain nor heat nor night holds back for the accomplishment of the course that has been assigned to him, as quickly as he may. The first that runs hands on what he has been given to the second, and the second to the third, and from there what is transmitted passes clean through, from hand to hand, to its end, even as among the Greeks there is the torch-race that they celebrate in honor of Hephaestus.

The phrase "neither snow nor rain nor heat nor night . . ." is familiar to New Yorkers: a slightly different, and not too literal, translation was used for an inscription over the width of the main U.S. Post Office in Manhattan (one city block wide). It reads "neither snow nor rain nor heat nor gloom of night stays these couriers from the swift completion of their appointed rounds." The Persian couriers, of course, did not walk rounds but ran a relay system, but the main idea is there.

The Romans adopted a similar system of relay stations. Originally, they used human runners to transport the messages.[15] Later, when the system became larger, they switched to couriers on horseback as in the Persian system. Suetonius, who lived from A.D. 70 to 150, described it in his biography of Augustus (63 B.C.–A.D. 14) in Book II of *The Twelve Caesars*:[16]

> To enable what was going on in each of the provinces to be reported and known more speedily and promptly, he at first stationed young men at short intervals along the military roads, and afterwards post-chaises [carriages]. The latter has seemed the more convenient arrangement, since the same men who bring the dispatches from any place can, if occasion demands, be questioned as well.

Each of the Roman relay stations kept a reserve of not fewer than 40 horses and riders.[17]

In an attempt to curb abuse, messengers, called *strators*, were issued special licenses from the Roman emperor that qualified them for the free exchange of horses at relay stations. Over the years, responsibility for the upkeep of relay stations became a hot political issue.[18] Roman rulers alternately strived either to delegate the responsibility to local communities, to reduce the tax burden on the state, or to transfer the responsibility back to the state, to secure more consistent maintenance. In the end, neither the state nor the local municipalities were willing to cover the expenses any longer, and the system perished.

The speed of the Roman relay system was approximately 80 km (50 miles) per day for regular mail, and twice that for express mail, although these numbers might be based on human runners instead of riders on horseback. In any case, the Roman system was never praised for its speed. Even the old historians poked fun at the system. Suetonius, for instance, wrote in his biography of Julius Caesar (100–44 B.C.) in Book I of *The Twelve Caesars*:[19]

> [He] often arrived at his destination before the messengers who had been sent ahead to announce his approach.

In the thirteenth century Marco Polo described another relay system that was used by the Mongol ruler Kublai Khan (1215–1294), grandson of the notorious Genghis Khan. Polo, who visited China between 1271 and 1295, described the system as follows:[20]   A.D. 1280

> Let us turn now to the system of post-horses by which the Great Khan sends his dispatches. You must know that the city of Khan-balik is a centre from which many roads radiate to many provinces, one to each, and every road bears the name of the province to which it runs. The whole system is admirably contrived. When one of the Khan's messengers sets out along any of these roads, he has only to go twenty-five miles [40 km] and there he finds a posting station, which in their language is called *yamb* and in our language may be rendered "horse post."
> ... Here the messengers find no less than 400 horses, stationed here by the Great Khan's orders and always kept in readiness for his messengers when they are sent on any mission. And you must understand that posts such as these, at distances of twenty-five or thirty miles, are to be found along all the main highways leading to the provinces of which I have spoken. ... The whole organization is so stupendous and so costly that it baffles speech and writing.

Later in his account Marco Polo points out that the 400 horses per post were not all present at the same time. At each time about 200 horses would be out in the meadows, regaining strength for a next tour of duty.

The speed of the Great Khan's messengers was apparently almost twice that of the Roman's:[21]

When the need arises for the Great Khan to receive immediate tidings by mounted messenger, as of the rebellion of a subject country or of one of his barons or any matter that many concern him deeply, I assure you that the messengers ride 200 miles [320 km] in a day, sometimes even 250. Let me explain how this is done. When a messenger wishes to travel at this speed and cover so many miles in a day, he carries a tablet with the sign of the gerfalcon as a token that he wishes to ride *poste haste*. If there are two of them, they set out from the place where they are on two good horses, strongly built and swift runners. They tighten their belts and swathe their heads and off they go with all the speed they can muster, till they reach the next post-house twenty-five miles away. As they draw near they sound a sort of horn which is audible at a great distance, so that horses may be got ready for them. On arrival they find two fresh horses, ready harnessed, fully rested, and in good running form. They mount there and then, without a moment's breathing-space, and are no sooner mounted than off they go again, taking the last ounce out of their horses and not pausing till they reach the next post, where they find two more horses harnessed as before.

. . . in extreme urgency, they can achieve 300 miles. In such cases they ride all night long; and if there is no moon, the men of the post run in front of them with torches as far as the next post.

In parallel with the horse post, also a relay system of human runners was employed.[22] These runners, however, did not always carry grave news of rebellions and uproar. Marco Polo notes dryly that the Great Khan had found ways to take advantage of it for more pleasurable uses as well:[23]

And in the fruit season it often happens that by this means fruit gathered in the morning in the city of Khan-balik is delivered on the evening of the next day to the Great Khan in the city of Shang-tu, ten days' journey away.

A.D. 1861 The *Pony Express*, which operated in the United States from April 1860 until October 1861, achieved comparable speeds to the Chinese horse post, but with more frequent switches. Each rider in the Pony Express relay rode approximately 150 km, and switched horses every 15 km. This system is said to have covered the 3,200 km distance from Missouri to California in about 10 days.

PIGEONS

Perhaps more inspiring than plain runners transporting messages, and just as old, is the description of a seemingly less reliable transmission
776 B.C. medium: the homing pigeon. It is said that the outcomes of the Olympic Games in ancient Greece, around 776 B.C., were sent to Athens by pigeons. But even in those days this must have been old news. As noted in a book
2900 B.C. by David Woods:[24]

. . . in the days of the Pharaohs the Egyptians announced the arrival of important visitors by releasing pigeons from incoming ships. This may have been common as early as 2900 B.C.

The writer Harry Neal noted another ingenious use of pigeons from a few
2350 B.C. centuries later. He stated that King Sargon of Akkad, who lived ca. 2350

6

Figure 1.1 Pigeon Post, Woodcut from A.D. 1481.
(Coll. Bibl. de Genève, [Fabre 1963], p. 44)

B.C. in Mesopotamia, had each of his messengers carry a homing pigeon.[25] If the messenger was attacked en route, he released the pigeon. The return of the pigeon to the palace was taken as a warning that the original message had been "lost," and that a new messenger should be sent, presumably via another route.

Homing pigeons were also used by the Romans, around the fourth century A.D. In 1641, John Wilkins referred to it as follows:[26]

> A.D. 350

> Lypsius relates out of Varro, that it was usual for the Roman magistrates when they went unto the theatre, or other such public meetings, whence they could not return at pleasure, to carry such a pigeon with them; that if any unexpected business should happen, they might thereby give warning to their friends or families at home.

The system was still in use some eight centuries later. Woods reports that in the twelfth century Genghis Khan (1167–1227) used a pigeon relay

A.D. 1200

7

system to communicate messages across Asia and much of Europe.[27] Figure 1.1 displays the use of carrier pigeons in a woodcut that appeared in 1481 in *Jean de Mandeville's Travels in the Orient*.

Another seven centuries later, in 1918, the British Air Force kept over 20,000 homing pigeons, handled by 380 pigeoneers. The system was organized by Colonel A. H. Osman. Woods quoted him as follows:[28]

> A small balloon was constructed with a metal [release-] band worked by clockwork. To this band was attached a small basket containing a single pigeon with a message holder on its leg, and to each basket was attached a small parachute. The balloons were liberated in favourable conditions of wind and at intervals automatically released from the special ring a single basket with a bird. These were dropped into Belgian and French territory when occupied by the Germans, and in French and Flemish a request was made to the finder to supply intelligence information that was needed, at the same time giving the finder hopefulness and cheer as to the ultimate success of the allies' cause and promising reward for the information supplied.

Woods adds a sobering note.

> The Germans tried to halt this activity by replacing captured pigeons with their own birds, and then arresting and shooting anyone foolish enough to sign his name and address to the note.

With this much history, it is not surprising that pigeons were still used in 1981 by a group of engineers at a Lockheed plant in Sunnyvale, California, to transmit negatives of drawings to a test station 40 km (25 miles) away. As Jon Bentley described it:[29]

> The pigeon took just half the time and less than one percent of the dollar amount of the car (the birds worked, literally, for pigeon feed). Over a 16-month period the pigeons transmitted hundreds of rolls of film and lost only two.

Pigeons and messengers have the advantage that a message need not be specially encoded, unless this is done for security. The problem is that the messages travel no faster than a horse can run, or than a bird wants to fly. Even the first ideas that were developed for alternative systems come very close to modern signaling methods.

Mirrors and Flags

It is easily confirmed that you can get anyone's attention quickly, even at large distances, by reflecting the sun into their eyes with a shiny surface. This could have been done also in antiquity, probably in a playful way, to amuse or to annoy. There are, however, indications that *heliographs* have a history of use for more serious signaling purposes as well.

HELIOGRAPHS

Consider the following passage from Xenophon's *Hellenica* (sometimes called *A History of My Times*), written in ca. 405 B.C.:[30]

8

On the fifth day as the Athenian ships sailed up, Lysander gave special instructions to the ships that were to follow them. As soon as they saw that the Athenians had disembarked and had scattered in various directions over the Chersonese—as they were now doing more freely every day, since they had to go a long way to get their food and were now actually contemptuous of Lysander for not coming out to fight—they were to sail back and *to signal with a shield* when they were half-way across the straits. These orders were carried out and as soon as he got the signal, Lysander ordered the fleet to sail at full speed. Thorax went with the fleet. When Conon saw that the enemy were attacking, he signaled to the Athenians to hurry back as fast as they could come to their ships. But they were scattered in all directions . . . *[emphasis added]*.

The phrase "to signal with a shield" is one of the earliest explicit mentions of a simple method of heliographic signaling, in this case with a burnished shield.

There are many other references to early signaling methods that may have been based on similar devices, but the oldest references are not too reliable. The writer Woods, for instance, stated that heliographs were used by the Romans between A.D. 26 and 37:[31]

A.D. 37

For nearly ten years during the reign of the wise but unpopular emperor Tiberius, Rome was ruled from the island of Capri. Each day he sent orders to the mainland by a type of "heliograph" which transmitted the sun's rays by means of a mirror of polished metal. Naturally this would not have been possible without a code, but no record exists of the means by which the emperor's commands were sent or received.

The original sources do not quite support this claim. There is a brief reference to a method of signaling in the biography of Tiberius (42 B.C.–A.D. 37) written by Suetonius, in Book III of *The Twelve Caesars*, but it is ambiguous. It is sometimes translated as:[32]

Often, he would stand at the highest tower and peer at the signals he had sent to him, so that when anything had happened, messages would reach him without delay.

In a later translation, however, the complete passage appears as:[33]

He thought, indeed, of taking refuge at the headquarters of some provincial army and had a naval flotilla standing by to carry him off the island; where he waited on a cliff top for the distant bonfire signals, announcing all possible eventualities, which he had ordered to be sent in case his couriers might be delayed.

Neither version seems quite right. A simple bonfire could have been used to give a straight warning signal that Tiberius would have wanted to monitor, but it could not easily be used to transmit "all possible eventualities." On the other hand, it is hard to imagine that a Roman emperor would trouble himself to learn a signaling code that is complex enough to transmit arbitrary messages.

Figure 1.2 Heliographic Device.
(Source: [Hennig 1908], p. 43)

Woods also reported that in the eleventh century the Moors made use of heliographs in Algeria.[34]

A.D. 1292 A first clear description of a heliographic signaling method was published in 1292 by the English author Roger Bako (often spelled Bacon, 1214–1292), in a work called *Opus Majus*.[35] There is, however, no record that it was actually used in this period.

A.D. 1598 Richard Hennig quoted a description of a heliograph from the sixteenth century author Khevenhiller. In *Annales Ferdinandei*, Khevenhiller described a device that had supposedly been used during the siege of a Hungarian fortress in A.D. 1598:[36]

> . . . with an art, as described by an Englishman, consisting of two mirrors and a magnet [a compass?], with which one can, at a distance of many miles, give signals to each other in moon-light.

Hennig questions the feasibility of the method. Yet, if the "magnet" was really a compass, it could have been used by the two correspondents to locate each other, before signaling began. On a clear night, the light of the moon can be reflected as easily as the light of the sun during a clear day, so the device may actually have worked.

A.D. 1810 The design of a heliographic device was not reliably documented until 1810.[37]

> Professor [Carl Friedrich] Gauss of Gottingen, Germany, invented a device to direct a controlled beam of sunlight to a distant station. It included "silvered and unsilvered mirrors" fixed at right angles to each other. The operator looked in the unsilvered mirror at the distant station. Then he turned both mirrors so the sun's image (reflected faintly from the plain surface of the unsilvered mirror) was superimposed over the distant station, automatically directing the beam from the silvered mirror in the same direction.

Though the device built by Gauss (cf. Figure 1.2) was meant to be used for geodetic survey work, it would later be used extensively by the British and the American armies as a so-called "wireless" field telegraph.

In 1869 Henry C. Mance adapted Gauss's design by adding a movable mirror that could be used to signal Morse code.[38] Since Mance was stationed in India at the time, the first body to adopt the new device in 1875 was the Indian government. It is said to have been in almost constant use by the British in India until roughly 1890.

In 1851 Charles Babbage, the builder of the so-called *analytical engine*, a precursor of the modern digital computer, also entered this arena with the invention of a "light-flashing machine," which he named an *occulting telegraph*. This is how Babbage described it.[39]

> I then, by means of a small piece of clock-work and an argand lamp, made a numerical system of occultation, by which any number might be transmitted to all those within sight of the source of light.

A copy of the device was presented to the Duke of Wellington.[40] In 1852, Babbage also sent descriptions to, among others, Louis Napoleon in France, and to representatives in the United States.[41] The American Congress later appropriated $5,000 for experiments with Babbage's telegraph.

Babbage also described another "sun-flashing" machine, which resembles Gauss's design more closely. The codes he proposed to use with such telegraphs, however, were only rudimentary.

The American army made an extensive use of heliographs in the 1880s, in combination with a Morse code. It is unclear if they were based on Babbage's proposal or Henry Mance's. In 1886 heliographs were used by General Nelson Miles, in his battles with native Americans in Arizona. He built a total of 27 signaling stations, 40 to 50 km (25 to 30 miles) apart. Between 1 May 1886 and 30 September 1886 a total of 2,276 mes- sages with 80,012 words were transmitted over this network.[42] The heliograph is said to have averaged some 16 words per minute.

FLAGS

Signals can, of course, also be given with coded flags. What would be the first recorded use of a flag signal?

The first reference is rather ambiguous. It can be found in the *The Lives of The Noble Grecians and Romans*, by the Roman historian Plutarch (A.D. 46–120), who referred to an event that took place in 410 B.C. In the chapter on Alcibiades he wrote:[43]

> Upon his first appearance, both sides formed a false impression; the enemy was encouraged and the Athenians terrified. But Alcibiades suddenly raised the Athenian ensign in the admiral ship, and fell upon those galleys of the Peloponnesians which had the advantage and were in pursuit.

Alcibiades had defected from the Athenian camp and fought against them in previous battles. So, when his battle ship appeared at a new battle scene, it was not clear which side he was going to take. The raising of the flag with the Athenian symbol cleared all doubt. This can hardly be considered a general method for communication, but it is not unlikely that flags of various kinds were already in use at this time to communicate standard battle orders from an admiral's ship to the fleet.

It would take a considerable time before flag signals were codified and standardized.

A.D. 900 There are indications that in the late ninth century A.D. the Byzantine Navy had started developing a more systematic approach. Very little documentation seems to have survived. Dvornik wrote:[44]

> During naval operations, the captains of the ships were expected to observe the "pamphylus" of the admiral, who gave orders by signaling from different sides and heights of the central flagship with banners of various colors, or with fire and smoke. A whole code of signals existed with which the commanders and their crews had to be acquainted. Part Nineteen of the strategic treatise ascribed to the Emperor Leo the Wise (A.D. 866–912) gives numerous instructions as to the kinds of signals to be used and how the signaling should be handled. Unfortunately, the need for secrecy prevented the author from explaining the various signals then in use.

In fourteenth century Europe, things were not much more advanced than in the time of Alcibiades. Woods wrote:[45]

A.D. 1337 Between 1337 and 1351 the British Navy lists two signals in their old "Black Book of the Admiralty." The first was to hoist a flag of council high in the middle of the mast, to notify all captains to come aboard the admiral's flagship for a meeting. Hoisting another flag aloft reported the sighting of the enemy.

By the late seventeenth century things still had not progressed much. A A.D. 1673 code book issued for the British Navy in 1673 defined 15 different flags, each with a single predefined meaning, which was probably not too different from what had been used since antiquity.

A.D. 1738 The first significant improvement was made in 1738, when the Frenchman de la Bourdonnais introduced a numerical code for flags. He proposed to use ten colored flags to indicate the numbers from zero to nine. With three sets of such flags, all separately colored, 1,000 code combinations could be made. The Frenchman Ignace Chappe (Claude Chappe's brother, see Chapter Two) wrote in 1824 that he considered it a regrettable mistake that the system of de la Bourdonnais had never been adopted by the French Navy.[46]

A.D. 1763 In 1763, another Frenchman, Sebastian Francisco de Bigot, the founder of the Marine Academy in Brest, published a new code book *Tactique Navale ou Traite des Evolutions et des Signaux*. The book, for the first time ever, specified a true protocol for the use of coded flags.

De Bigot's book had three parts. The first, and largest, part listed 336 distinct flag signals for signaling predefined events or commands from ship to ship. It introduced some important protocol rules, such as the definition of a "preparatory signal flag" for synchronization, the requirement that a receiver acknowledge all signals received by repeating them, and

12

the use of "repeater vessels" to allow for broadcasting signals to an entire fleet. The second part of the book, *Table de Manieres*, contained an alphabetical index of all signals listed in the first part. Each signal was given a number, allowing for a quick cross-referencing of related signals. The third part of the book gave standard maneuvering diagrams for ships. As Woods noted:[47]

> Thus the book permitted a captain to look up an unknown signal in the index of part 2, locate the meaning from part 1, and study the evolution from the diagram in part 3. Cannon, flares, and lights were supplied for transmitting an identical code during night or fog.

Although the book was translated and published in England in 1767, it took more then two decades before the British Navy developed a comparable system with numeric codes. In 1790, the British admiral Lord A.D. 1790 Richard Howe became commander-in-chief of the British Channel Fleet, and introduced a new signal book, which became known as *The Howe Code*.[48] Howe's code used ten colored flags to represent the numbers from zero to nine, and six additional flags to represent a small number of special control codes, e.g., for acknowledgements, and terminations. The numerical flags were used in combination with a small dictionary of 260 numbered entries, which was extended to 340 entries in 1799.

The range of the dictionary was extended considerably in 1800 by Admiral Sir Home Popham.[49] Popham's new signal book, *Telegraphic Signals of Marine Vocabulary*, was adopted officially by the British Royal Navy in 1803. In Popham's code, the ten colored flags from the Howe code were A.D. 1803 designated to represent either the numerals from zero to nine, or the letters A to K in a single flag hoist, the letters I and J sharing a flag. Fifteen combinations of two flags gave the remaining letters of the alphabet. The code also included an index of 3,000 numbered sentences and phrases, in three series. Each series had its own indicator flag; the signals in each series were made with combinations of three flags, hoisted together.

Fifty copies of Popham's code book were issued to the British fleet at Cadiz in early September 1805.[50] The battle of Trafalgar, which took place the A.D. 1805 next month, put the new code to its first test. Flag signaling codes were used extensively by both the French and the British, as indicated by the following description.[51]

> Accordingly he [French admiral Villeneuve] hoisted the signal to weigh anchor, and at six in the morning of 19 October the [British] frigate Sirius, waiting outside Cadiz, signaled to the fleet below the horizon "Enemy have topsails hoisted." An hour later it hoisted signal no. 370, "Enemy ships are coming out of port." The hoists were made to the next frigate in the signaling chain, Euryalus, which in turn signaled no. 370 to Phoebe with the accompanying admonition—superfluous in a service schooled to such discipline—"Repeat signals to lookout ships west." And so no. 370 traveled down the chain, from Phoebe to Naiad, Naiad to Defence (a line-of-battleship), Defence to Colossus and Colossus to Mars, standing in Nelson's line of battle itself, 77 km (48 miles) from the mouth of Cadiz harbour. The news reached Nelson at 9:30. He

Figure 1.3 Wig-Wag Flag Signaling.
(Source: [Hennig 1908], p. 45)

immediately ordered "General chase southeast" and steered to place the fleet between Cadiz and the Straits of Gibraltar. The opening move of the battle of Trafalgar had begun.

Just before the battle, Nelson signaled a final instruction that would become famous in Britain: "England expects that every man will do his duty." Since it was not one of the predefined phrases, it had to be spelled out with individual flag hoists. Of the nine words, eight were in the code book and could be signaled with single hoists of three flags each. The word "duty," however, was not in the code, and had to be spelled out with single- and double-flag hoists.

After the battle, Popham's code became known as the *Trafalgar Code*, an A.D. 1813 indication that it was considered a success. In 1813 Popham issued new signal books, extending the range to 6,000 predefined sentences and phrases, and 60,000 words.

WIG-WAG

All the flag signaling methods mentioned so far clearly dealt with ship-to-ship communications, and were not intended to be used on land. In 1856 an American army doctor named Albert James Myer (1827–1880) changed that with a system he called *wig-wag signaling*. He proposed a

14

method of signaling with either flags or torches, which allowed for two basic motions, that is, a wave of the flag or torch to the left or to the right. Myer's code also defined the acknowledgement of messages, using special codes for signaling "not understood," or "understood."

The wig-wag method was adopted by the American Army in January 1860. Myer even obtained a U.S. patent, No. 252, for his system titled *An improved system of signaling.*[52] The patent issued on 29 January 1861. Even though the simpler Morse code already existed, it did not replace Myer's code until 1886, some twenty-five years later.

A.D. 1860

Flag signaling was standardized in 1857 with the publication of a first international code. It was last revised in 1934.

A.D. 1934

So far, we have seen four different methods for sending messages over a long distance: runners, pigeons, heliographs, and flags. Each of these methods has a much longer history than one would expect. At least two of these methods led to the development of sophisticated, semi-permanent, signaling networks, such as the courier relay systems of the Persians and the Romans, and the heliograph networks used by the Americans in Arizona.

There are two other signaling methods that we have not discussed in detail yet, each also with a remarkably long history: fire or light signals, and semaphores. Both of these methods would reach a level of sophistication that was not reached by any other method.

Fire Beacons

Many Americans can quote the lines of Longfellow's ballad celebrating the ventures of the American patriot Paul Revere (1735–1818):[53]

> One if by land, and two if by sea
> And I on the opposite shore will be
> Ready to ride and spread the alarm
> Through every Middlesex village and farm.

The poem refers to a simple code that had been used in 1775 by Revere during the Revolutionary War. Here is how Revere described it in a letter he wrote later to Dr. Jeremy Belknap:[54]

> If the British went out by water, to show two lanterns in the North Church steeple; and if by land, one as a signal, for we were apprehensive it would be difficult to cross the Charles River or get over Boston Neck.

This was, of course, not the first time that a light signal was used to encode a message. A first reference to the systematic use of fire signals to transmit messages can be found in descriptions of the siege of Troy by the Greek army, which is now assumed to have taken place in approximately 1184 B.C. At least three different sources, Homer, Aeschylus, and Vergil, describe such signaling methods, sometimes in elaborate detail.

1184 B.C.

One of the oldest sources is Homer's *Iliad*, written in approximately 700 B.C. It contains the following passage:[55]

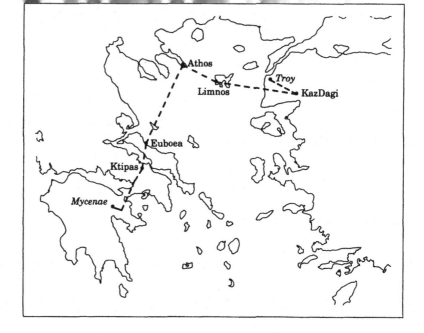

Figure 1.4 The Line of Beacons from Troy to Mycenae.

Thus, from some far-away beleaguered island, where all day long the men have fought a desperate battle from their city walls, the smoke goes up to heaven; but no sooner has the sun gone down than the light from the line of beacons blazes up and shoots into the sky to warn the neighbouring islanders and bring them to the rescue in their ships.

Two other passages can be found in the play *Agamemnon*, written by the Greek dramatist Aeschylus, who lived 525–456 B.C. Aeschylus described how fire beacons were used to signal the fall of Troy to Mycenae, over a distance of roughly 600 km. This is how the play begins:[56]

Watchman—I pray the gods a deliverance from these toils, a remedy for my year-long watch, in which, couching on my elbows on the roofs of the Atreidae, like a dog, I have contemplated the host of the nightly stars, and the bright potentates that bear winter and summer to mortals, conspicuous in the firmament. And now I am watching for the signal of the beacon, the blaze of fire that brings a voice from Troy, and tidings of its capture; ...

A little further, the line of beacons is described in detail.[57]

Chorus—And at what time hath the city been sacked?
Clytaemnestra—I say in the night that hath now brought forth this day.
Chorus—And what messenger could come with such speed?
Clytaemnestra—Vulcan [Hephaestus], sending forth a brilliant gleam from

Table 1.1 Aeschylus's Line of Beacons.

Location	Modern Name	Altitude (m)	Distance (km)
Troy	Troy	100	0
Mt. Ida	Kaz Dagi	1774	55
Lemnos	Skopia at Limnos	430	154
Mt. Athos	Athos	2033	70
Macistus	Kandilion at Euboea	1209	177
Messapius	Ktipas	1020	30
Cithaeron	Elatias	1410	25
Mt. Aegiplanetus	Mt. Jeraneia	1370	30
Arachnaean Hgt	Arna	1199	50
Mycenae	Mycenae	150	20

Ida; and beacon dispatched beacon of courier-fire hitherward. Ida, first to the Hermaean promontory of Lemnos, and third in order Athos, mount of Jove [Zeus], received the great torch from the isle, and passing over so as to ridge the sea, the might of the lamp as it joyously traveled, the pine-torch transmitting its gold gleaming splendor, like a sun, to the watch towers of Macistus. And the watchman omitted not his share of the messenger's duty, either by any delay, or by being carelessly overcome by sleep; but the light of the beacon coming from afar to the streams of the Euripus gives signal to the watchmen of Messapius, and they lighted a flame in turn and sent the tidings onward, having kindled with fire a pile of withered heath.

And the lamp in its strength not yet at all bedimmed, bounding over the plain of the Asopus, like the bright moon to the crag of Cithaeron, aroused another relay of the courier fire. And the watch refused not the light that was sent from afar, lighting a larger pile than those above mentioned; but it darted across the lake Gorgopis, and having reached mount Aegiplanetus, stirred it up in unscathing strength, they send on a mighty beard of flame, so that it passed glaring beyond the headland that looks down upon the Saronic frith, then it darted down until it reached the Arachnaean height, the neighboring post of observation, and thereupon to this roof of the Atreidae here darts this light, no new descendant of the fire of Ida.

Such, in truth, were my regulations for the bearers of the torch fulfilled by succession from one to another; and the first and the last in the course surpassed the rest. Such proof and signal do I tell thee of my husband having sent me tidings from Troy.

Later in the story, Clytaemnestra's enthusiasm about her husband's return apparently diminishes somewhat. When Agamemnon finally returns to Mycenae, he is murdered by Clytaemnestra and her lover.

The locations of the beacon stations can be found on modern maps, although some of the names have changed. Richard Hennig, in 1908, calculated the approximate distances between the stations that Aeschylus names.[58] Volker Aschoff also listed the approximate altitudes and verified the feasibility of a communication across this line.[59] The information is summarized in Table 1.1.

The inclusion of Mount Athos in the chain is the hardest to understand. It appears that a beacon placed at the 792 meter high Mt. Kochylas at the island of Skyros could have replaced the beacon at Athos, and perhaps also the one at Lemnos, by signaling directly to Mount Ida. Nevertheless, with the given altitudes, each beacon along the line that Aeschylus specified, would indeed have been visible from its neighboring stations. Aschoff calculated that on a clear night a stack of wood of roughly 5 to 10 meters high suffices to produce enough brightness to bridge the longest link in the chain, from Athos to Macistus.[60] This is well within the realm of possibility. It is not likely, though, that such a system could have been used for anything other than the transmission of a pre-arranged signal.

The Roman poet Vergil, who lived 70–19 B.C., described another use of fire signals during the siege of Troy. This is from *The Aeneid*:[61]

And now from Tenedos set free
The Greeks are sailing on the sea
Bound for the shore where erst they lay
Beneath the still moon's friendly ray
When in a moment leaps to sight
On the King's ship the signal light
And Sinon, screened by partial fate
Unlocks the pine-wood prison's gate
The horse its charge to air restores
And forth the armed invasion pours

Thessander, Sthenelus, the first
Slide down the rope: Ulysses curst
Thoas and Acamas are there
And great Pelides youthful heir
Machaon, Menelaus, last
Epeus, who the plot forecast
They seized the city, buried deep
In floods of revelry and sleep
Cut down the warders of the gates
And introduce their banded mates.

The "pine-wood prison" is the Trojan Horse in which the eight Greek soldiers were hiding, waiting for Sinon to release them so that they could unlock the gates of Troy from the inside.

The use of beacons or fire signals is mentioned in many sources. The Biblical book of Isaiah, written between 742 and 701 B.C., says, for instance:[62] **742 B.C.**

One thousand shall flee at the rebuke of one; at the rebuke of five shall ye flee: till ye be left as a beacon upon the top of a mountain, and as an ensign on a hill.

588 B.C. Similarly, in the book of Jeremiah, from approximately 588 B.C.:[63]

O, ye children of Benjamin, gather yourselves to flee out of the midst of Jerusalem, and blow the trumpet in Tekóa, and set up a sign of fire in Beth-Kérem; for evil appears out of the North, and great destruction.

Similar references can be found also in the Talmud.[64]

The use of beacons must have been a standard part of daily life; at least it is described as such in many places. Herodotus casually refers to it a few times in his book *The History*. For example, he describes an event that **481 B.C.** took place in 481 B.C., like this:[65]

Of all these things [the loss of three ships to the Persians], the Greeks who were stationed at Artemisium were informed by beacon fires from Sciathus; when they did learn of them, they took fright and changed their anchorage from Artemisium to Chalcis, to keep guard over the Euripus, while they left day-watchmen on the heights of Euboea.

And in another book from this series, he describes how the Persian general Mardonius communicated with Xerxes, some 300 km away:[66]

> A terrible longing had seeped into his [Mardonius's] heart to take Athens a second time. It was partly arrogant pride and partly that he saw himself proving to the King (who was in Sardis), through beacon fires across the islands, that he had taken Athens.

Thucydides, another Greek historian, living from 460 to 399 B.C., referred to beacons in a similarly casual way. In the *History of The Peloponnesian War*, he wrote:[67] 440 B.C.

> Beacons were lit to warn Athens of an enemy attack, and a panic broke out which was as great as any in the course of the war. For the people in the city thought that the enemy had already sailed into Piraeus, and in Piraeus people thought that they had taken Salamis and were just on the point of sailing into the harbour.

Such matter-of-fact references return a few more times. For instance:[68]

> The Athenians were at Sestos with eighteen ships. Informed by the fire signals and observing also that many fires were suddenly appearing on the shore held by the enemy, they realized that the Peloponnesians were sailing in, and set off that very night.

And the more intriguing statement:[69]

> The Peloponnesians, however, having spent the time up till midday in laying waste the land, sailed away again, and about nightfall were informed by fire signals that a fleet of sixty Athenian ships was approaching from the direction of Leucas.

Could it be that the actual number of ships was part of the message transmitted? Alas, Thucydides does not elaborate. In one place, he does note that the beacon fires were not always reliable:[70]

> Fire signals of an enemy attack were made [from Plataea] to Thebes [for assistance against a plot of captives to escape from the city]; but the Plataeans in the town also displayed a number of fire signals from their own walls, having them all ready made for this very purpose, so as to make the enemy's signals unintelligible, to stop help coming from Thebes, and to prevent the Thebans from having a true idea of what was happening, until their own men who had gone out had escaped and got into safety.

All systems described thus far seem somewhat ad hoc, being primarily used to send a single predefined alarm, victory, or attack signal. Three things are still lacking that are essential for something that we could recognize as telegraphic correspondence: (1) a permanent installation, or network of signaling points, spread out over a larger area, (2) a capability for two-way communication, and (3) an encoding system that allows for

19

the transmission of either single letters or arbitrary words and phrases with a single sign.

Watchmen and Stentors

The first mention of a permanent system of signaling using fires or beacons can be found in a work that has been ascribed to the school of Aristotle (384–322 B.C.). In *Peri Kosmon* (The World Around Us), Book 6, either Aristotle or one of his students writes about a system that was used in the Persian empire around 500 B.C.:[71]

500 B.C.

> The organization, however, was so good, especially that of the fire-watches that passed on fire signals along rows, from the border of the kingdom to Susa and Ekbatana, so that the king would know within one day everything that took place in Asia Minor.

The city of Susa, which is today called Shûsh in southwestern Iran, was the ancient Persian capital where King Darius I had his palace during his reign from 521 to 486 B.C. The city was at the eastern endpoint of the Persian Royal Road that ran west about 2,600 km (1,600 miles), to Sardis in modern-day Turkey. Herodotus reported that there were no less than 111 relay stations along this road.[72] He, however, also indicated that the Persians preferred the reliability of well-trained couriers to fire signals.[73]

Elsewhere, Xenophon (431–355 B.C.) referred to a curious variant of a relay system.[74]

> It was at night that the Paralus arrived at Athens. As the news of the disaster was told, one man passed it on to another, and a sound of wailing arose and extended first from Piraeus, then along the Long Walls until it reached the city. That night no one slept.

This may be a first reference to a system of human stentors, or shouters, that passed news across roads or fields, from one person to the next. A more explicit description of such a system was given by Diodorus Siculus, in the first century B.C., describing events that took place in Persia, roughly two centuries earlier.[75]

315 B.C.

> Although some of the Persians were distant a thirty days' journey, they all received the order on that very day, thanks to the skillful arrangement of the posts of the guard, a matter that it is not well to pass over in silence. Persia is cut by many narrow valleys and has many lookout posts that are high and close together, on which those of the inhabitants who had the loudest voices had been stationed. Since these posts were separated from each other by the distance at which a man's voice can be heard, those who received the order passed it on in the same way to the next, and then these in turn to others until the message had been delivered at the border of the satrapy [province].

A little later, in the same book, Diodorus Siculus also refers to other organized systems for long-distance communications, also in use around this time.[76]

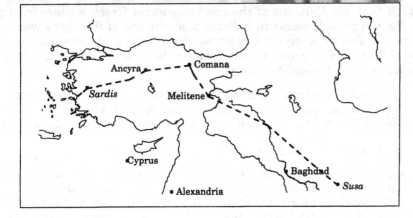

Figure 1.5 The Persian Royal Road from Sardis to Susa.

He [Antigonus] himself established at intervals throughout all that part of Asia of which he was master a system of fire signals and dispatch carriers, by means of which he expected to have quick service in all his business.

The clear suggestion here is that at least three systems were in use at the same time: calling posts, fire signals, and couriers. Presumably these could have dealt with three different types of messages. Short, high-priority messages could be sent during the day by calling post, and by night with fire signals. Other messages could travel by mounted courier.

The Romans later also used all three systems for long-distance communications. We have already discussed the Roman courier system. Julius Caesar (100–44 B.C.) referred to the other two systems in his *Bellum Gallicum*. First, he described the use of calling posts:[77]

52 B.C.

Quickly the news reaches all parts of Gaul, because whenever something important happens, they announce it by loud calls across fields and plains. These calls are heard by others, that have been positioned in rows and these pass them on to the next, and so on. Then, what happens at sunrise at Genabum [Orleans], is heard before sunset near Arverner, at a distance of 160,000 double-steps [approx. 240km (150 miles)].

Caesar also mentioned the systematic use of fire signals:[78]

. . . the alarm was quickly given by fire signals, in accordance with orders issued beforehand, and troops hastened up from the nearest redoubts.

Plinius the Elder (A.D. 23–79) stated that the Carthaginian general Hannibal, who lived 247–183 B.C., made elaborate use of fire signals and watch towers during his campaigns. He wrote:[79]

Even today, in Spain one can still see Hannibal's watch towers, and the earthen towers erected at mountain ridges.

Plutarch (A.D. 46–120), one of the most important Greek writers from the early Roman period, seems to indicate that the use of fire signs was common in the Roman army, not even worthy of much elaboration. In *The Lives of The Noble Grecians and Romans*, he describes how the Roman general Sertorius trained his army:[80]

73 B.C.

> . . . and [he] brought them to make use of the Roman armour, taught them to keep their ranks, and observe signals and watchwords; and out of a confused number of thieves and robbers he constituted a regular, well-disciplined army.

In his description, Woods goes even further. He wrote:[81]

> During most of the Greek and Roman wars there were special corps of signalists or telegraphers within their armies, known as πυρδευται (*pyrdeitai*). The word frequently has been translated as "fire-bearers." More literally it is "fire-movers," "fire-shakers," or perhaps . . . "fire-swingers" from πυρ, the word for "fire" and δευω, the verb "to move" or "to shake." Marcellinus [third century A.D.] mentions "speculatores" and "vexillarii" who observed and reported signals in the Roman navy.

According to Shaffner and Hennig, Vegetius states in *De Re Militari* that the Roman generals were accustomed to communicating by telegraph.[82] Aschoff is more guarded in his interpretation.[83] The assumption is based on the following intriguing quote from Vegetius:[84]

> When troops are separated, they announce to their colleagues, with fires during the night, and with smoke during the day, anything that cannot be otherwise communicated. Many also mount wooden beams at the towers of fortifications or cities, sometimes pointing upwards sometimes downward, to indicate what takes place. [Latin: *Aliquanti in castellorum aut urbium turribus adpendunt trabes, quibus aliquando erectis aliquando depositis indicant quae geruntur.*]

It is tempting to recognize a semaphore system in this description, but, as Aschoff points out, other explanations are also possible. Several authors point to illustrations on the Victory Columns erected by the Roman emperors Trajan (A.D. 53–117) and Marcus Aurelius (A.D. 121–180) in Rome.[85] The clearest illustration appears at the base of Trajan's Column, dating from A.D. 113 (Figure 1.6). It shows what appears to be a series of six guard houses. Three of the houses have a Roman soldier posted in front, and a large torch mounted through an opening near the roof.[86] The illustration lead Dvornik to a far-reaching conclusion:[87]

A.D. 113

> On the famous columns of the Emperors Trajan and Marcus Aurelius, on which their victories are depicted, we see soldiers signaling with flaming torches from the towers of the limes as a warning of the approach of the barbarians. This can be considered sufficient evidence that fire signals were introduced at last on a large scale in the Roman army during the imperial period.

Although the sequence could well depict a communication chain, more conservative explanations are equally plausible. There is little else to be found in Roman art and literature that could substantiate the claim that a

Figure 1.6 Guard House on Trajan's Column.
(Source: [Hennig 1908], p. 15)

telegraph system existed in early Rome.

Is there, then, any reliable indication that telegraphic systems existed? This question brings us to the first explicit descriptions of telegraphs in antiquity: devices that allowed for true long-distance communications.

The First Telegraphs
Many problems have to be solved before a telegraphic device can be built that can be used for two-way communications. Messages have to be

encoded, and some type of protocol has to be established between sender and receiver to deal minimally with the basic problems of synchronization ("after you?", "no, after you!"), visibility ("repeat please"), and transmission speed ("not so fast!"). When did people first build such devices?

The first person who we reliably know developed a telegraph was Aeneas (not the Aeneas from Vergil's *Aeneid*). Aeneas was a well-known author in ancient Greece, who lived around 350 B.C. and wrote works on military strategy. Only part of his main work, *The Art of War*, still exists, and unfortunately it does not contain the description of his telegraph.

350 B.C.

We do have a clear description of Aeneas's design by the historian Polybius (ca. 200–118 B.C.). In *The Histories* Polybius first described, in crystal-clear prose, the limitations of plain beacon fires.[88]

> I think that as regards the system of signaling by fire, which is now of the greatest possible service in war but was formerly underdeveloped, it will be of use not to pass it over but to give it a proper discussion. It is evident to all that in every matter, and especially in warfare, the power of acting at the right time contributes very much to the success of enterprises, and fire signals are the most efficient of all the devices which aid us to do this. For they show what has recently occurred and what is still in the course of being done, and by means of them anyone who cares to do so even if he is at a distance of three, four, or even more days' journey can be informed. So that it is always surprising how help can be brought by means of fire messages when the situation requires it. Now in former times, as fire signals were simple beacons, they were for the most part of little use to those who used them. For the service should have been performed by signals previously determined upon, and as facts are indefinite, most of them defied communication by fire signals. To take the case I just mentioned, it was possible for those who had agreed on this to convey information that a fleet had arrived at Oreus, Peparethus, or Chalcis, but when it came to some of the citizens having changed sides or having been guilty of treachery or a massacre having taken place in the town, or anything of the kind, things that often happen, but cannot all be foreseen—and it is chiefly unexpected occurrences which require instant consideration and help—all such matters defied communication by fire signal. For it was quite impossible to have a preconcerted code for things which there was no means of foretelling.

In the next section, Polybius describes Aeneas's solution to this problem, dating back to around 350 B.C. This is how he described it, over 2,100 years ago.[89]

> Aeneas, the author of the work on strategy, wishing to find a remedy for the difficulty, advanced matters a little, but his device still fell far short of our requirements, as can be seen from his description of it. He says that those who are about to communicate urgent news to each other by fire signal should procure two earthenware vessels of exactly the same width and depth, the depth being some three cubits[90] and the width one. Then they should have corks made a little narrower than the mouths of the vessels and through the middle of each cork should pass a rod graduated in equal sections of three finger-breadths, each clearly marked off from the next. In each section should be written the most evident and ordinary events that occur in war, e.g., on the

Figure 1.7 Synchronous Telegraph, ca. 350 B.C.
(Coll. Musée de la Poste, Paris)

first "Cavalry arrived in the country," on the second "Heavy infantry," on the third "Light-armed infantry," next "Infantry and cavalry," next "Ships," next "Corn," and so on until we have entered in all the sections the chief contingencies of which, at the present time, there is a reasonable probability in wartime. Next he tells us to bore holes in both vessels of exactly the same size, so that they allow exactly the same escape. Then we are to fill the vessels with water and put on the corks with the rods in them and allow the water to flow through the two apertures. When this is done it is evident that, the conditions being precisely similar, in proportion as the water escapes the two corks will sink and the rods will disappear into the vessels. When by experiment it is seen that the rapidity of escape is in both cases the same, the vessels are to be conveyed to the places in which both parties are to look after the signals and deposited there. Now whenever any of the contingencies written on the rods occurs he tells us to raise a torch and to wait until the corresponding party raise another. When both the torches are clearly visible the signaler is to lower his torch and at once allow the water to escape through the aperture. Whenever, as the corks sink, the contingency you wish to communicate reaches the mouth of the vessel he tells the signaler to raise his torch and the receivers of the signal are to stop the aperture at once and to note which of the messages written on the rods is at the mouth of the vessel. This will be the message delivered, if the apparatus works at the same pace in both cases.

Not many would have trouble reproducing the device from this description. It appears that precisely this system was used for the communications of the Roman troops at Carthage, on the Tunesian coast of North Africa, and Sicily in the second century A.D., long after Polybius. This is how Polyaenus described it in his work *Strategematon* from this period:[91]

They [the Carthaginians] must watch and when they see a fire signal in Sicily, they should let the water flow from the water-clock in Carthage. When they see another fire signal, they should stop the flowing of water and see which circle it had reached. When they had read the inscription they should send in the quickest way the things they had been asked for by these signals.

A set of nine specific inscriptions used for this purpose was also given by Polyaenus: "We need warships, cargo boats, money, machines for besieging, food, cattle, arms, infantry, cavalry." The shortest distance between Sicily and Carthage, however, is close to 150 km, which makes it hard to interpret correctly what type of signal could have been used to bridge such a large gap. It almost certainly could not have been a simple torch signal, not even if shot up into the air with arrows or slings.[92]

Polybius continues his account with what may be the first technical critique of a telegraphic device in recorded history. He wrote:[93]

This is a slight advance on beacons with a preconcerted code, but it is still quite indefinite. For it is evident that it is neither possible to foresee all contingencies or, even if one did, to write them on the rod. So that when circumstances produce some unexpected event, it is evident that it cannot be conveyed by this plan. Again none of the things written on the rod are defined statements, for it is impossible to indicate how many infantry are coming and to what part of the country, or how many ships or how much corn. For it is impossible to agree beforehand about things of which one cannot be aware before they happen. And this is the vital matter; for how can anyone consider how to render assistance if he does not know how many of the enemy have arrived, or where? And how can anyone be of good cheer or the reverse, or in fact think of anything at all, if he does not understand how many ships or how much corn has arrived from the allies?

Polybius hints here at a method for encoding the alphabet into signals, so that arbitrary messages can be spelled out. From other sources we know that such a device had been developed by Cleoxenus and Democleitus.[94] Polybius proceeds by describing this design, with some important alterations.[95]

> The most recent method, devised by Cleoxenus and Democleitus and perfected by myself, is quite definite and capable of dispatching with accuracy every kind of urgent message, but in practice it requires care and exact attention. It is as follows: We take the alphabet and divide it into five parts, each consisting of five letters. There is one letter less in the last division, but it makes no practical difference. Each of the two parties who are about to signal to each other must now get ready five tablets and write one division of the alphabet on each tablet, and then come to an agreement that the man who is going to signal is in the first place to raise two torches and wait until the other replies by doing the same. This is for the purpose of conveying to each other that they are both at attention. These torches having been lowered, the dispatcher of the message will now raise the first set of torches on the left side indicating which tablet is to be consulted, i.e., one torch if it is the first, two if it is the second, and so on. Next he will raise the second set on the right on the same principle to indicate what letter of the tablet the receiver should write down.

Note that there were no spaces or punctuation characters (none were used in written Greek at the time) and that the Greek alphabet contained only 24 letters. Polybius chose not to use the 25th spare letter code, but instead designed an out-of-band code for synchronization: one torch in each group raised simultaneously. It would be a long time before anyone else paid this much attention again to the design of a signaling code!

There is still a question as to how much of this design was due to Polybius, and how much had already been present in the descriptions of Cleoxenus and Democleitus. There is, fortunately, an independent description of this telegraph, written between A.D. 200 and 250 by Sextus Julius Africanus. From the differences we can reasonably deduce what the additions of Polybius were.

In the system described by Sextus Julius Africanus in his book *Kestoi*, the alphabet was divided into three groups of eight letters each.[96] The sender used three different torches, one for each group. By raising a torch between one and eight times, the corresponding letter from that group would be signaled.[97] There was also an alternative way of transmitting the signals by using more torches or fires, as was illustrated in 1796 by Edelcrantz in his treatise:[98]

> Polybius and Julius Africanus record its use by the Greeks and Romans, using kettles with burning twigs or straw in oil, indicating letters in such a way that 1 to 8 fires in the first series encoded the first 8 letters of the alphabet, and similarly, fires in the next two series were used to encode the remaining 16 letters. One, two, or three separate fires lit at a distance were used to indicate the number of the series intended.

The improvements to this system that were due to Polybius were in all likelihood the more systematic usage of a smaller number of torches, and,

Figure 1.8 Polybius´s Torch Telegraph, ca. 150 B.C.
(Coll. Musée de la Poste, Paris)

as described in the next section, the use of special screens and viewing tubes to block out peripheral light.[99] Polybius continued:[100]

> Upon their separating after coming to this understanding each of them must first have on the spot a "viewing tube" with two cylinders, so that with the one he can observe the space on the right of the man who is going to signal back and with the other that on the left. The tablets must be set straight up in order next the tubes, and there must be a screen before both spaces, as well the right as the left, ten feet in length and of the height of a man so that by this means the torches may be seen distinctly when raised and disappear when lowered. When all has been thus got ready on both sides, if the signaler wants to convey, for instance, that a hundred of the soldiers have deserted to the enemy, he must first of all choose words which will convey what he means in the smallest number of letters, e.g., instead of the above "Cretans a hundred deserted us," for thus the letters are less than one half in number, but the same sense is conveyed. Having jotted this down on a writing-tablet he will communicate it by the torches as follows: The first letter is kappa. This being in the second division is on tablet number two, and, therefore, he must raise two torches on the left, so that the receiver may know that he has to consult the second tablet. He will now raise five torches on the right, to indicate that it is kappa, this being the fifth letter in the second division, and the receiver of the signal will note this down on his writing tablet. The dispatcher will then raise four torches on the left as rho belongs to the fourth division, and then two on the right, rho being the second letter in this division. The receiver writes down rho and so forth. This device enables any news to be definitely conveyed.

28

The "viewing tubes," referred to here, although sometimes translated as "telescopes," did not magnify, but merely limited the field of vision.[101]

How hard would it be to use a telegraph like this? Polybius had a few words to say about this as well.[102]

> Many torches, of course, are required as the signal for each letter is a double one. But if all is properly prepared for the purpose, what is required can be done whichever system we follow. Those engaged in the work must have had proper practice, so that when it comes to putting it in action they may communicate with each other without the possibility of a mistake.

Volker Aschoff reported that students from the Technical University of Aachen in Germany successfully reproduced Polybius's torch telegraph.[103] They achieved a quite reasonable signaling rate of up to eight letters per minute on short messages, without using modern telescopes.

Well aware of the importance of his description, Polybius concluded with the following observation.[104]

> In offering these observations I am acting up to the promise I originally made at the outset of this work. For I stated that in our time all arts and sciences have so much advanced that knowledge of most of them may be said to have been reduced to a system. This is, then, one of the most useful parts of a history properly written.

According to the Roman historian Titus Livius (64 B.C.–A.D. 17), torch telegraphs as described by Polybius and his predecessors were used by Philip of Macedonia (238–179 B.C.) in his war against the Romans in 207 B.C. 207 B.C. Livius wrote:[105]

> From there, in order that he [Philip of Macedonia] might meet every movement of his enemies, he sent men into Phocis, Euboea and to Peparethus, to select heights from which signal fires might be visible. For himself he placed a watch-tower on Mountain Tisäon, whose peak rises to a great height, so that by fires on distant heights he might in an instant receive a message as to where his enemies were active.

Implicit in this description is the realization that letter telegraphs, just like beacon fires, can be used to cover very long distances by using stations as relays in chains. That principle was already recognized by Julius Sextus Africanus when he wrote in *Kestoi*:[106]

> . . . then they signal what they have received to those who operate the next fire signals post, and these in the same manner pass it further, towards those who operate the last signal post.

Many of the principles laid out so clearly in the third and second century B.C. would not be rediscovered until the seventeenth century A.D.

The 2000-Year Gap
It is hard to believe that for almost two millennia people were any less curious about the construction of practical methods for long-distance

communication than they were at the time of the Egyptians, Babylonians, Greeks, and Romans, but the sobering fact is that throughout this period only occasional references were made to simple beacon fires or messenger systems. All progress that had been made was forgotten.

We find a first new reference to a telegraphic system in the ninth century A.D. It was developed by Leo the Mathematician in Byzantium, during the reign of Theophilus (A.D. 829–842). Francis Dvornik described this system as follows:[107]

A.D. 842

> He [Leo] constructed two identical clocks which kept exactly the same time. One was placed at the last station of the fire signals near the frontier [in Loulon], and the other near the imperial palace [in Constantinople]. Twelve incidents likely to occur, and which would have to be communicated through seven relays to headquarters at the imperial palace, were assigned to each of the twelve hours and written on the faces of both clocks. Upon receiving intelligence that the enemy was about to cross the frontier, the commander of the frontier post lit his fire signal when the clock showed the hour of one, and thus the watches in the palace knew at what time [day?] the invasion had begun.

Reportedly, this system was used until well into the tenth century A.D. To make a system like this work at all, there must have been a method to compensate for the 22-minute time difference between Loulon and Constantinople, and the shortening of the time available for nighttime signaling during the summers. Even with those problems solved, it must have been hard to construct clocks that could be kept in sufficient synchrony, and hard to cope with the average half-day delay before an urgent message could be sent. Considering also the limited code space, it is hard to see this as an improvement over Polybius's system.

Three hundred years later we find the following passage in *Usatges*, a book written by Berengars I in 1176:[108]

A.D. 1176

> When the sovereign is attacked, or when he discovers that a king or monarch advances to fight him, he will inform his constituents either by proclamation, or by messengers, or in the usual way, by fire signals.

The use of the phrase "in the usual way" (German: *auf die gewohnte Weise*) seems to indicate that the use of fire beacons was still the standard way of communicating signs of alarm, victory or attack.

Another three hundred years later there still hadn't been much progress. The text of an enactment of the Scottish Parliament from the year 1455, for instance, reads:[109]

A.D. 1455

> One bale of faggot shall be the notice of the approach of the English in any manner; two bales that they are "coming indeed;" and four bales blazing beside each other, to say that they are "coming in earnest."

The first sign of improvement came in the early sixteenth century. In this period, the French, Spanish and Venetian navies started using simple flag signaling methods for ship-to-ship and for ship-to-shore communications. Precious little is known about the devices or codes that were used,[110] but

Figure 1.9 Sixteenth Century Spanish Map (Detail).
(Source: [Sider 1992], Fig. 24)

on old maps from this period peculiar disc-shaped devices suspended from towers can be seen that in all likelihood served signaling purposes (Figure 1.9). Almost identical signaling devices were used in Holland until well into the nineteenth century.[111]

The improvements in signaling apparently did not spread very rapidly through Europe. In 1569, for instance, the British erected a signal house A.D. 1569 on a platform battery in Portsmouth, as the endpoint of a classic line of beacons that stretched from Portsmouth to London. It was this line of beacons that notified London of the approach of the Spanish Armada in 1588.[112] If the Spanish did indeed have better signaling methods, it does not seem to have helped them in this instance.

At the start of the seventeenth century a discovery was made that would change the art of signaling decisively.

TELESCOPES

In 1608 Dutch spectacle-maker Hans Lippershey accidentally aligned two A.D. 1608 lenses of opposite curvature and of different focal lengths in his workshop in Middelburg. He discovered that this combination of lenses distorts the image in a wonderfully useful way: the telescope was born. Galileo was able to reproduce the effect, based on a description he had received from

Holland. By the end of 1609, he had succeeded in building a 30-power telescope, allowing him to discover, for instance, the moons of Jupiter. In 1610 he published his findings in *Siderius Nuncius* (The Starry Messenger).

The invention of the telescope made a considerable difference in the development of telegraphs. Since large objects could now be spotted from 15 to 30 km (10 to 20 miles) away, it didn't take much imagination for the inventors of those days to consider all kinds of new telegraphic schemes. Some of these systems are referred to in Edelcrantz's treatise, as follows:[113]

> Also notable is an idea from an unknown person that is contained in a letter to Schottus. He proposes to establish communication between Mainz and Rome by erecting 5 poles on a hill at such a distance from each other that they can easily be distinguished from 5 to 6 [German] miles away with a telescope. A pulley is attached to the top of each pole to hoist a stick, a sheaf of straw, or other objects to the top. If the alphabet is divided into 5 groups of letters, an object is first raised to indicate the group number. After the first object is lowered, another one is raised to indicate the number of the letter within the group. The art is the same as that of the Greeks but adapted to daytime use. The inventor, however, seems to be the first to have suggested the use of telescopes.

Edelcrantz refers to Gaspard Schottus, who lived from 1608 to 1666. The letter that Schottus quoted in 1664 was written by Philipp Ernst Vegelin von Claerberg, an official at the court of the Prince of Nassau.

Edelcrantz continues with a more interesting reference to a method that even predates the one described by Schottus.

> Someone named Kessler, who lived at the beginning of the last century [i.e., the seventeenth century], suggested using letters cut from the bottom of barrels, using them to spell out words that would be readable at great distances.

Someone named Franz Kessler (ca. 1580–1650) did in fact write a book called *Unterschiedliche bisshero mehrern Theils Secreta oder Verborgene, Geheime Kunste* (Various until now mostly hidden, secret arts), which was published in Oppenheim in September 1616. The description of Kessler's method given by Edelcrantz is not quite accurate, though. Kessler was one of the first authors to describe a working system based on the use of a telescope and a light signaling device.

In the preface to Kessler's book written by Hans Dietrich von Bry, a bookseller from Oppenheim, the method is introduced as follows:[114]

> Then it is not a small matter that two good friends in case of emergency, or otherwise at their pleasure, can communicate their wishes to each other, without meeting or go-between, and also at one or two miles distance can have their discourse or conversation, which in case of a siege or in other emergencies can be used to advantage to save an entire city or fortress, as will also be learned in more detail from the [following] description.

Figure 1.10 Kessler's Device.
(Coll. New York Public Library, New York)

Kessler himself then refers to the telescope as a useful novelty from Holland. Apparently the word *telescope* had not been adopted yet.[115]

> With the help of a long perspective, and in recent years in Holland newly discovered Tubular Spectacles [German: *Rohren Brillens*], used outside in the field, with which one can see best in time of peace, and the most secure at times of war.

Kessler then describes how the alphabet can be compressed into fifteen essential characters, each of which can be associated with a number between one and fifteen in a pre-arranged random order, to make it harder for others to detect what is being signaled. Kessler stresses that the code can and should be changed frequently if secrecy is required.

To use this code, in addition to "tubular spectacles," one needs:[116]

> At night a burning light or a torch suffices; by day a mere stick with a white piece of cloth or paper.

Kessler then details the nighttime signaling method. For this one needs:

> . . . two square boxes, or common round barrels. They must, however, also on the inside, be covered with lead. In the middle of the barrel one must place a long hook. The bottom of the barrel must have a square door, about a quarter

ell [15 cm] long and wide, so that, through this door, one can hang from the hook several pitch-crowns of appropriate size.

The barrel is placed on its side, with the bottom facing the signaler, as illustrated by Kessler in Figure 1.10. The other side is open, but equipped with a shutter that can be lifted or lowered to produce the light signals: one flash for the letter "d," two flashes for an "i," and so on.

Kessler realized well that the same encoding would work for waving a flag, or for giving sound signals with bells, or hammers, or by knocking on walls.[117]

He gives much attention to a related problem, which seems to indicate that, unlike many other inventors from this period, he really did use the signaling method he describes. The question is how one could locate a remote receiver or sender in the middle of the night, before the signaling begins. To solve that problem Kessler built a large disc, marked in degrees from 0 to 360, with a compass on it, and with a pointing device attached to the center. The pointing device was a simple stick with two flat pieces of metal at the ends, each with a small slit in it. The idea was that at daylight one would accurately locate the remote correspondent, mark the angle on the disc, using the compass for an absolute reference of orientation. Then, at night, at a predetermined hour, the barrel and the disc would be lined up with the remote location, and signaling could begin. Curiously, Kessler states that the receiver only really needed the disc, not the barrel, which implied that he had not thought of things like message acknowledgement or error control. The method is reminiscent of signal-lights flashing Morse codes, as they are used in the Navy even today.

Several less sophisticated methods from the same period seem to have been popular; sufficiently so for the Dutch writer Wynant van Westen to remark in his booklet, *Mathematische Vermakelyckheden* (Mathematical Amusements), published in Arnhem in 1636, that these signaling devices were of most use to spies, since they made it so much easier to intercept the supposedly secret communications of an adversary.

A.D. 1636

Mentioned in many sources is a description from the Marquis of Worcester, in his book *Century of Inventions*, which was published in 1663. He claimed:[118]

A.D. 1663

> . . . a method by which, at a window, as far as [the] eye can discover black from white, a man may hold discourse with his correspondent, without noise made or notice taken; being according to occasion given, or means afforded, *ex re nata*, and no need of provision beforehand; though much better if foreseen, and course taken by mutual consent of parties.

There is again no mention that a large-scale use of this method was ever contemplated.

Another telegraphic device mentioned by Edelcrantz is a letter telegraph developed by the Englishman Robert Hooke (1635–1703).[119] Hooke's device would prove to be a seminal step in the development of telegraphy.

34

Nonetheless, it appears to have been only of passing interest to Hooke himself.

The Art of Conveying Intelligence

The only record of Hooke's invention is the text of a lecture he gave on 21 May 1684 to the Royal Society with the title *On Showing A Way How To Communicate One's Mind At Great Distances*. The design he describes there has some unique features that had not been described before. Even though the device itself appears never to have been applied in practice, it provided a rich inspiration for many others. The text of Hooke's speech gives a unique view of the communication problem as it was seen by this seventeenth century scholar:[120]

A.D. 1684

> That which I now propound, is what I have some years since discoursed of; but being then laid by, the great siege of Vienna, the last year, by the Turks, did again revive in my memory; and that was a method of discoursing at a distance, not by sound, but by sight. I say, therefore, 't is possible to convey intelligence from any one high and eminent place, to any other that lies in sight of it, though 30 or 40 [English] miles distant in as short a time almost as a man can write what he would have sent, and as suddenly to receive an answer as he that receives it hath a mind to return it, or can write it down in paper. Nay, by the help of three, four, or more of such eminent places, visible to each other, lying next it in a straight line, 't is possible to convey intelligence, almost in a moment, to twice, thrice, or more times that distance, with as great certainty as by writing.

In the next paragraph Hooke refers to telescopes, still as a recent invention. The term "tubular spectacles" had now been abandoned.

> For the performance of this, we must be beholden to a late invention, which we do not find any of the ancients knew; that is, the eye must be assisted with telescopes, of lengths appropriated to the respective distances, that whatever characters are exposed at one station, may be made plain and distinguishable at the other that respect it.
>
> First. For the stations; if they be far distant, it will be necessary that they should be high, and lie exposed to the sky, that there be no higher hill, or part of the earth beyond them, that may hinder the distinctness of the characters which are to appear dark, the sky beyond them appearing white: by which means also, the thick and vaporous air, near the ground will be passed over and avoided; for it many times happens that the tops of hills are very clear and conspicuous to each other, when as the whole interjacent vale, or country, lies drowned in a fog. Next, because a much greater distance and space of ground becomes visible, insomuch that I have been informed by such, who have been at the top of some very high mountains, as particularly at the top of the pike of Teneriff, that island of the Grand Canaries, which lies above 60 [English] miles distant, appears so clear, as if it were hard by; and I myself have often taken notice of the great difference there is between the appearing distance of objects seen from the tops and bottoms of pretty high hills, the same objects from the top appearing nearer and clearer by half, and more than they do when viewed from lower stations of the hills; and this not only when the space between them was land, but where it was nothing but sea. I have taken notice also of the

Figure 1.11 Hooke's Device.
(Source: [Hooke 1726])

same difference from the prospect of places from the top of the column at Fish-street Hill, where the eye is, in good part, raised above the smoky air below.

After more on air quality, and the type of telescopes that would be required, Hooke continued:

Next, there must be certain times agreed on, when the correspondents are to expect; or else there must be set at the top of the pole [the first mention of the word "pole" in the description], in the morning, the hour appointed by either of the correspondents, for acting that day; if the hour be appointed, pendulum clocks may adjust the moment of expectation and observing. And the same may serve for all other intermediate correspondents.

Other than Kessler or the Marquis of Worcester before him, Hooke had a clear view of how his system could be used to set up a longer chain of signaling stations.

Hooke then describes his encoding method in detail.

> Next, there must be a convenient apparatus of characters, whereby to communicate any thing with great ease, distinctness, and secrecy. There must be therefore, at least, as many distinct characters as there are necessary letters in the alphabet that is made use of . . . and those must be either day characters or night characters: if they are to be made use of in the day-time, they may all be made of three slit deals [boards or planks], moving in the manner I here shew, and of bigness convenient for the several distances of the stations for which they are made, that they may be visible through the telescope of the next station. Any one of which characters may signify any one letter of the alphabet, and the whole alphabet may be varied 10,000 ways; so that none but the two extreme correspondents shall be able to discover the information conveyed, which I shall not now insist on, because it does more properly belong to Cruptography [Hooke's spelling].

Hooke's encoding by arbitrarily mapping letters of the alphabet to symbols is similar to Kessler's. It is not certain, however, that Hooke knew about Kessler's book. Also interesting is the detailed attention that even the earliest developers of signaling systems seem to have given to cryptography. To Hooke's credit, though, he was one of the few who realized that it was a separate topic, and need not be confused with the design of the basic signaling method.

Hooke next explains how the night characters can be made, but here he is not very explicit.

> If the characters are for the night, then they may be made with links [Oxford dictionary: torches formerly used for lighting/guiding people along streets], or other lights, disposed in a certain order, which may be veiled, or discovered, according to the method of the character agreed on; by which, all sorts of letters may be discovered clearly, and without ambiguity.

Next, Hooke comes to the actual apparatus that he is proposing for displaying the day characters.

> There may be various contrivances to facilitate and expedite the way of displaying and exposing these characters to view, and of withdrawing, or hiding them from the sight; but this I here shew, I conceive, will be as easy and simple as any: all which may be exposed at the top of a high pole, and by two small lines moved at the bottom, so as to represent any character.

> By these contrivances, the characters may be shifted almost as fast, as the same may be written; so that a great quantity of intelligence may be, in a very short time, communicated.

The characters are suspended from a frame, where they can be obscured behind a screen when moved to the left, or displayed when moved to the right, with the help of lines attached to each character, each line going down to an operator standing at the bottom of the frame.

In the next paragraph, Hooke explicitly describes the use of control codes that can be used in true two-way communication, for instance, to signal acknowledgements or error conditions. As far as we know, Hooke was the first person who realized that such codes were necessary for effective communication.[121]

> There will also requisite several other characters, which may, for expedition, express a whole sentence, to be continually made use of, whilst the correspondents are attentive and communicating. The sentences to be expressed by one character [symbol] may be such as these . . . I am ready to communicate [synchronization]. I am ready to observe [idem]. I shall be ready presently [delay]. I see plainly what you shew [acknowledgement]. Shew the last again [an error code]. Not too fast [rate control]. Shew faster [idem]. Answer me presently. *Dixi*. Make haste to communicate this to the next correspondent [priority]. I stay for an answer; and the like. All which may be expressed by several single characters, to be exposed on the top of the poles [instead of suspended below them, like the other characters], by themselves, in the following manner, so as no confusion may be created thereby.

The meaning of the word *Dixi* is not clear. It was set in a different font, and may not have represented a separate code. It could, however, also be Latin for "I have said," meaning "end of message." From the other ten code words, at least eight are control codes that can be found in most modern data communication protocols, and some of these (i.e., the rate control codes) only in the most recent designs. For the first design that included control codes at all, it was not a bad choice indeed.

Hooke summed up his lecture as follows, anticipating his critics:

> There may be many objections brought against this way of communication; and so many the more, because the thing has not yet been put in practice. But, I think, there can hardly be any so great, as may not easily be answered and obviated.
>
> There may be many uses of this contrivance, wherein it will exceed any thing of this kind yet practiced, but I shall not now spend time to enumerate them; only in two cases, it may be of inestimable use. The first is for cities or towns besieged, and the second is for ships upon the sea; in both which cases, it may be practiced with great certainty, security, and expedition.

The telegraph design of Hooke would never be put to practice, but it A.D. 1690 inspired many of his successors.[122] In 1690, a curious variant of Hooke's method, developed by the Frenchman Guillaume Amontons was described in a letter written by Abbé Fénelons, the Archbishop of Cambrai, to the secretary of the Polish king Johann Sobieski:[123]

> Monseigneur has told me that he was in Meudon and from there sent a secret message via windmills to Belleville and from there to Paris. The answer was given to him similarly by signals, that were attached to the wings of the

windmill and read in Meudon with a telescope. The signals were letters from the alphabet, displayed one after the other, at the rate of the slowly turning mill. As soon as each letter appeared, it was recorded in a table by the observer at the observatory in Meudon. The inventor [Amontons] stated that by increasing the distances, with signals and fire signs one could quickly and cheaply send messages from Paris to Rome; but, I believe, he agreed with me, that this invention is more a curiosity than a practical form of traffic.

A method attributed to Amontons is also described in the *Encyclopaedia Britannica* of 1797, but this time much more systematically, and without the mention of windmills.[124]

> His method was this: let there be people placed in several stations, at such a distance from one another, that by the help of a telescope a man in one station may see a signal made in the next before him; he must immediately make the same signal, that it may be seen by persons in the station next after him, who are to communicate it to those in the following station, and so on.
>
> These signals may be as letters of the alphabet, or as a cipher, understood only by the two persons who are in the distant places, and not by those who make the signals. . . .
>
> Amontons tried this method in a small tract of land before several persons of the highest rank at the court in France.

The signaling methods of Hooke and of Amontons were apparently quite well-known in the eighteenth century. They are referred to in letters to *Gentleman's Magazine* from 1794, discussing Claude Chappe's telegraph designs.[125] They are also mentioned in Edelcrantz's treatise.[126] In footnote 29, for instance, Edelcrantz remarked:[127]

> Apart from Linguet, one usually credits the invention to both Amontons and to Hooke, but there is no real evidence to support this.

NEW LENS DESIGNS

The telescopes of the seventeenth century could produce superb images, even at high magnification levels. The restriction to single-element lenses, however, meant that the telescopes had to be made quite long to achieve optimal image quality.[128] Christiaan Huygens, for example, showed in 1656 that Saturn's "ears," as they were called by Galileo, were actually rings. He used a telescope of almost six meters long.

This problem was not solved until 1747, when Leonhard Euler A.D. 1747 (1707–1783) discovered that one could use the flaws of one lens to correct those of another, by using multiple lens elements in a compact design. Euler's goal was primarily to improve the quality of the microscope, by reducing flaws such as chromatic and spherical aberration, but the principles applied equally to the telescope. Shortly afterwards, in 1750, the Swede Samuel Klingenstjerna (1698–1765) made an extensive study of the color separation properties of different types of glass. And in 1757 all A.D. 1757 this new knowledge was combined in the construction of the so-called "Dollond telescope," by John Dollond (1706–1761) in England, with much improved image quality and resolution. It became the standard for many years to come, and was used in the optical telegraphic systems that followed within a matter of years.

The Non-Inventions

Before the attempts to build a better telegraph were successful, quite a few non-designs would be pursued. Most of these non-designs were efforts to exploit the simple observation that two magnetized objects will align themselves when held close together. The idea was that if two small magnets can do this at a few centimeters distance, two stronger magnets should be able to do this a few decimeters apart, and with some further study, special magnets might be able to allow communication from one city to the next. Figuring out who would be talking to whom, with a number of such magnets in use in different cities, was another one of the details to iron out in field studies. The important thing was that one knew quite definitely in which direction to search.

A.D. 1553 In 1553 a young Giambattista della Porta (1535–1615) published his *Magia Naturalis* which, for better or worse, became a standard reference for later scholars. Porta described several telegraphic instruments, one resembling a heliograph, another an acoustical device where people would shout messages through so-called "speaking tubes."[129] They are duly referred to by Edelcrantz in his treatise.[130] The book also contains brief mention of cryptographic systems of substitution ciphers. This, and his more encompassing *De Furtivis Literarum Notis*, published in 1563, gained Porta recognition as one of the founders of modern cryptography.[131] Especially in *Magia Naturalis*, however, Porta frequently allows his pen to be guided by his enthusiasm. The 1589 edition of *Magia Naturalis*, for instance, contains the following statement that inspired many of Porta's contemporaries and successors:[132]

> And to a friend that is at a far distance from us, and fast shut up in prison, we may relate our minds; which I doubt not may be done with two Mariner's Compasses, having the Alphabet writ about them.

Porta did not have such a method; he only thought there had to be one. To illustrate on what shaky grounds Porta's claim stood, the sentence that immediately follows the one about Mariner's Compasses, but rarely included in the quote, is:

> Upon this [also] depends the principle of perpetual motion, and more admirable things, which I shall here let pass.

A flurry of "inventions" soon followed. The first victim seems to have been A.D. 1600 Daniel Schwenter. In 1600 he published a book, titled *Steganologia et Steganographia*, under the assumed name of Johannes Hercules de Sunde, in which he describes a communication system based on the deflection of two magnetized compass needles.[133] Schwenter divided the alphabet into groups of four letters, each group assigned to a section of the compass. By moving a needle between one and four times into one of its sections, the sender could indicate a specific letter within the corresponding group.

In 1617 the Italian Famianus Strada published the first edition of his *Pro-* A.D. 1617
lusiones Academicae which also became a standard reference work. He
described the new invention in elaborate detail:[134]

> Therefore try the experiment, if you desire a friend who is at a distance to
> know anything to whom no letter could get, take a flat smooth disc, describe
> round the outside edges of the disc stops, and the first letters of the alphabet,
> in the order in which boys learn them, and place in the centre, lying horizon-
> tally, a dial-pin that has touched the magnet, so that, turned easily from
> thence, it can touch each separate letter that you desire.
>
> After the pattern of this one, construct another disc, described with a similar
> margin, and furnished with a pointer of iron—of iron that has received a
> motion from the same magnet. Let your friend about to depart carry this disc
> with him, and let it be agreed beforehand at what time, or on what days, he
> shall observe whether the dial-pin trembles, or what it marks with the indica-
> tor. These things being thus arranged, if you desire to address your friend
> secretly, whom a part of the earth separates far from you, bring your hand to
> the disc, take hold of the movable iron, here you observe the letters arranged
> round the whole margin, with stops of which there is need for words, hither
> direct the iron, and touch with the point the separate letters, now this one, and
> now the other, whilst, by turning the iron round again and again throughout
> these, you may distinctly express all the sentiments of your mind.
>
> Strange, but true! The friend who is far distant sees the movable iron tremble
> without the touch of any one, and to traverse, now in one, now in another direc-
> tion; he stands attentive, and observes the leading of the iron, and follows, by
> collecting the letters from each direction, with which, being formed into words,
> he perceives what may be intended, and learns from the iron as his interpreter.

It wasn't just a one-way system. Strada continued:

> Moreover, when he sees the dial-pin stop, he, in his turn, if he thinks of any
> things to answer, in the same manner by the letters being touched separately
> writes back to his friend.
>
> Oh, I wish this mode of writing may become in use, a letter would travel safer
> and quicker, fearing no plots of robbers and retarding rivers. The prince, with
> his own hands, might despatch business for himself. We, the race of scribes,
> escaped from an inky sea, would dedicate the pen to the Shores of Magnet.

Each new inventor guarded the secret mechanism of his device with his
life and more often than not refused to demonstrate it to anyone other
than the king of whatever country he happened to live in. Needless to
say, these kings quickly got wary of all the non-devices, and they soon
learned to reject such requests, which in turn made it harder for those
who were studying more realistic solutions.

In 1632 Galileo referred to the popularity of these non-inventions in his A.D. 1632
Dialogus de Systemate Mundi. In it, he has Sagredo say:[135]

> You remind me of a man who wanted to sell me a secret art that would allow
> me to speak to someone at a distance of 2–3 thousand miles, by means of the
> attraction of magnetized needles. When I told him that I would be delighted to

purchase the device, if only I was allowed to try it first, and that I would be satisfied if I could do so from one corner of the room to another, he answered that at such a short distance the effect would barely be visible. At that point I said farewell to the man and I told him I had no interest to travel to Egypt or Moscow before I could try the device, but if he wanted to move there I would be happy to remain in Venice and give the signals from here.

There were also more serious attempts, some of which contained concepts that would be rediscovered only hundreds of years later. Telegraph design became a popular pastime in the late eighteenth century.

A.D. 1782 On 8 June 1782, for instance, Dom Gauthey submitted two proposals to the Academy of Sciences in Paris. One was said to be an improvement of an early system used by Dupuis (about which more shortly). The other was a variation of an acoustical method that had been described earlier by Giambattista della Porta. Gauthey's variation of Porta's method was to replace the shouting of messages through metal tubes with the blowing of air puffs,[136] or the tapping of a code on the outside of the tubes with a hammer.[137] The tapping comes remarkably close to a Morse code, but no specific method of encoding is mentioned by Gauthey.

Gauthey called his machine a *télélogue*. Ignace Chappe wrote in 1824 that Gauthey had stipulated that his methods could not be disclosed unless they were adopted.[138] His original plans were kept sealed at the Academy of Sciences in Paris for almost half a century. The seals were broken on 6 February 1826, perhaps prompted by Ignace Chappe's publication, but Gauthey was long dead by then, and the plans received no further attention.[139]

A.D. 1784 A new device of a charming simplicity was proposed in 1784 by the Swiss watchmaker Christin. His invention was to connect the stations that wished to communicate with a system of shafts and gears.[140] The parties could signal each other by rotating a letter wheel. This device would probably have worked, although not over very large distances.

A.D. 1786 In 1786 the German professor Johann Bergstrasser (1732–1798) (sometimes also spelled as "Bergstraesser") constructed an optical telegraph line between Feldberg, Homberg and Phillippsruhe. Not much is known about the precise type of telegraph he used. Bergstrasser did, however, publish an influential study of communication methods in 1785, titled *Synthematographik*, referenced respectfully by Edelcrantz.[141] If the telegraph built by Bergstrasser was one of those he described in his book, it was no real competition for either Chappe's or Edelcrantz's later designs. There are indications that it was based on light flares. An eyewitness of an experiment performed by Bergstrasser in 1786 said:[142]

> I have seen your experiment of the fourth [4 April 1786] near Bergen, at a distance of roughly three hours, and saw both signals, the first consisting of two, and the second of three flares [German: *Raketen*].

A.D. 1787 The Czech musical director Jóseph Chudy developed a more interesting optical telegraph in 1787. His design consisted of a row of five lights that

42

Table 1.2 Long-Distance Communication Methods.

Method	First Recorded Use		Last Recorded Use	
Pigeons	Egypt	2900 B.C.	California	A.D. 1981
Runners/Couriers	Egypt	1928 B.C.	Pony Express	A.D. 1860
Beacons/Torches	Troy	1184 B.C.	England	A.D. 1588
Calling posts	Persia	400 B.C.	Germany[143]	A.D. 1796
Heliographs	Greece	400 B.C.	Arizona	A.D. 1886
Flags	Greece	400 B.C.	Maritime use	today

could individually be turned on or off, giving 2^5 possible code combinations. With a telescope, the code could be read from a distance and passed on from station to station.

Chudy's design would not get much attention. When Chappe's telegraph did, Chudy decided to publicize his contribution in the best way he could: by writing an opera. The premiere of this opera, *Der Telegraph oder die Fernschreibmaschine* (The Telegraph or the Telewriter), took place on 3 January 1796 in the city of Buda, today part of Budapest.

The most interesting part of Chudy's design is the use of the five-bit binary code, some hundred years before a similar five-bit code by the French telegraph operator Emile Baudot was adopted as International Telegraph Alphabet No. 2. Chudy was, however, not the first to develop such a five-bit binary code, even if we discard the torch telegraph of Polybius (see the Bibliographic Notes below).

In 1788, finally, the Frenchman Charles Francois Dupuis constructed a A.D. 1788 private telegraph line between Ménil-Montant and Bagneux, a few kilometers apart. The line was used until 1792 for a correspondence between Mr. Dupuis and a Mr. Fortin (sometimes spelled "Fortui"). No precise description of the telegraph itself has been preserved, other than a terse observation that it was an improvement of the design of Guillaume Amontons from 1690.[144] According to Chappe, Dupuis abandoned his design when the Chappes submitted their proposal to the Legislative Assembly in 1792.[145] Dupuis was a member of that body.

The success of Chappe's telegraph unmistakably started a new era in the history of long-distance communications.

Summary

There are many ways to transmit information over long distances, also without the help of electricity. Most of them have not only been tried, they have been applied throughout history on a remarkably large scale.

Table 1.2 summarizes the methods that have been applied, and gives the approximate dates of the earliest and the latest recorded use. Each type of system was initially used as a point-to-point communication method, e.g., a single messenger running a distance. In due time, though, most systems developed into sophisticated relay systems, with permanent posts at fixed distances, covering a fairly wide area. It should perhaps not be surprising that almost all methods have remained in use virtually up to the present day, give or take a few hundred years.[146]

There is just one class of systems that did not fully develop until the late eighteenth century A.D., but then dominated the landscape for nearly half a century: the optical semaphores. The remainder of this book is devoted to the people who first built them.

Bibliographic Notes

Most of the writings of historians such as Herodotus, Plutarch, Polybius, Thucydides, or Xenophon are available in modern translations, for example, in the Penguin Classics or Viking Library series. Nothing, of course, can equal the reading of these original texts. The bibliography on p. 210 of this book contain the details on the translations that we have used.

Systems of messengers and couriers on horseback are said to have existed also in China as early as the Chou Dynasty (1122–256 B.C.). Very few documents describing these systems have survived though. For a discussion see, for instance, [Dvornik 1974, p. 277], or [Olbricht 1954]. The relay systems that were used by the Mongol ruler Kublai Khan (sometimes spelled Kubilai Khan) were described in Marco Polo's *Travels*. Excerpts can also be found in [Dvornik 1974, p. 290–291].

Fire, smoke, and drum signals are also known to have been used until quite recently by African and Australian tribes, and by native Americans. It seems likely that the history of the usage of these methods dates back much further than we could ever hope to find written records. Good descriptions can be found in [Mallery 1879] and [Hodge 1910].

Outstanding surveys of early communication methods can also be found in [Bergstrasser 1785], [Bockmann 1794], [Chappe 1824], [Shaffner 1859], [Hennig 1908], [Appleyard 1930], [Hennig 1936], [Still 1946], [Michaelis 1965], [Woods 1965], [Herbarth 1978], [Aschoff 1984], and of course also in [Edelcrantz 1796]. The most thorough studies among these, roughly in order of importance, are [Aschoff 1984], [Hennig 1908], [Bergstrasser 1785], and [Woods 1965].

More details on naval flag signaling systems and their use at the battle of Trafalgar is contained in [Keegan 1988], and can also be found, in Swedish, in [Cyrus 1912].

Many of the fifteenth and sixteenth century maps that appear to show ball- or disc-semaphores in Spain were published in [Sider 1992]. Several of the maps show a semaphore tower on mount *Montjuich*, near the city of Barcelona. City records from Barcelona indicate that towers at this location have been used for signaling since at least A.D. 1073, when construction on a new stone signaling tower was begun. The first mention of the word *pomo*, which could refer to a ball or disc, in relation to this signaling post dates from 1534, see [Voltesbou 1940, Chapter 7]. The description from 1534, which is by far the oldest known reference to this type of semaphore, includes mention of a signaling code that details how the balls or discs are

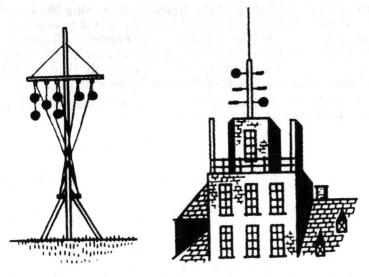

Figure 1.12 Dutch Semaphores—Nineteenth Century.
(Source: [Ringnalda 1902], p. 1)

to be displayed from a mast at different heights. In [Ringnalda 1902] and also in [Michaelis 1965] similar looking semaphores are reproduced, which were used for telegraphy around 1831 in Holland (cf. Figure 1.12). A variant of the naval telegraph that was used by the British in the early nineteenth century also appears to match this design. See, for instance, Plate II-1 in [Woods 1965] for a telegraph that was deployed between 1808 and 1814. It also uses series of discs or balls suspended from masts. More details on the use of disc telegraphs in the Netherlands and in Curacao in the nineteenth century can be found in Chapter Five of this book.

More about the early non-devices for communication based on magnetized needles can be found in [Fahie 1884]. Fahie lists over twenty works of sixteenth and seventeenth century authors, describing variations of telegraphs that were supposedly based on the use of magnets.

The principle of encoding up to 32 items with five symbols of two types only was described in 1641 by John Wilkins (1614–1672). In a summary he referred to his description as follows:[147]

> It is more convenient, indeed, that these Differences should be of as great Variety as the Letters of the Alphabet; but it is sufficient if they be but twofold, because Two alone may, with somewhat more Labour and Time, be well enough contrived to express all the rest. Thus any two Letters or Numbers, suppose A B being transposed through five Places, will yield Thirty two Differences, and so consequently will superabundantly serve for the Four and twenty Letters, as was before more largely explained in the Ninth Chapter.

45

Wilkins based himself on Sir Francis Bacon (1561–1626), who in 1623 described a binary encoding of the alphabet, also using the letters A and B.[148] The earliest reference to binary encoding is said to appear in a work from around 1605 by the English mathematician Thomas Harriot (1560–1621).[149] The credit for inventing a binary arithmetic based on this encoding, finally, was claimed in 1697, and first published in 1703, by the German mathematician Gottfried Wilhelm Leibniz (1646–1716).

Robert Hooke's lecture from 1684, finally, is included in [Hooke 1726], which was published after his death.

(Source: [Belloc 1888], p. 97)

Chapter Two
Claude Chappe

Claude Chappe was an unusual man. Under the most unlikely circumstances, in the middle of an eighteenth century revolution, he managed to build a telegraph network that spanned the entire country of France, with branches leading into Holland, Germany, Italy, and Spain. His success in France inspired similar work in almost every other European country. Optical telegraph lines of many different designs sprang up in Sweden, Norway, Finland, Denmark, England, Poland, and Russia, almost as quickly as the word about Chappe's success could spread.

What characterized Claude Chappe was not luck, but an admirable drive and a relentless dedication to perfection, even under adversity. He faced the violence of the French Revolution, with many people around him literally losing their heads over lesser causes than Chappe advocated. He also faced sometimes severe competition from others who claimed to have built a better telegraph, or a different one, or who simply claimed to have done it all before. Although some of the latter claims may have been partly justified, as we shall see, it was perseverance and dedication that made the difference between Chappe and his predecessors.

Of Barons and Kings

Claude Chappe was born on Christmas day 1763, in a little town called Brûlon, about 200 km (130 miles) southwest of Paris, in what is today called the Sarthe Department.[1]   A.D. 1763

At this time, France was still ruled by King Louis XV, living in splendor at the Royal Palace in Versailles, and entertained by mistresses such as Madame de Pompadour. Failing the entertainment of a mistress, the

1. The notes to this chapter start at p. 251.

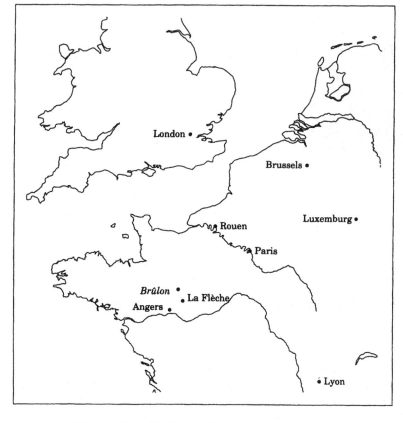

Figure 2.1 Brûlon—Chappe's Birthplace.

French king could resort to the musical entertainment of performers such as the young Mozart.[2] The French revolution (1789–1799) was still safely a couple of decades away.

Chappe was born into a fairly influential family. His grandfather was a baron. According to the rules of nobility, though, that title could only be passed to the eldest son of the family. In this case, that was Claude's uncle Jean Baptiste Chappe d'Auteroche, about whom we will learn more shortly. Claude's father, Ignace Chappe d'Auteroche (1724–1783), although not himself a baron, was clearly still a man of influence. He worked for a while as a parliamentary lawyer, and at one time received an appointment as *Directeur des Domaines* of the French king in Rouen.

On 13 February 1762, when he was 37 years old, Ignace Chappe d'Auteroche married 31-year-old Marie-Renée de Vernay de Vert.[3] Within the next eleven years the couple had ten children, three of whom died as infants. The names of the seven surviving children, and the dates they were born, are:

Ignace Urbain Jean	26 November	1762
Claude	25 December	1763
Marie Marthe	26 December	1763
Pierre Francois	11 August	1765
Sophie Francois	4 March	1767
René	3 September	1769
Abraham	6 May	1773

The eldest son, Ignace Urbain Jean, was born at Laval; all other children were born at Brûlon. Marie Marthe was, of course, Claude's twin sister. We can assume that Claude was born close to midnight, and Marie Marthe shortly thereafter. The birth register in Brûlon names Claude Nouët as Claude Chappe's godfather. Nouët was a former cavalier in the royal army, and a well-respected friend of the family.

We know very little of what happened to the two sisters, but all four of Claude's brothers, Ignace, Pierre, René, and Abraham, at one time or another became involved in the construction and maintenance of the later Telegraph Administration.

The young Claude Chappe was raised for the church, and studied to become an *Abbé Commendataire*. He first attended the *College de Joyeuse* in Rouen. Later, he moved to a seminary at La Flèche, about 30 km (18 miles) southeast of Brûlon.[4] When he graduated from the seminary in around 1783, Claude obtained two religious benefices, Saint-Martin de A.D. 1783 Châlautre and Baignolet, which provided him with ample funds and few obligations.[5]

During his religious training, Claude showed a strong interest in science. He became acquainted with a group of physicists in Paris, and later joined the prestigious *Société Philomatique*.[6] Chappe performed many experiments in physics, and, starting in 1789, published the results in several A.D. 1789 papers, some written jointly with other physicists.[7]

Some say that even before 1789 Claude had started performing experiments with telegraphy, attempting to communicate with his brother Ignace who attended a seminary school in Angers, southwest of La Flèche.[8] No record to substantiate that claim can be found today, though. It seems improbable, given that the distance between La Flèche and Angers is about 48 km (30 miles). The various optical telegraph designs developed later by Chappe and others could not have covered that distance. In a book published in 1824, Ignace Chappe recalls that:[9]

> The Chappes corresponded routinely with each other, using this device [the synchronized system—to be discussed], at a distance of 3 leagues.

The 3 leagues (14.5 km) would clearly not have covered the distance from La Flèche to Angers, but it is approximately the distance from Brûlon to Parcé, a small town near La Flèche. Brûlon and Parcé were the two sites used in the first reliably documented experiments, as we shall see below.

A FAMOUS UNCLE

The piety of Chappe's youth and his remarkable career as an engineer and inventor may be easy to explain. He almost duplicated the life of his uncle, Abbé Jean Baptiste Chappe d'Auteroche (1722–1769). This uncle was also first ordained as a priest, but later acquired some fame as an astronomer, earning him a membership in the French Academy of Sciences. He worked on cartographical maps of France with César Francois Cassini de Thury, the director of the Paris Observatory and the third generation in a line of famous astronomers and cartographers. In 1752, Chappe's uncle published a translation of the *Tables* of the English astronomer Edmond Halley (of Halley's comet). He first obtained independent recognition in 1761, with the publication of *Voyage en Siberie*. In this book, which can still be found in most good libraries, the Abbé Chappe described the passage of the planet Venus in front of the sun in the early morning hours of 6 June 1761. To make the observation, he had traveled to the Russian city of Tobolsk.

A.D. 1752

A.D. 1761

The life of Claude's famous uncle had a peculiar end. A new transit of Venus had been predicted for 3 June 1769, and Jean Baptiste decided to travel to Baja California for the best view. He did so despite reports of contagious diseases ravaging that part of the world at the time. He faithfully made the observation, and as a truly dedicated scientist decided to stay on another two weeks to observe also a lunar eclipse predicted for 18 June 1769. In those two extra weeks he caught yellow fever and died 1 August 1769. He was buried in the village of Saint-Joseph, in California. On 14 November a eulogy was read for him at the Academy of Sciences in Paris. The book describing his observation of the transit of Venus was published by a friend well after his death.

A.D. 1769

Some of this passion for religion and science must have rubbed off on the young Claude Chappe. Abraham Chappe later wrote that the first book Claude read in his youth was the famous *Voyage en Siberie*. He added:[10]

> Reading this book greatly inspired him, and gave him a taste for the physical sciences. From this point on, all his studies, and even his pastimes, were focused on that subject.

Because of his astronomer uncle, Claude may also have become familiar with the properties of telescopes. A good quality telescope later became one of the most important devices for turning an optical telegraph from a curiosity into a practical device.

The First Experiments

On 14 July 1789 the French Revolution began in earnest with the storming of the Bastille in Paris, and the rules of life changed. In the next few months, Louis XVI and Marie Antoinette were evicted from the Palace in Versailles and moved to Paris. A range of traditional privileges held by the nobility and the religious orders was abolished by a new Legislative Assembly. As a small side effect, Claude Chappe lost his religious benefices on 2 November 1789, and had to return to Brûlon newly unemployed.

In the turmoil of the revolution, Claude's brothers had also lost their jobs and had returned home to Brûlon.[11] Together they decided to set up a shop to work on telegraphs.

This decision to start working on telegraphs was not as unusual as it may seem. Proposals for telegraphs of all different kinds, ranging from the most frivolous and impractical to serious precursors of the later electrical telegraphs, were being pursued by many.

One of the more practical proposals came from De Courrejolles, a captain in the French navy.[12] In February 1783, De Courrejolles was engaged in battle with the English fleet, at what is described as the Turkish or Ionic Isles, about 145 km (90 miles) northeast of Cap Francois. He found himself surrounded by an English squadron commanded by Admiral Hood. De Courrejolles had a simple optical telegraph erected at a mountain top on the coast of one of the islands, and used it to monitor the enemy's movements. Every change in position was reported by the telegraph. Using this information De Courrejolles was able to overrun a squadron commanded by the then Captain (later Admiral) Nelson, and force the English fleet to retreat.[13] Inspired by this success, De Courrejolles submitted a proposal to the French Minister of War to have the army adopt optical telegraphs for signaling purposes. Though De Courrejolles was unsuccessful at that time, he may well have paved the way for Chappe.

No precise information has survived on the type of semaphore used by Courrejolles. An indication that it may have resembled one of Chappe's later designs is that Courrejolles later accused Chappe of plagiarism, as we shall see below.

THE SYNCHRONIZED SYSTEM

The brothers Chappe spent the winter of 1790–1791 experimenting with telegraph designs. In March 1791, they were ready for a first public demonstration of the telegraph they had constructed. The telegraph design used in this first experiment was described by the Chappes as a "pendulum system." It is usually referred to as the *Synchronized System*.

For the first experiments, two telegraphs were used, possibly merely two modified pendulum clocks. One was placed on a terrace at the former location of a castle in Chappe's hometown Brûlon, and the other at the window of a private house in Parcé, a little town at a distance of roughly 16 km (10 miles), and about halfway between Brûlon and La Flèche. The Brûlon location, referred to in most documents as "the castle," was in reality a regular house, built on the spot where a larger castle used to stand. The castle was destroyed in 1774.[14] The house that replaced it, and where the experiment took place, was itself also destroyed by fire in 1793.

Unfortunately, we do not have an accurate description of the working of the pendulums that were used in the first experiment, and the information we have leaves many questions unanswered. The most reliable record that has survived is a description given by Ignace Chappe, which reads as follows.[15]

Figure 2.2 Dubious Representation of the Synchronized System.
(Source: [Figuier 1868])

The first telegraphic correspondence that we performed was done with two pendulum clocks, that were kept in perfect synchrony; the face of the clocks was divided into ten parts, each part designating a different numeral [French: *un chiffre de la numération ordinaire*]. When the pointer of one clock passed over the number one wanted to indicate, a sound was made, announcing to the correspondent that the number which also his pointer indicated at the moment that the sound was heard, was significant. By representing the words in a dictionary with successive numbers one could thus transmit any thought.

An illustration of the telegraph that was supposedly used in this first experiment (Figure 2.2) is reproduced in virtually every source, with the notable exception of Chappe's book. Ignace Chappe does not present drawings for any of the early designs, and it appears that his verbal description is at odds with the ones that others used.

The most popular illustration shows not 10 but 16 divisions of the clock face, each one indicated not with a number but with a symbolic code that very closely resembles the symbols used by Robert Hooke in his experiments in 1684.[16] Probably based on this illustration, many later writers have suggested that Chappe borrowed some of his ideas from Hooke. It is not known with certainty where the dubious illustration first originated.[17]

As Chappe indicated, to operate correctly, the hands of the clocks of neighboring stations had to be synchronized. The Chappes had an original solution to this problem:[18]

> To transmit a phrase, the two clocks (separated by 400 meters in the first experiments) were set in motion, at the same instant. A sound was made, by striking a casserole [stewpan], at the moment that the pointer was over that part of the clock-face that corresponded with the number of the code one wished to signal.

The two pointers rotated by the pull of falling weights. We can imagine that a first sound signal at the sending station was used to indicate to the telegraph operators at what precise moment the weights had to be released to start the pointers rotating. Each new signal could then be used to transmit a single code symbol, until either the message was completed or the weights would hit the floor and the pointers stopped.

The initial experiments were held over distances up to ca. 400 meters (1300 feet), behind the parental house in Brûlon.[19] At this distance, the sound signals could still easily be heard, but it was clear also at that time that it would eventually have to be replaced if longer distances were to be covered. Abraham Chappe later wrote that Claude performed many experiments to find a good alternative, including the use of electrical signals traveling through conducting wires. He records that an optical method was only chosen[20]

> . . . after having tried, unsuccessfully, electricity, various acoustical methods, the use of smoke produced by different types of combustible materials, etc.

The idea to use an electrical signal had to be abandoned when no adequate insulators could be found for the wires. Ignace Chappe wrote in 1824 that the signals could also be given visually, with the help of large black and white surfaces that could be flipped at the moment that otherwise the sound signal would have been given. Of course, a proper application of any of these alternative synchronization methods could have replaced the whole telegraph, but the Chappes did not realize it at the time.

The first experiment took place on 2 March 1791 before a collection of respected officials from the two towns. The following sworn affidavit of the experiment was given by the eyewitnesses at Parcé.[21]

> Today, 2 March 1791, at 11 A.M., we, the undersigned municipal officers from Parcé, district Sablé, département of Sarthe, in the presence of MM. Francois Delauney de Fresney, Julien Delauney de la Motte, Léon Delauney, Prosper Delauney, René Taillay, Jean-André Tellot, royal notary and elected representative of the département de la Mayenne, all inhabitants of Laval; Etienne Eutrope Brossard, royal notary at Avoise, Jean-Baptiste-Joseph Gillier de la Chererollais, curator of Saint-Pierre de Parcé.

At the invitation of Mr. Claude Chappe, we have gone to the house of Mr. Ambroise Perrotin, in the aforementioned city of Parcé, to observe the result of an invention intended to communicate and correspond in the shortest amount of time.

First, we were led into a room of the said house, by the said Mr. Claude Chappe, and we found there a pendulum clock, and a telescope pointing in the direction of Brûlon, 4 leagues distant from Parcé.

Next, the said Mr. Claude Chappe aimed the telescope directly at Brûlon, announcing that even though the weather was rainy, his correspondent at Brûlon would proceed by initiating a transmission that would be dictated to him by the municipal officers at that site; and while continuously keeping his eye at the telescope, he successively, within the space of four minutes, dictated to Mr. Pierre Francois Chappe, his brother, various characters, unknown to us. By translating these characters, the following phrase was produced: *Si vous réussissez vous serez bientôt couvert de gloire* [If you succeed you will soon bask in glory].

Done and attested to in Parcé, at the house of the said Mr. Perrotin, before midday, at said day and year. [Followed by a list of signatures.]

It is curious that the affidavit mentions that the message was encoded in "characters, unknown to us" (French: *caractères, à nous inconnus*), although Ignace Chappe indicates that the encoding was done in numerals. It could also be that the phrase indicated unknown "encodings" rather than unknown "symbols," but it isn't clear from the text.

The matching affidavit from the eyewitnesses at Brûlon is also preserved. It gives some extra clues about the method of signaling used in this test.

Today 2 March 1791, at 11 A.M., we, municipal officers at Brûlon, district Sablé, département of Sarthe, have accompanied MM. Avenant, vicar, and Jean Audruger de la Maisonneuve, doctor, from Brûlon, to the castle of said Brûlon, at the invitation that was given us for the purpose of witnessing, and confirming the authenticity of an invention of Mr. Claude Chappe, nephew of the celebrated Abbé of the same name, intended to correspond and transmit news in a very short period of time.

First, we went with Mr. René Chappe, brother of Mr. Claude Chappe, to the terrace at the castle, and there we found a pendulum clock and a movable tableau, with two sides, one being white and one black.

Next, Mr. René Chappe informed us that Mr. Claude Chappe was at that time at Parcé, at a distance from Brûlon of 4 leagues, to receive what he was about to transmit. He asked us to dictate a phrase to him, or any series of phrases of our choosing. In response, Mr. Chenou, doctor, proposed the following phrase: *Si vous réussissez vous serez bientôt couvert de gloire.* Immediately, said Mr. René Chappe, after pointing out to us that the weather was rainy, and that the atmosphere was obscured by a light mist, contemplated said phrase, and proceeded to transmit it while moving the tableau in various ways, which lasted four minutes. He then told us that the said phrase had actually been transmitted to Parcé; as an inspection of the notary report, drafted by the municipal officers at that location would demonstrate.

Done and attested to in Brûlon, at said castle, at midday, at said day and year. [Followed by a list of signatures.]

Since the phrase of nine words, or 55 letters, was transmitted in just four minutes, it can be ruled out that the pendulum ran at a normal speed.[22] In that case the second hand of the clock could have indicated no more than one code per minute. If a dictionary of, say, 1000 words was used, every word would have been required one, two, or three digits to encode. This would mean that between 9 and 27 (3 × 9) codes were transmitted in 240 seconds. If this is correct, the pointer on the clock rotated through the code space of the 10 available numbers once every 10 to 30 seconds.

Interesting also is the mention of the movable tableau that was being manipulated by René Chappe during the experiment. It means that synchronization was no longer done by striking a stewpan, but was given visually with black and white surfaces. Abraham Chappe wrote in 1840 that the tableau was 1.66 × 1.33 meter, and mounted on an axis 4 meters above the ground.[23]

The experiment was repeated, with the same witnesses, at 3 P.M. of the same day, and a third time at 10:30 A.M. the next day, 3 March 1791. The phrase from the second test, transmitted by Claude Chappe in Parcé to his brother Pierre-Francois at Brûlon, was: *L'Assembleé nationale récompensera les experiences utiles au public.* [The national assembly will reward experiments that are useful to the public.] This time the phrase took 6 minutes and 20 seconds to transmit. Though the phrase was probably not made up by Chappe himself, it perfectly illustrates what his ultimate ambition was, even at this early stage. From the third test we only know that the phrase that was transmitted contained 25 words; it was not recorded how long it took to transmit it.

THE POLITICS OF INVENTION

Claude Chappe used the affidavits within a few months to support a first request to the Legislative Assembly to permit and support the construction of a true telegraph line. The request specifically asked for permission to perform further experiments at the *Barrière de l'Etoile* in Paris. This is where the hard road to success really began for Chappe. Understandably, it was much harder to secure government funding for the construction of a telegraph network than it was to develop a working telegraph in the first place. What sets Chappe apart from his many contemporary inventors was his stamina in solving this part of the problem adequately. He simply refused to give up until the network was a fact.

Even the request to perform experiments in Paris, rather than to continue experiments in Brûlon, was probably, and appropriately, pursued more for its political than for its technical merits. In another astute political move, the same year that the first experiments were held Claude's brother Ignace volunteered for, and was elected to, the new Legislative Assembly in Paris. He became a Deputy to the Assembly on 1 October 1791, A.D. 1791 representing Sarthe. He also became a member of the Committee for Public Instruction, which had an important advisory role in the consideration of new inventions. Through Ignace, and the Committee of Public Instruction, Claude Chappe would be able to gain access to the Legislative

Assembly to defend his proposals personally. The first request, however, just like De Courrejolles's earlier attempt, was unsuccessful. Chappe succeeded only in obtaining permission from the local commune near the *Etoile* to erect his telegraph.

It is not certain what type of telegraph Chappe was planning to build at this site. According to Abraham Chappe, writing in 1840, the materials for its construction were stolen before any tests could be done.[24]

A.D. 1792 Not in the least discouraged by these experiences, on 22 March 1792 Claude Chappe submitted a new proposal to the Legislative Assembly. He wanted to have his design evaluated in a serious experiment. With help from his brother Ignace, Claude obtained permission to address the Assembly in Paris on 24 March 1792 to explain his plan. The text of his address has been preserved.[25]

Mr. President,

I have come to offer to the National Assembly the tribute of a discovery that I believe to be useful to the public cause. This discovery provides a simple method for rapidly communicating over great distances, anything that could be the subject of a correspondence. The report of an event or an occurrence could be transmitted, by night or by day, over more than 40 miles in under 46 minutes. This transmission takes place almost as rapidly over a much larger distance (the time required for the communication does not increase proportionally with the distance). I can, in 20 minutes, transmit over a distance of 8 to 10 miles, the following, or any other similar phrase: "Lukner has left for Mons to besiege that city. Bender is advancing for its defense. The two generals are present. Tomorrow the battle will start." These same phrases are communicated in 24 minutes over a distance twice that of before; in 33 minutes they cover 50 miles. The transmission over a distance of 100 miles requires just 12 minutes more. Among the many useful applications for which this discovery can be used, there is one that, under the present circumstances, is of the greatest importance. It offers a reliable way of establishing a correspondence by which the legislative branch of the government could send its orders to our frontiers, and receive a response from there while still in session.

My assertions are not just based on a simple theory. Many successful experiments, held at a distance of 10 miles, in the Sarthe department, are for me a certain guarantee that this can be accomplished. The attached affidavits, drawn up at two municipalities, in the presence of a range of witnesses, attest to its authenticity. The obstacle that seems to me to be the most difficult to overcome is the popular suspicion that usually confronts those who pursue projects such as these. I could never have escaped from the fear that has overtaken them, if I was not sustained by the conviction that I should, as every French citizen, today more than ever, contribute to his country what he can.

I ask, Sirs, that the Assembly submit to one of its committees the examination of this project that I have the honor to announce to you, so that they can appoint delegates to observe the results of an experiment readily performed at a distance of 8 to 10 miles, and convince themselves that the same can be accomplished at any distance. I will perform this experiment, and in addition, at any distance that is requested, and I ask only, in case of success, to be reimbursed for the expenses that are made.

Figure 2.3 Destruction of the Panel Telegraph
(Source: [Figuier 1868])

Curiously, the proposal does not detail a specific method, nor does it contain any mention of the word *telegraph*. It is said, that at this time Chappe called his device a *tachygraphe*, i.e., a "rapid writer," although also that term is not used here.[26]

As requested, the proposal was promptly delegated to a committee. About six months passed in which Chappe worked feverishly to make certain that he would be ready when called upon to perform the experiment.

THE PANEL TELEGRAPH

Not satisfied with the use of the pendulum system, Chappe had started experimenting with a different design. He built a rectangular wooden frame with five sliding panels (in French *persiennes*) that could be displayed or obscured individually with pulleys. The five panels trivially produced a five-bit binary code, with $2^5 = 32$ possible combinations, more than three times as many codes as used in the first design.

To avoid further mishaps, Chappe also moved from the *Etoile* to the quieter park of *Ménilmontant* in the town of Belleville, just to the northeast of Paris. But it was to no avail. Before any tests could be performed, the telegraphs were destroyed by an angry mob. The system was suspected to be a subversive instrument, meant to send signals to the enemy, which at this time included royalists, Austrians, Prussians, and Englishmen. Ignace Chappe described the events as follows:[27]

This new experiment carried some risks for those involved: a crowd had formed in the Parc Saint-Fargeau [at Ménilmontant]; the telegraph was set on fire, and when the workers returned to the park to continue their work, the crowd had to be prevented from throwing them into the fire as well. The experiment could not be continued . . .

It is intriguing to see how close Chappe came to the shutter systems that the Swedes and the British later adopted. In 1794, Abraham Edelcrantz would perform virtually the same experiments as Chappe, comparing semaphore arms to tilting shutters, and arrived at different conclusions. Still, Ignace Chappe, describing Edelcrantz's system in 1824, considered his shutter system an independent invention. He wrote:[28]

M. Endelcrantz [the name is misspelled consistently by Chappe], author of the Swedish telegraph, felt the correctness of these observations [i.e., about the necessity of tests]; he has made a large number of experiments to develop an idea that was entirely unknown before him: the usage of shutters that can either block light or permit it to pass through.

There is not even a mention in Ignace's account that the shutter system resembles the original panel system.

On 12 September, shortly after the destruction of the panel telegraphs, Chappe wrote another letter to the Legislative Assembly, describing his difficulties, but also announcing that he could be ready to perform a demonstration within two weeks. But his timing was poor. The Legislative Assembly was disbanded that month, and replaced with a National Convention. Ignace Chappe was not re-elected to the new body, so part of Claude's influence was lost in the transition.

A.D. 1792 The National Convention temporarily had more important things on its agenda than new proposals for telegraphs. On 10 August 1792, a mob had stormed the royal palace at the Tuileries, where the king and his family had, in effect, been kept hostage since their eviction from the Versailles palace three years earlier. After a short scuffle, King Louis XVI and Marie Antoinette were then imprisoned at the ominous "Temple" dungeon on 13 August. In its first session, on 21 September 1792, the National Convention sanctioned these decisions and it voted unanimously to abolish the monarchy and to establish a French Republic.

Apparently Claude Chappe was not too impressed with all this upheaval. He was not one to keep a low profile. On 9 October he resubmitted his proposal to the National Convention, which decided to delegate it to a fresh new committee. Then, on 15 October 1792 Chappe sent another letter to the convention, asking for official authorization to rebuild his telegraphs. Also that request was delegated to a committee.

A.D. 1793 The story again did not end there. The infamous "Reign of Terror" was about to begin. On 21 January 1793 King Louis XVI was beheaded, and in April of that year the Committee of Public Safety started its persecution of all those suspected of opposing the revolution. On 1 February war was declared on Britain and the Netherlands, and on 7 March also on

Spain. Miraculously, the telegraph study was not discarded as utterly irrelevant under those circumstances.

THE SEMAPHORE TELEGRAPH

Around this time Claude Chappe concluded that the panel telegraph had been a false start, and he changed designs once more. As Ignace noted:[29]

> Some time later [we] established with certainty that elongated objects were better visible than the sliding panels adopted before.

The semaphore telegraph that Chappe designed next consisted of a large horizontal beam, called a *regulator*, with two smaller wings, called *indicators*, mounted at the ends, seemingly mimicking a person with wide-outstretched arms, holding a signal flag in each hand. The angles of the indicators, and independently also the position of the large regulator beam, could be varied in increments of 45 degrees, sufficient for the encoding of hundreds of symbols, as we will see shortly (see p. 79).

Chappe had found a few allies in the legislative bodies, the most prominent of whom was deputy Charles-Gilbert Romme (1750–1795).[30] On 1 April 1793 Romme intervened at the Convention on Chappe's behalf. He gave a speech that strongly supported Chappe's proposals, saying:[31]

> Many memoranda on this subject [i.e., telegraph proposals] have been presented to the Legislative Assembly, and have been delegated to the Committee for Public Instruction; just one of those truly merits attention. Citizen Chappe offers an ingenious method to write in the air, using a small number of symbols, simply formed from straight line segments, easily distinguished from one another, that can be executed rapidly and clearly over great distances.

Romme duly noted the potential importance of the invention for military purposes in this revolutionary period, and proposed to allocate 6,000 francs immediately to fund the construction of the telegraphs for the proposed experiments. This time the proposal was not delegated, but simply accepted. Two deputies, Joseph Lakanal and Pierre Claude Francois Daunou, were appointed official observers for the Convention on 6 April. A few days later a third observer, Louis Arbogast, was added. As it turned out, Joseph Lakanal, a well-respected scientist at the time, was also a strong ally of Chappe. Arbogast, a professor of mathematics, and Daunou, a jurist and historian, were more conservative, but also somewhat less influential than Lakanal.[32]

Ignace Chappe, though no longer an elected representative, was still actively involved in the lobby to have the proposal approved. It is recorded that at this moment the term *tachygraphe* was first replaced with the term *télégraphe*, or "far writer," as a result of a conversation between Ignace Chappe and Count André Francois Miot de Mélito, who was then *Chèf de Division à l'Interieur*.[33]

The danger of having telegraphs demolished by mobs still existed. On 2 July 1793 Joseph Lakanal filed a report to the Convention on Chappe's

Figure 2.4 The Semaphore Telegraph.
(Coll. Musée de la Poste, Paris)

behalf, requesting officially that the mayors of the three communities where the first telegraphs were being erected would be ordered to take measures for the protection of the telegraphs. The proposal was accepted. The three locations that had been selected were the park Ménilmontant in Belleville, the heights of Ecouen at 15 km north of Belleville, and the town of Saint-Martin-du-Tertre, another 11 km further north.

On 12 July 1793 the official test was held, with all three observers from the committee present. Daunou was at the Belleville station with Claude Chappe; Lakanal and Arbogast were at Saint-Martin-du-Tertre, which was operated by Abraham Chappe. At 4:26 P.M. the first signals were exchanged, and within 11 minutes thereafter Daunou completed the transmission of the following message:

> Daunou has arrived here. He announces that the National Convention has just authorized his Committee of General Security to put seals on the papers of the deputies.

The answer from Lakanal arrived 9 minutes later. It was probably the result of some painstaking earlier deliberations between Lakanal and Arbogast, since it didn't really respond much to Daunou's enthusiasm for the new seals. It said:

> The inhabitants of this beautiful region are worthy of liberty by their respect for the National Convention and its laws.

Communication continued a while longer, until the intermediate station at Ecouen signaled that it was unable to dispatch any further messages.

Lakanal's report to the Convention was submitted on 25 July 1793, and read the next day. In the report, Lakanal emphasized the accuracy and security of the telegraphic transmissions. He noted that several transmission errors were made during the experiment, but that they were easily recognized and corrected.

Things moved quickly from here on. On 26 July 1793 the decision was made to establish a French state telegraph. On 4 August 1793 the Convention appropriated 58,400 francs for the construction of a first line of fifteen stations from Paris to Lille, at the frontier with the Austrian Netherlands (now part of Belgium), about 190 km (120 miles) north of Paris. On 24 September 1793, the Convention gave blanket permission to the Chappes to place telegraphs in any belfries, towers, or emplacements of their choosing. They also had permission to remove any trees that interfered with the line of vision between the stations. Permission was also granted for Chappe to hire personnel, and to draft the first rules and regulations for the French telegraph.

Claude Chappe was given the title of *Ingénieur Télégraphe*,[34] with the military rank of an engineering lieutenant,[35] a salary of 600 francs per month, and the permanent use of a government horse. The name *stationaire* was introduced for the telegraph attendants, a name that would continue to be used until 1862. At Chappe's request, his brothers Ignace, Abraham, and Pierre Francois were appointed as administrators of the line to Lille, at 500 francs per month each. The office boys assigned to them received a modest 125 francs.

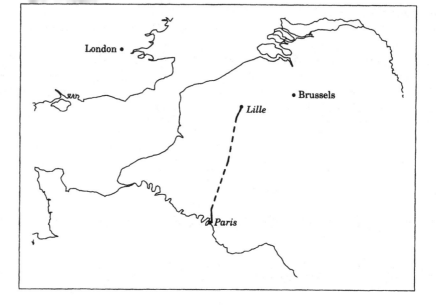

Figure 2.5 The First Line from Paris to Lille (1794).

Success

The Chappes now started working on the design of the mechanics of the stations. To construct the controls of the telegraph, an intricate system of pulleys and ropes, Claude Chappe consulted Abraham Louis Bréguet (1747–1823), a well-known watchmaker at the time. For the design of the all-important code tables, it is often said that he relied on Léon Delauney, a cousin of the Chappes who had been a staff member of the French Consulate in Lisbon, and was experienced in diplomatic ciphers and codes.[36] According to the affidavits from the first experiments in 1791, Léon Delauney and his brother Prosper had been involved in the experiments from the very start in Brûlon.

To make sure that a communication with Lille could be established, even if that city were to fall under a siege by the enemy while the work was in progress, Claude Chappe sent his brother Abraham to Lille with instructions to remain there until the line was completed. The conditions under which Abraham Chappe had to work in the year that followed are recorded in letters he sent to Claude.[37] Funds appropriated by the Convention were always slow in coming, and the Chappes understandably had a hard time convincing workers to stay on the job without pay, sometimes for weeks on end. Abraham noted in one of his letters that the people in Lille were starting to avoid him, and were treating him with increasing hostility.

A.D. 1794 On 30 April 1794 all stations along the line to Lille were manned and preparations for the first trial transmissions began. An early logbook

Figure 2.6 Construction of a Telegraph Station.
(Source: [Belloc 1888], p. 91)

reveals that the telegraph line was routinely transmitting texts of decrees from the National Convention from Paris to Lille, at least as early as 17 May 1794.[38]

On 16 July 1794, less than one year after the decision of the Convention to build a line, the connection between Paris and Lille was formally declared open. There were two stations in the city of Paris itself, the first at the Louvre, and the second at the St. Pierre tower on the MontMartre. The next three stations along the line were the ones from the experiment: Belleville, Ecouen, and Saint-Martin-du-Tertre. The remaining stations were Ercuis, Clermont de l'Oise, Fouilleuse, Belloy, Boulogne la Grasse, Parvillers, Lihons, Dompierre, Guinchy, Hamelincourt/Brévillers, Théluch, Carvin, and Lille (tour Saint-Pierre).

On 15 August 1794 the first official message passed along this line from Lille to Paris, reporting the recapture of the city of LeQuesnoy from the Austrians and Prussians by the French generals Sherer and Marescot. The message arrived in Paris within a few hours after the recapture had taken place, and, of course, the delegates were impressed.[39] Two days later, delegate Bertrand Barère de Vieuzac described the sentiment in a speech to the Convention, as follows:

> Modern peoples by printing, gunpowder, the compass and the language of telegraph signs, have made vanish the greatest obstacles which have opposed the civilization of men, and made possible their union in great republics. It is thus that the arts and sciences serve liberty.

Two weeks later, on 30 August 1794, the telegraph was used again to report happy news: the recapture of Condé.[40] The message read as follows, being restricted to the words that occurred in the vocabulary:

> *Condé être restituer à la Republique. Reddition avoir eu lieu ce matin à six heures.* [Condé is restored to the Republic. Surrender took place this morning at six o'clock.]

These first two messages firmly established the reputation of both the optical telegraph and of its creator. More reports of victories followed in 1794 and 1795 as the French advanced north into Holland, and Chappe looked better with every piece of good news that arrived in Paris. Soon Claude Chappe was being hailed as a "benefactor of the motherland." The future of the French telegraph network was virtually guaranteed. On 3 October 1794 a decision was made to build a second line, originally intended to connect Paris to Landau via Metz and Strasbourg.[41] Construction on the new line started the same year, but incurred many delays. It took four years before the connection with Strasbourg was established, and by that time it was decided not to extend the line further.

In December 1794 Chappe moved his workshop from No. 23 Quai d'Orsay to No. 9 Rue de l'Université, the new headquarters for the Telegraph Administration, known as l'Hôtel Villeroy.

MONGE'S DESIGN
Despite the success, Chappe still was not satisfied with the performance of the semaphore telegraph. The time to transmit messages was longer than he had expected, and the relatively poor visibility of the stations caused too many transmission errors. There is a note from Abraham Chappe written just two days after the first message was successfully transmitted, announcing the recapture of LeQuesnoy, in which he complains to Claude that far too many service interruptions occur, making effective use of the

Figure 2.7 Gaspard Monge's Design.
(Source: [Chappe 1824])

telegraph almost impossible. According to the logbooks, the transmission of the second important message, about the recapture of Condé, was also hit by an unscheduled interruption lasting one hour. Fortunately, enough of the message had arrived at the time of the interruption that Claude Chappe decided to deliver it to the Convention immediately, without waiting for its completion.

A number of ways were considered to alleviate the problems. First, Claude Chappe decided to have extra stations built along the line from Paris to Lille. These auxiliary stations could be included in the transmission chain when visibility was low, for instance, in early morning fog. Second, he proposed to enlarge the regulator from roughly 4 meters to close to 15 meters to improve its visibility. Third, he consulted French mathematician Gaspard Monge (1746–1818) about the problem. Monge recommended increasing the number of arms (often also called "wings" or "indicators") from two to seven to increase the code space and hence the speed of transmission (Figure 2.7).

Monge designed a code for a seven-indicator semaphore, and several sources report that many telegraphs of this type were built for the Paris to Strasbourg line. But neither Monge's seven-indicator telegraphs, nor the enlarged two-indicator semaphores would ever be used.[42] Chappe finally came to the conclusion that the problem with the semaphore telegraph was not its size or the number of indicators, but an inadequate signaling A.D. 1795 code. Between 1794 and 1795 he developed a new coding system that alleviated much of the problem.

Despite the early successes, there was little that the Chappes could take for granted. Especially the first lines were constructed to establish communication with cities that were at risk of being besieged by the enemy, which meant that they lead close to enemy territory. During the construction of the station at Brévillers, on the line to Lille, Prosper Delauney wrote to Claude Chappe on 22 April 1794, almost casually:[43]

> Until yesterday, every afternoon and all morning yesterday, the cannons fired constantly; we can hear them clearly because the attack, we have been told, comes from Cambrai, which is no more than 6 leagues from here.

Ignace Chappe also described the atmosphere during this construction in gloomy terms.[44]

> It is remarkable how difficult it was to survive the second phase of our efforts, the establishment and the organization of the line from Paris to Lille; how much energy, exhaustion, and resources we had to spend to overcome the unforeseen obstacles, returning endlessly, in a project of a kind that had never been attempted before; the fear and the worries caused by the uncertainty if the project could succeed at all: the death of the project could always be read on everyone's face!

A.D. 1798 This aspect of the work would never change. In 1798, for instance, the funds for payment to workers on a new line from Paris to Brest, commissioned by the French Navy, were repeatedly delayed. Attempts were made to pay in kind, instead of in cash, but that also failed. Claude Chappe made desperate pleas for money, as recorded in a series of notes sent to Paris (cf. Figure 2.8):[45]

> *18 Ventôse An VI—Des fonds, des fonds, encore une fois, des fonds, autrement nous ne pouvons rien faire. Adressez-les à Port-Malo . . .*
> [9 March 1798—Funds, funds, once more, funds, or we cannot do anything. Send them to Port-Malo . . .]
> *30 Ventôse An VI—Point encore de fonds, nous perdons depuis près de huit jours un temps extrêmement précieux . . . cette situation me désespère . . .*
> [21 March 1798—No more funds, we have lost almost eight days at an extremely important time . . . this situation makes me desperate . . .]
> *14 Prairial An VI—Je fais tout pour assurer le prompt succès de l'établissement que je dirige; de l'argent, ou point de ligne de Brest.*
> [3 June 1798—I do everything to assure the prompt success of the organization I direct; money or there will be no line to Brest.]

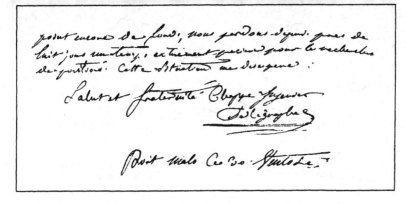

Figure 2.8 Claude Chappe's Appeal for Funds, 21 March 1798.
(Source: [Belloc 1888])

The line to Brest was nonetheless completed in seven months.

Beginnings of a Network
The beginnings of a network became visible around 1800. Telegraph stations were built roughly 10 km (6 miles) apart. To simplify the administration and the reliability, each line was divided into short, autonomous segments called divisions. At the start and end of every division all messages were to be completely decoded and recorded in logbooks by an inspector, before being passed on. The operators at intermediate stations were allowed to know only a small subset of the telegraph code: the control codes that preceded and followed the actual messages, and the occasional error codes that could be inserted into them. They did not know the code used for enciphering the actual messages. That authority rested solely with the inspectors of the lines, and the director and assistant directors of the Telegraph Administration.

At the start of 1805 there were four main branches, stretching out into the north, south, east, and west of France. The main lines constructed in this period are given below. The distances given are map distances, and most likely underestimate the actual distances along the trajectories of the lines as they were built. The dates in the leftmost column of the table indicate when construction began. The last column gives the period the line was in active use. Some of the longer lines took several years to be completed. Note, for instance, that the line from Lyon to Turin was built directly across the Alps, and took three years to complete.

1794	Paris to Lille	190 km	(1794–1847)
	Paris to Landau/Strasbourg	128	(1798–1852)
1798	Lille to Dunkerque	64	(1798–1801)
	Paris to Brest	210	(1798–1853)
1799	Strasbourg to Huningue	96	(1799–1800)

Figure 2.9 The Semaphore Telegraph Network, ca. 1805.

1803	Lille to Brussels	96	(1803–1814)
	Lille to Boulogne	80	(1803–1816)
1804	Paris to Dijon to Lyon	370	(1804–1852)
1804	Lyon to Turin	250	(1807–1814)
	Turin to Milan	100	(1809–1814)
1805	Lyon to Toulon	305	(replaced in 1821)

For a short period after the treaty Amiens from March 1802, most lines of the network, except the line from Paris to Brest, were shut down for lack of both the motivation and the funds to operate them. The line to Brest, by virtue of being funded through the navy, was spared this fate, and remained in operation as the only remaining line for more then one year. In May 1803, however, England resumed its war with France, and the telegraph network was quickly restored to its original size.

The Chappes were now arguably at the peak of their success. The construction on the line to Milan, for example, was begun at the explicit request of Napoleon Bonaparte, who had seized power in 1799 and declared himself emperor in 1804. Between 1800 and 1804, however,

Figure 2.10 Claude Chappe, ca. 1804.
(Source: [Koenig 1944], p. 432)

Claude Chappe became increasingly despondent. He was especially upset when others started attacking his designs, claiming credit for having invented the telegraph earlier. These critics included Bréguet, who had helped with the mechanics of the first stations in 1794, and Bétancourt, who together with Bréguet had made an unsuccessful attempt in 1797 to have Chappe's design replaced with their own.[46] A third critic was Captain De Courrejolles, who we met earlier, and who had also been unsuccessful in promoting his own design for an optical telegraph in 1783.

Despair
Towards the end of 1804, Claude Chappe fell ill during a routine inspection tour of some of the new lines that were under construction. He suspected food poisoning, and pointed an accusing finger at his adversaries. When Chappe returned to Paris after a sickness of several months, he sank into a depression from which he did not recover. On Wednesday

Figure 2.11 Chappe's Tombstone from Vaugirard.
(Source: [Belloc 1888], p. 135)

A.D. 1805 23 January 1805 he committed suicide by jumping into a well outside the Telegraph Administration at l'Hôtel Villeroy in Paris.[47] According to some newspapers, a short note was found, written in a quivering hand:[48]

> *Je me donne la mort pour éviter l'ennui de la vie qui m'accable; je n'ai point de reproches à me faire.* [I give myself to death to avoid life's worries that weigh me down; I'll have no reproaches to make myself.]

Five days later, on 28 January 1805, Chappe's death was reported in the French newspaper *Le Moniteur* as follows:[49]

> Mr. Claude Chappe, the inventor and administrator of the telegraph, died Wednesday last, at the age of forty-two; a true loss for the arts. It has been said, with reason, that the art of signaling existed long before him. But, in fairness, what he added was to expand this art into an application so simple, so methodical, so certain, and so universally adopted, that he can be regarded its true inventor.

70

Abraham Chappe commemorated the accomplishments of his brother in a letter to the editor of the *Journal de Paris*. The letter was dated 7 Pluviôse An XIII (27 January 1805), and was published six days later. It ended ambiguously:[50]

> He is dead, like his uncle the Abbé Chappe, a victim of his passion for the sciences and for his country. May their successors learn to imitate their example, and not to fear the fate of those who went before them!

In the letter, Abraham also referred to the accusations of Bréguet, Bétancourt, and De Courrejolles, that had driven Claude to such despair. It seems that at least De Courrejolles's accusation was unfounded. Claude's other brother Ignace later wrote in his book:[51]

> . . . two different types of telegraph have been experimented with. One was placed at the Louvre, the other at the pavilion in the middle of the Tuileries. This last one, of which Mr. De Courrejolles claims that it resembles his own design, was designed by Monge; it was, however, never used. Mr. De Courrejolles has acquired too much fame at the Turkish isles to have any need to claim the paternal rights to a child that died at birth.

Chappe was buried in a cemetery at Vaugirard, near Paris. The front of the tombstone that was placed at his grave shows a snake eating its tail (a symbol of eternity), encircling the words *Claude Chappe 1765–1805*. The back has a small vertical sempahore sign in the middle (the code for "idle"), and a picture of a telegraph below it showing the station sign of Lille. At the top is a reference to one of the first messages sent: *Reprise de Condé sur les Autrichiens 1793*. The tombstone seems to have been made in haste: Claude Chappe was not born in 1765, but in 1763, and Condé was not retaken in 1793, but in 1794.

The Network Expands

After Claude Chappe's death the remaining brothers continued working for the Telegraph Administration, with the strong support of the government. Napoleon Bonaparte understood the potential of Chappe's system. Immediately after seizing power in 1799, he used the telegraph network to send the reassuring message:[52]

> *Paris est tranquille et les bons citoyens sont contents.* [Paris is quiet and the good citizens are content.]

He later also made use of the telegraph in his campaigns, in attempts to outwit the enemy by having fast notification of their intentions.

In 1801 Napoleon commissioned Abraham Chappe to develop a telegraph that could signal across the English Channel, to facilitate a possible invasion of England. In preparation for this, he ordered the line to Calais extended to Boulogne. Abraham designed a large semaphore with two arms. It was tested in June and July of 1801 between Belleville and Saint-Martin-du-Tertre, the two terminal stations on the first experimental line from 1793. The distance between these two stations roughly

Figure 2.12 Button from Claude Chappe's Uniform (left)
Seal of the Telegraph Administration (right).
(Coll. Musée de la Poste, Paris)

matches the shortest distance across the English Channel. The test proved to be successful. A telegraph of this design was installed for a
A.D. 1804 short time in Boulogne, around 1804, but since Napoleon changed his mind about the invasion of England, it was never used as intended.

A.D. 1808 In 1808, Napoleon requested a report from the Minister of the French Navy, Vice-Admiral Decrès, which reads as follows:[53]

> Send me a memo on the establishment of signals and telegraphs similar to those near Spain and Cadix [Cadiz], so that I can learn within moments what happens at Toulon on the channel, at Cape Finistère, and at Cape Saint-Vincent. Make the memo short and clear, so that it tells me which new telegraphs you will have erected. Are they [based on] combinations of the letters of the alphabet, as in the land telegraph, or [flag] signals? Can one send, via these telegraphs, an order to the squadron in Cadix [Cadiz] to perform a manoeuvre, or to prevent an squadron from leaving Toulon or Brest?

A year later Napoleon became impatient with the slow progress in the construction of the line to Milan. The following angry note, directed at
A.D. 1809 Minister of Interior Mr. Crétet, was written on 16 March 1809:[54]

> Mr. Crétet, I wish that you complete without delay the establishment of the telegraphic line from here to Milan, and that in fifteen days one can communicate with that capital.

The emperor promptly received his guarantee from Crétet that the line would be completed within weeks. Of course, it took another few months before it could actually be done.[55]

Figure 2.13 Mobile Semaphore Telegraph
Used in the Crimean War 1853–1856.
(Source: [Belloc 1888])

In 1812 Abraham Chappe was commissioned again by Napoleon, this time A.D. 1812
to develop a mobile version of Chappe's telegraph that could be deployed
during the invasion of Russia in that year. His design was still in use in
1853 when the Crimean War took place.

The brothers Chappe had achieved a position of power and relative
independence in the administration and operation of the telegraph network. When Louis XVIII was restored to the throne in 1814, the three A.D. 1814
brothers Ignace, Pierre, and Abraham were given the rank of *Chevaliers
de Légion d'Honneur.*[56]

The network of optical telegraphs meanwhile continued to grow.

1809	Brussels to Antwerp	40 km	(1809–1813)
	Antwerp to Vlissingen	72	(1809–1811)
1810	Antwerp to Amsterdam	128	(1810–1813)
	Milan via Turin to Venice	241	(1810–1814)
1813	Metz to Mainz	225	(1813–1814)
1816	Lille to Calais	80	(1816–1852)
1821	Lyon to Toulon	305	(1821–1852)
1823	Paris to Bordeaux	507	(1823–1853)
	Bordeaux to Bayonne	160	(1823–1853)

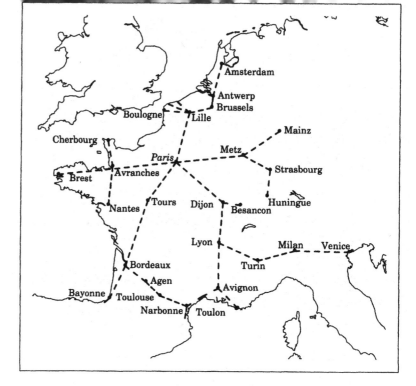

Figure 2.14 The Semaphore Telegraph Network
Overview of Lines Constructed between 1794 and 1846.

	Avranches to Nantes	157	(1823–1853)
1825	Paris to Lille	190	(expanded)
1828	Avignon to Perpignan	209	(1828–1853)
1833	Avranches to Cherbourg	108	(1833–1853)
1834	Bordeaux to Toulouse	205	(1834–1853)
	Toulouse to Narbonne	127	(1834–1853)
	Narbonne to Montpellier	84	(1834–1853)
	Montpellier to Avignon	80	(1834–1853)
1840	Boulogne to Calais	32	(1840–1852)
	Narbonne to Perpignan	54	(1840–1853)
	Calais to Boulogne	40	(1840–1853)
	Dijon to Besancon	72	(1840–1852)
1844	Bordeaux to Agen	145	(replaced)
1845	Boulogne to Eu	100	(1845–1853)
1846	Bayonne to Behobie	30	(1846–1853)

The connection between Metz and Mainz was also established at
Napoleon's request, and disappeared with his fall in 1814. The connection

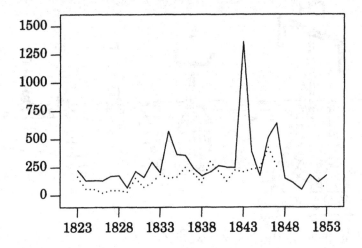

Figure 2.15 Message Traffic between Paris and Bayonne
Solid: Messages from Bayonne to Paris (1823–1853)
Dotted: Messages from Paris to Bayonne (1823–1847).
(Data from: [Massie 1979])

from Lille to Calais from 1816 replaced the earlier line from Lille to
Boulogne, but only the last four or five stations along the line were
affected by this switch. In 1840 the connection to Boulogne was restored
with the construction of an extra line segment long the coast to Calais,
and in 1845 that line was extended further south to the city Eu. The line
from Dijon to Besancon, finally, was originally intended to reach Strasbourg via Huningue, to provide an alternate route through the network,
but the full line was never completed.

Figure 2.15 shows the amount of traffic carried on a typical line from this
network, between Paris and Bayonne, over the 30-year period it was in
use (9 April 1823 to 24 March 1853).[57] Traffic averaged a few hundred
messages per year, with most traffic flowing towards Paris.

FRAUD
Every attempt was made to guard the secrecy of transmissions on the telegraph network. There was clearly money to be made by speculators if, for
instance, they could find a way to transmit news from the stock market in
Paris to other parts of the country faster than the daily papers.

A curious case of fraud was discovered on the Paris to Bordeaux line.[58]
Two bankers, the brothers Francois and Joseph Blanc, had bribed the telegraph operators at a station just behind Tours to introduce a specific pat-
tern of errors into the transmissions, to signal the direction in which the
stock market was moving in Paris to an accomplice in Bordeaux. The

Figure 2.16 Transmission Line.
(Source: [Koenig 1944], p. 435)

telegraph operators near Tours received their instructions from Paris by ordinary (stage-coach) mail, in the form of packages wrapped in either white or grey paper, indicating whether the stock market in Paris had gone up or down. The fraud had been in operation for two years when it was discovered in August of 1836.

A.D. 1836

The reason that the telegraph station at Tours was chosen for this fraud lies in the administration of the telegraph network itself. At each division station, such as Tours, all incoming messages were decoded by a telegraph director. The messages were purged of transmission errors, and then re-encoded and passed on. On the French telegraph network only the directors and inspectors were allowed to know the code for message signals. The operators, or *stationaires*, knew only the limited set of control codes used for error corrections, clock synchronizations and the like (see also Chapter Six).

NETWORK NODES

Avranches in Bretagne was another division station where four lines met at a single network node. Each line was terminated at a separate telegraph, and each message received was decoded before it was passed on, by hand, to the operators of the appropriate connecting line. The same method was also adopted in Paris where four telegraph lines terminated at the headquarters of the Telegraph Administration, located at 103 Rue de Grenelle since 1840. The four faces of the telegraph tower on this building each carried a separate telegraph, mounted on the outside walls.

76

Figure 2.17 Telegraph Lines in Paris, ca. 1852.
(Coll. Musée de la Poste, Paris)

In 1823 Ignace Chappe retired at a pension of 4,255 francs per year. A.D. 1823 Pierre-Francois Chappe also retired and received 2,252 francs. They were succeeded by their younger brothers, René and Abraham, though nominally placed under the supervision of a new general administrator appointed by King Louis XVIII, Count Kerespertz. Ignace died on 25 January 1829, 66 years old. Claude Chappe was then reburied next to his brother on 19 June 1829 at the cemetery Père Lachaise in Paris.[59] A.D. 1829

René and Abraham remained in charge of the Telegraph Administration until 1830. During the July revolution of that year, René Chappe refused A.D. 1830 to transmit messages on the optical telegraph network for the new government, considering himself bound by his oath to the king.[60] The refusal made it painfully clear to the government how much power the two remaining Chappe brothers still had over the telegraph network. Shortly thereafter, that power was eliminated when both Réne and Abraham were forced to retire.

Pierre-Francois died 20 February 1834 in Allonnes near Le Mans at the age of 64. Abraham died 26 July 1849, 76 years old, and was buried in Brûlon. René, the longest surviving Chappe brother, died in Brûlon on 6 November 1854. He was 85 years old.

Only two of the five Chappe brothers ever married. Pierre-Francois married Marie Blondel de Manneville and had three children, only one of whom survived: a daughter named Cornélie Emilie born in 1800. Abraham Chappe married the same Cornélie Emilie, his niece, in 1825, and had one child, Pierre-Emile, in 1826. Pierre-Emile, in turn, married in 1855 and had two daughters and two sons. These two sons, Pierre and Francois, each also married and had six children in all (two for Pierre, and

Figure 2.18 Statue by M. Damé—Destroyed in 1942.
(Photo: Agence Roger-Viollet, Paris)

four for Francois). The two male descendants of the Chappe brothers among these, named Christian and Claude, were both killed in World War I, leaving no male descendants alive today.[61]

A.D. 1852 By 1852 the French network of optical telegraphs had grown to 556

Figure 2.19 The Letterhead Used for Telegrams.
(Source: [Belloc 1888], p. 177)

telegraph stations, covering roughly 4800 km (3000 miles). The network connected 29 of France's largest cities to Paris. With two operators on duty at each station, the network employed well over 1,000 people, including nearly forty telegraph inspectors and twenty directors.[62]

In 1859 Claude Chappe's dubious tombstone was removed from Vaugirard A.D. 1859 and presented to the Telegraph Administration, which had it cut into two slabs. The two halves of the stone, front and back, were placed in the entrance hall of the new headquarters at No. 103 Rue Grenelle in Paris, where they remain today.

In 1893, at the first centennial of the telegraph, a copper statue of Claude A.D. 1893 Chappe by M. Damé was erected in Paris, at the intersection of Boulevard Saint-Germain and Boulevard Raspail, near the Rue du Bac where Chappe had his first workshop. Alas, the statue did not survive long enough for a bicentennial celebration. It was melted down for ammunition during World War II, and was never replaced.

How the Telegraph Worked
The mechanical construction of the telegraph was thoroughly studied by the Chappes before a final design was chosen. In Ignace Chappe's words:[63]

> ... a telegraph appears to be such a simple device to construct that few people have studied it seriously.

Several authors have given detailed information on the design, although the measurements given are rarely in precise accordance.[64] The measurements below are taken from Shaffner, as the earliest source. The telegraph consisted of an iron support column, 4.55m (15 ft) high, with a movable wooden regulator of $4.25 \times 0.35 \times 0.05$m attached to the top. At the ends of the regulator beam were two movable indicators, each 1.80×0.30

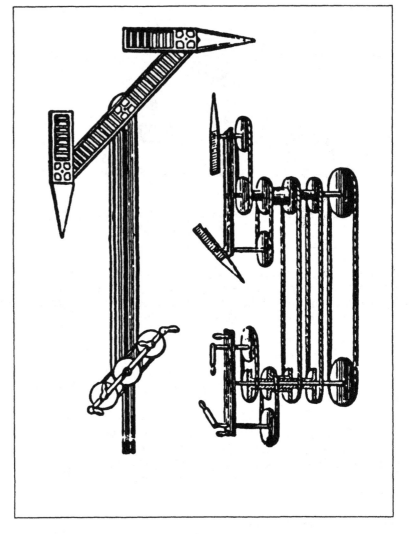

Figure 2.20 Semaphore Telegraph Mechanics.
(Source: [Koenig 1944], p. 434)

× 0.025m, counterbalanced with lead weights on steel rods. The indicators were mounted asymmetrically on the regulator beam, the longest end measuring 1.65m. The distance from the center of the regulator to the center of each indicator was set at 2m, so that when both indicators were turned inward they were 0.70m apart.

A large control handle, about one meter long, was placed at the bottom of the support beam. The control handle exactly reproduced the position of the semaphore outside. It rotated the regulator with two cords, running across double pulleys to the beam. To allow the cords to be shortened and lengthened for proper tension, the cords were interrupted in the middle by iron bars with tension screws. The indicators were moved, also via pulleys and cords, in such a way that their angle with the regulator stayed fixed, and could be set independently of the position of the main regulator. The angles of the indicators were further secured with spring-loaded tooth-in-notch mechanisms. The regulator itself could be secured (at night or during storms) with a large bolt in the support beam.

To reduce both weight and wind resistance, the indicators were made from a brass grating with copper slats. Half the slats were set to the right, the other half to the left, to distribute the wind forces evenly, and to avoid reflections. Both the regulator and the indicators were painted black to produce a maximum contrast against the sky.

THE FIRST CODE

Much attention was also given to the definition of workable signaling codes and station instructions, to secure maximum visibility and a minimum number of operator errors.

Ignace Chappe noted that it was virtually impossible to prevent transmission errors when messages had to be passed down long chains of telegraphs. He ridiculed those who thought they could design new telegraphs without considering the subtleties of signaling across longer chains.[65]

> Those who think they have invented a telegraph that can be used without preliminary instructions for the telegraph operators, are mistaken; they have probably never performed experiments with more than two or three stations.

The original code for the synchronized system (the pendulum telegraph), possibly developed with the help of Léon Delauney in 1791, consisted of a code book of 9,999 entries.[66] The clock face of the pendulums had 10 divisions on them, leading naturally to a decimal encoding. Delauney placed the most frequently used words and phrases at the top of the encoding list, giving them the shortest encodings. The first nine entries, for instance, were the numerals from 1 to 9, which were encoded in one signal. The next 89 entries, numbered from 10 to 99, were encoded in two subsequent signals. Similarly, the entries from 100 to 999 required three, and the remaining entries, from 1,000 to 9,999, four subsequent signals.

According to the description later given by Ignace Chappe, and discussed also by Jacquez in 1893, the Chappes continued to use a code very similar to this on the semaphore telegraph until 1795. Several drastic variations were considered before the decision was made to adopt it though.

In an undated manuscript titled *Mémoire relatif à une découverte dont l'objet est de communiquer rapidement à de grandes distances, tout ce qui peut faire le sujet d'une correspondance* [Memorandum on an invention for communicating quickly over great distances, everything that could be the subject of a correspondence], Claude Chappe motivated the initial choice

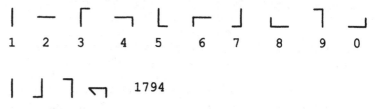

Figure 2.21 Basic Code for Numerals, ca. 1794 (top)
And the Number 1794 as Transmitted (bottom).

of signals for the semaphore system. The memoire was probably written in late 1793. It reads as follows:[67]

> With ten characteristic, and two secondary, signs, I will now introduce a system of combinations that reduces the language of signals to a very simple [method of] expression. One should consider these characters as a form of numerical shorthand, which aims to represent words in the smallest possible number of signs.

The ten "characteristic" signs were formed with the regulator in either a horizontal or a vertical position, and at most one of the indicators tilted 90 degrees, leaving the other indicator idle.

Claude proposed to use these ten characteristic signs to encode numbers from one to 20, by prefixing each with one of two possible "secondary" signs. These secondary signs, also called the right and the left *oblique* position, were formed by placing the regulator at a 45 degree angle with the horizon. If the characteristic sign was preceded by a right oblique, the number was odd, if it was preceded by a left oblique, it was even. Compared to a purely decimal system, the base-20 system allowed for a smaller number of signals to be used per word or phrase from a numbered dictionary or code-book. It was, however, never adopted. The code used on the Paris to Lille line in 1794 was still based on a decimal encoding, as in the synchronized system, using the ten characteristic signs to represent the numbers from one to ten (see Figure 2.21).

To separate variable-length code groups from each other in a longer transmission, the last sign in each group was made with the unused indicator turned slightly away from the regulator. The undated manuscript gives the required angle as 22.5 degrees, rather than 45 degrees, to clearly distinguish this "termination" sign from other possible semaphore positions. It is not known if this smaller angle was also used in the code that was adopted in 1794.

Apart from these correspondence signals, of which the meaning—other than the numeral value of the code—was unknown to anyone below the level of telegraph inspector, there were fourteen service or *control* signals known to all operators. These signals were always set with both indicators turned, avoiding the codes that were used for the correspondence

Figure 2.22 The Telegraph at Montpellier.
(Coll. Musée de la Poste, Paris)

signals. They were used to signal the following conditions:

o Start of transmission
o End of transmission
o Suspension of transmissions for one hour
o Suspension of transmissions for two hours
o Synchronization, meant to allow the stations along the telegraph line to resynchronize their clocks
o Conflict, to indicate that two messages from opposite directions had arrived simultaneously at one station
o Priority, to indicate the precedence of one of the conflicting messages
o Acknowledgement, indicating the reception of a correctly deciphered message at the final destination
o Error, to cancel the last transmitted sign
o Idle, indicating the closing of the station or line
o Minor failure, to indicate a small problem with the telegraph, or the temporary absence of the operator

Figure 2.23 Instructions for Use of the Error Signal.
(Coll. Musée de la Poste, Paris)

o Major failure, to indicate a more serious problem disabling the telegraph, requiring outside help
o Rain or fog restricting visibility, and
o Night transmission.

The last signal was probably included only with an eye towards future
extensions of the telegraph system on which transmissions at night were
foreseen. As far as we know, no effective system of night signaling was
ever used on the Chappe telegraphs.[68]

The precise signaling code that was used on the Paris to Lille line is still
somewhat of a mystery. In a letter dated 5 July 1794 Claude Chappe
writes that he just completed two code books regulating the corre-

spondence on the new line, together with a set of detailed instructions on the use of the telegraph, which he delivered to the Committee for Public Safety.[69] No code books, however, have been preserved that completely match the descriptions. It is understandable that, to safeguard the secrecy of the correspondence signs, very few of such books would have been prepared.

In the Paris Postal Museum an undated code book has been preserved that could be either an adapted version of Delauney's first code, or a proposal for a new code that remained unused. It contains two sets of 88 pages, each with four columns of 88 entries, not all of which are defined. From the $2 \times 88 \times 4 \times 88$, or 61,952, possible code combinations, only 45,056 were filled in. Possibly, this code required that the semaphore be set in one of 88 positions to form each sign. That number was increased to 92 or 94 in the code that Chappe adopted in 1795.

THE REVISED CODE

Based on the first year of experience with the Paris to Lille line, Claude Chappe developed a new code in 1795.

From the beginning, the regulator and the indicators of the telegraph were set only at angles that varied in increments of at least 45 degrees. This allowed for eight positions for each indicator and four for the regulator, giving $8 \times 8 \times 4 = 256$ possible combinations. It was also realized from the beginning that the positions where the indicators either extended the position of the regulator, or were hidden behind it, were almost indistinguishable. By excluding the positions that extended the regulator beam, the number of indicator positions was reduced to seven each, leaving $7 \times 7 \times 4 = 196$ possible combinations for the telegraph as a whole. Since the available code space was still large enough, the meaningful signs were further restricted to only those where the regulator beam was either placed horizontally or vertically. This limited the number of possible signs to $7 \times 7 \times 2 = 98$. These 98 combinations were further reduced to either 92 or 94 signals. After retiring from the Telegraph Administration, Abraham Chappe summarized this signaling system in a letter dated 24 January 1844. He explained this last restriction as follows:[70]

> From these 98 signals 4 or 6 are reserved for special indications, so that 92 or 94 signals remain for the correspondence.

The code that was adopted in 1795 consisted of two parts, called *divisions*. According to Abraham Chappe's letter, the first division defined 94 different signs encoding the alphabet, the numbers from zero to nine, and some frequently used syllables. Each code from this division was set, following the rules for the formation of signals to be explained shortly, and then confirmed, or *closed*, by folding in the two indicators. The resulting two double-closed positions (horizontal and vertical closed) were not counted among the 94 signals from the code books, but among those that were reserved for "special use," as indicated by Abraham Chappe.

The second division of the code consisted of a code book of 94 pages with 94 signs (called *series*) each, defining more syllables and commonly used words.[71] Each entry from this code table was again transmitted as a code pair. The first sign of the pair now gave a line number from the code book, and the second sign gave the page number. Care was taken that the second sign could never be a "double closed" sign, to make sure that the codes from the first and the second division were different.

The complete code of $94 + 94 \times 94 = 8,930$ words and phrases comes close to the size of Delauney's original code with 9,999 entries, but was presumably somewhat simpler to use.

In 1799, four years after the new code was adopted, Chappe extended his code by adding a few extra divisions in separate code books. The extra divisions contained codes for additional words and phrases, names of places and people, etc. In his summary from 1844, Abraham Chappe described a total of five different divisions. The codes in the third division were preceded by a separate horizontal, double-closed signal; those in the fourth division were preceded by a vertical double-closed signal; and those in the fifth division by a signal that was borrowed from the first division. All codes from the first and second division, therefore, required two signs; those from the third and fourth division required three signs, and those from the fifth division four.

There are indications that the codes were revised once more in 1809, but remained stable thereafter.

FORMING A SIGNAL

By restricting the regulator beam to only a horizontal or vertical position potentially half of the code space remained unused. Diagonal semaphore positions did, however, occur during the formation of signals. From the first code on, in 1794, each sign was always set in two separate movements. The first step was used for the formation of the signal proper, the second step for its confirmation, or completion. To form a signal, the regulator beam was first tilted to the right or to the left, with both indicators folded in. Only then could the indicators be turned to assume their new position. Moving the regulator back into a horizontal or vertical position was called *carrying the signal to completion*. The tilted positions of the regulator were called the *right oblique* and the *left oblique*.

By definition, a signal was meaningless as long as the regulator beam was tilted—a safeguard against the confusion caused by quickly changing arm positions during the formation of signals. With these rules, then, the transmission of a complete code from the fifth division of the code books required a total of eight movements of the telegraph. The more frequently occurring codes from the first division, however, required just three movements: (1) setting the signal on an oblique, (2) carrying the signal to completion, and (3) folding in the indicators to close the signal.

Correspondence (message) signals were always formed on the left oblique, and service (control) signals always on the right oblique. Of course, what

Figure 2.24 Uniform of a Telegraph Inspector.
(Coll. Musée de la Poste, Paris)

was the "left" oblique to one operator, looked like the "right" oblique to another, thus providing a wonderful source of confusion.

All signals on the semaphore telegraph were passed one at a time, in strictly synchronous fashion. The operators were required to check their neighboring stations every few minutes for new signals, and reproduce them as quickly as possible. The operator then had to verify that the next station in line reproduced the signal correctly, and set an error signal if it failed to do so. Each signal received had to be recorded in a logbook, as soon as it was carried to completion. Since no symbolic or numeric code system for representing the semaphore positions was described, this was done in the form of little pictograms, displaying the relative positions of regulator and indicators. If the signal was a control signal, the hour and minute of its arrival was also recorded in the logs.

The instructions that were given to the operators of the semaphore

Figure 2.25 Flocon's Design, Reconstructed Station near Narbonne.
(Source: [Galfano 1990], p. 13)

telegraphs have been preserved. They detail precisely what the operator had to do to detect and recover from transmission errors, how to resolve conflicts between messages traveling in opposite directions, and how to deal with low visibility and unscheduled delays. Translations of the original texts are reproduced in Appendix B. The instructions are also discussed in Chapter Six.

In 1837 Gabriel Flocon, an administrator of the French telegraph network, introduced a new coding method, where the heavy regulator beam always remained fixed in a horizontal position.[72] A separate, small, indicator wing was added in the middle to represent what would have been the position of the regulator. This version of the telegraph was called the *télégraphe horizontale*. Abraham Chappe wrote in his letter from 1844 that this variant had been installed on short line segments only, such as Perpignan to Bayonne and Dijon to Besancon. One of the Flocon stations near Narbonne, at Jonquières, was reconstructed in 1987, and can still be visited today (see Figure 2.25).

Table 2.1 Transmission Times.

Destination	Stations	Time (sec)	Time/Station (sec)
Calais	27	180	6.7
Brest	80	480	6
Lille	22	120	5.5
Strasbourg	45	390	8.7
Lyon	50	540	10.8
Total	224	1710	7.6

TRANSMISSION SPEED

Edelcrantz says in his treatise from 1796 that initial reports gave the speed of the French telegraph as 20 seconds per symbol.[73] Most other sources, however, rated the speed at 30 seconds per symbol, noting that at higher speeds the number of transmission errors increased too much.

The end-to-end speed of the telegraph lines is reported in various places, but not always consistently. In early 1819, John Macdonald quoted the numbers shown in Table 2.1 from a "recent French paper," counting telegraphs on the lines from Paris to various destinations, and the time it took to send a first sign from Paris to five destinations.[74]

The line to Lille had been extended from 17 to 22 stations by the time these data were collected. Of course, the transmission times in the table above were not averages that could be sustained for all signs throughout a message. The overall average of 7.6 seconds per sign per station is therefore best interpreted as a lower bound. The usual quote of two to three symbols per minute, or 30 to 20 seconds per sign, also matches the clock-times recorded in logbooks from this period.[75]

Rollo Appleyard, most likely basing his report on figures from the earlier book written by Alexis Belloc, wrote:[76]

> At Paris, when this system had been perfected, they could receive communications from Lille in two minutes, from Calais in four minutes five seconds, from Strasbourg in five minutes fifty-two seconds, from Toulon in twelve minutes fifty seconds, from Bayonne in fourteen minutes, and from Brest in six minutes fifty seconds.

Shaffner reported somewhat better results, quoting roughly six seconds per station:[77]

> Chappe said that when the weather was fine, and the fogs and haziness of the atmosphere are not a hindrance to vision, the first signal of a communication ought not to occupy more than 10 or 12 minutes in passing from Toulon to Paris, cities situated 215 leagues or 475 miles [765 km] apart, and connected by a telegraph line of 120 stations; but Chappe added that if we suppose a continuous correspondence between Paris and Toulon, there would ordinarily arrive at Toulon but one signal a minute.

Of course, transmitting complete messages one signal at a time would take time. Whether or not a message would get through correctly on the first try depended on the weather, and thus on the time of year. M. Vasseur, studying the reliability of message transmissions over a four-year period (1836–1839) for a private optical telegraph line connecting Antwerp and Brussels, noted that messages would get through on the first try an average of 97 percent of the time in the month of August 1838 (the best month), but only 16 percent of the time in the month of December 1839 (the worst one).[78] In related studies it was found that during the winter messages could take up to three days to reach their destination.[79] Despite all this, messages traveled faster on these networks than they had ever done before; after all, in the winter a rider on horseback also has trouble getting through. Macdonald reflected the excitement of the new phenomenon in the following note, written in 1819:

> It was lately stated, in their [the French] papers, that 3000 messages could be conveyed in one day from Paris to any extremity of France; and also that answers could be received to them.

The claim seems exaggerated. Even if one sign would have taken roughly eight seconds to traverse a station, in eight hours of daylight a maximum of only 3600 signs could have been given, with full-time operation. Each message surely consisted of more than just a single sign, requiring at least signals for identifying the sender and the receiver, and multiple signals for encoding the communication itself.

The Competition

Even during the growth of the optical telegraph network in France, Chappe's design did not go unchallenged. Chappe managed to win each such challenge decisively. In 1794, for instance, the designer of a competing telegraph design, called the *Vigigraph*, obtained permission to construct a line between Paris and Le Havre. But the line went unused and was discarded after only a few months.

In 1796, when the Chappe system was fairly well established, Gottfried Huth (1763–1818), a German professor, published a curious booklet titled *A treatise concerning some acoustic instruments and the use of the speaking tube in telegraphy*, which included a translation of a work on acoustical instruments from 1763 by the Frenchman J. H. Lambert.[80] In his own additions to the translation, Huth criticized the Chappe system for being obviously restricted to fair weather and day-time use. As an alternative, Huth proposed a system where men with so-called "speaking tubes," or megaphones, would be placed on towers, roughly five km apart, so that they could shout messages to each other. Huth's suggestion was based on the legend that Alexander the Great had used a megaphone of enormous proportions to shout messages to his troops during battles.[81]

Huth realized that he had to think of an original name for his system to set it apart from the Chappe system. He wrote:

The fundamental difference therefore deserves, and will ultimately require, a different name for the telegraph based on speaking tubes. But what name would be more appropriate than the word derived from the Greek: "Telephon," or far-speaker [German: *Fernsprecher*].

The name would stick, though not to this invention. As far as we know, Huth's proposal was never put into practice.

In 1809 Napoleon decided to experiment with a quickly improvised communication line that consisted simply of men equipped with colored signal flags. It is possible, though, this was only a stop-gap measure to bridge the distance from his military headquarters in Vienna to the nearest optical telegraph station in Strasbourg. The flag signaling line was abandoned when Napoleon left Vienna.

A more serious challenge to Chappe's design would come in 1831 when a private citizen, Alexander Ferrier, opened a public telegraph line between Paris and Rouen, funded by stockholders. He charged 20 francs per 100 French miles (444 km). Ferrier's telegraph consisted of two rotating pointers, placed five meters (16 feet) apart, each pointer with a 30 cm (one foot), counterbalanced, disc mounted at the end.[82] Each pointer could be set in one of eight positions. At night, each pointer carried two lights, one in the center, one at the disc. Ferrier advertised that he could transmit at least 10 messages per hour over 100 French miles, allowing an average of 12–15 words per message. The first station of Ferrier's line was placed on the Boulevard MontMartre, another in a private house on the MontMartre itself. The line failed to make a profit, though, and was abandoned within one year. Ferrier then moved to Brussels to try his luck there.

More private telegraph companies appeared and disappeared over the years. Fearing a proliferation of communications networks that would be hard to control in the long run, the French government soon moved to ban the establishment of private telegraphs.[83] A bill to that effect was passed on 14 March 1837 in the Chamber of Deputies (the lower house). It was confirmed by the Chamber of Peers (the upper house) and became law on 17 April 1837:

> Anyone performing unauthorized transmissions of signals from one place to another, with the aid of telegraphic machines or by any other means, will be punished with an imprisonment of one month to one year, and a fine of 1,000 to 10,000 Francs.

Virtually the same law is in effect today. In the current text the term *telegraphic machines* has been replaced with *telecommunications apparatus* and the fine has been increased to 3,600 to 36,000 Francs. [84]

The End

Even at the peak of their success, around 1824, the Chappes made it clear that they were not satisfied with the way the network was being used. Ignace Chappe wrote in the introduction to his book:[85]

Why is its use restricted to the transmission between a relatively small number of cities, of news that is usually of little importance?

Instead, argued Chappe, the telegraph network could be exploited profitably, for instance, by quickly reporting market prices from all over Europe to Paris, so that traders could instantly buy goods at whichever location they were offered for the lowest price, and sell them where the price was highest. Such use, wrote Ignace, could establish Paris as the trade capital of Europe. Whatever the reasons may have been, it was never done. Perhaps, as Chappe noted somewhat bitterly, the reason was simply this:

> The use of novel methods that modify established habits, often hurts the interests of those who profit the most from the older methods. Few people, with the exception of the inventors, are truly interested in helping projects succeed while their ultimate impact is still uncertain. . . . Those in power will normally make no effort to support a new invention, unless it can help them to augment their power; and even when they do support it, their efforts are usually insufficient to allow the new ideas to be fully exploited.

A final, and, of course, for good reason fatal, competition to Chappe's optical semaphore network came from the electrical telegraph. It took many years, however, for the advocates of the electrical telegraph to prove its superiority. As early as in 1838 Samuel Morse visited France to demonstrate his telegraph to the French Academy of Sciences. Morse bid on a contract to install an electrical telegraph line along the railway from Paris to Saint-Germain. But, when Morse left France again in February 1839, he had not succeeded in winning that contract. The French government had decided that the installation and exploitation of the telegraph network was too important to be trusted to a private company, and the plan to install an electrical line was abandoned.[86]

In 1840, one of the staunchest defenders of optical telegraphy, Dr. Jules Guyot, traveled to England to study the electrical novelties. Upon his return he published an article in the *Courier Francais* that appeared 5 July 1841. It argues convincingly:

> . . . with the aerial telegraph you can transmit your dispatches from station to station; under no circumstances will the Government fail to receive news from scenes of conflagrations or the theater of war.

The electrical telegraph, on the other hand, was clearly less useful. Its reliance on the existence of an uninterrupted, physical connection between stations could prove to be a fatal flaw:

> Every sensible person will agree that a single man in a single day could, without interference, cut all the electrical wires terminating in Paris; it is obvious that a single man could sever, in ten places, in the course of a day, the electrical wires of a particular line of communication, without being stopped or even recognized.

To settle the matter once and for all, Guyot concluded:

Figure 2.26 Foy-Bréguet's Electrical Telegraph.
(Coll. France Telecom CNET, Paris)

. . . what can one expect of a few wretched wires under similar conditions? . . .
Assuming that the electrical telegraph functions well in winter and poorly in
summer, or that it functions well at all times, it cannot seriously be considered
suitable for the needs of the Government, and the day is not far distant when
this truth will be clearly demonstrated.

Funds for the first experimental electro-magnetic telegraph line between
Paris and Rouen were appropriated in 1844 and the line went into service
on 18 May 1845.[87] The test proved successful, and on 3 July 1846 the
French government made the historic decision to begin replacing optical
telegraph lines with electrical ones. The first one chosen was the oldest
line of the network, the line from Paris to Lille.

Alphonse Foy, the chief administrator of the telegraph network at this
time, ordered the construction of a version of the electrical telegraph that
would be backward compatible with the French optical telegraphs. The
design was made by the engineer Louis Bréguet, grandson of the famed
Abraham Louis Bréguet who had assisted Claude Chappe with the construction of his first telegraphs fifty years earlier. Bréguet designed a little wooden cabinet, displaying a Chappe regulator, with two indicator
wings, that could transmit the familiar Chappe codes as electrical
signals.[88] Curiously, the Foy-Bréguet telegraph duplicated only the
Chappe indicators and not the regulator. A competing electrical telegraph
design by Dr. Pierre-Antoine Joseph Dujardin did contain small replicas of
both indicators and regulator, but, perhaps because it required an

additional wire to control the regulator, it was not selected.

The attempt to duplicate part of Chappe's vocabulary on the Foy-Bréguet telegraph was quickly abandoned. By 1852 the same device was still in use, but with a much simplified character encoding, using one indicator combination for each letter of the alphabet. The telegraphs were finally replaced with Morse telegraphs in 1855.

One of the last messages transmitted over an optical telegraph line reported the fall of Sebastopol in 1855.

Bibliographic Notes

The first publications on Chappe's designs were newspaper articles. The telegraph was debated in 1794 in a series of letters sent to *Gentleman's Magazine*, reproduced in Appendix A. Chappe's design is also discussed in Edelcrantz's Treatise from 1796, see Chapter Four.

Claude Chappe himself published several papers in physics, [Chappe 1789a, 1789b, 1790, 1791, 1792, 1793]. On the optical telegraph, though, he left only some handwritten notes and letters. An undated manuscript written by Claude Chappe was preserved entitled *Mémoire relatif à une découverte dont l'objet est de communiquer rapidement à de grandes distances, tout ce qui peut faire le sujet d'une correspondance* [Memorandum on an invention for communicating quickly over great distances, everything that could be the subject of a correspondence]. The manuscript must have been written after 1792, since it discusses a code for the semaphore telegraph which was first used in that year, and before early 1794, since the proposed code differs from the one that was adopted at that time.

Many letters written by the Chappe brothers between 1792 and 1798 have been preserved. They provide a valuable source of information about the hardships that the Chappes had to endure, especially during the construction of the first line from Paris to Lille in 1793 and 1794. The letters were collected and annotated by Gérard Contant in [Contant 1993].

In 1798 a letter by Claude Chappe appeared in several French newspapers, including *Le Moniteur Universel* and *Republicain*. In the letter Claude defended his semaphore design against a simplified variant that had been advanced starting in 1796 by Abraham Louis Bréguet (1747–1823) and Augustin Bétancourt (1760–1826). When the attempts of Bréguet and Bétancourt to get their alternative design adopted failed, their friend Ange Marie Eymar wrote a letter of complaint to the newspapers on their behalf. Chappe's letter was a response to this first letter of Eymar. The complete exchange contained three more letters, two by Eymar and one by Chappe. Three of the letters were later republished under the title *Lettres sur le nouveau télégraphe* [Chappe 1798].

The most detailed contemporary information on Chappe's designs is contained in a book by Claude's brother Ignace, *Histoire de la télégraphie*. It was published in 1824, a year after Ignace retired from the Telegraph Administration. In 1840, well after Ignace's death, Abraham Chappe had the book reprinted, and wrote a new long preface for it, comparing, among

Figure 2.27 Remains of a Chappe Tower at La Queue-les-Yvelines.
(Photo: Gerard J. Holzmann, 1993)

others, the advantages of the optical telegraphs to those of acoustical systems.

Reproductions of many original documents, including letters written by Abraham Chappe to his brother Claude during the construction of the first telegraph line from Paris to Lille, can be found in [Belloc 1888].

A first biography of Claude Chappe was written by Ernest Jacquez, at the time a librarian at the Post and Telegraph administration in Paris, and secretary of the committee preparing the celebrations for the first centennial of Chappe's system, [Jacquez 1893]. Under the direction of Jacquez's committee, the Frenchman A. Kermabon also prepared a series of 49 maps, documenting the detailed trajectories of the lines of the optical telegraph network, [Kermabon 1892]. More biographical information on Claude Chappe and his uncle Abbé Jean Baptiste can be found in [Brevost et al. 1959], [Appleyard 1930], and [FNARH 1991].

A good description of the operation and construction of Chappe's telegraphs is given in [Shaffner 1859]. The general history of the French optical network is traced in many books, most notably [Hennig 1908], [Koenig 1944], [Still 1946], [Wilson 1976], [Herbarth 1978], and, more recently, in Alexander Field's article [Field 1994]. A more dubious source, containing many inaccuracies that have left an unfortunate trail in later works, is [Figuier 1868], published by the prolific writer of popular science books Louis Figuier. Numerous misleading copper engravings from [Figuier 1868] have been reproduced in later works, often without mention of the source.

At the bicentennial celebrations of the first experiments, in 1993, the FNARH or *Fédération Nationale des Associations de Personnel des Postes et Télécommunications pour la Recherche Historique* (National Federation of Organizations of PTT Personnel for Historical Research) published an excellent collection of articles on various aspects of the Chappe system, [FNARH 1993]. The FNARH is located in Nancy, France.

In 1968 a reconstruction of the Chappe telegraph that once stood at Haut-Barr in the Alsace was completed. It was once part of the line from Paris to Strasbourg. In 1987 the reconstruction was begun of a second station at Jonquières near Narbonne, originally on the line to Perpignan. This telegraph is of the type introduced by Gabriel Flocon in 1837, with a fixed regulator beam and three indicators, the third indicator taking the place of the movable regulator in the original version. The reconstruction was completed on 12 May 1989. A replica of a telegraph that was based on original construction drawings discovered in Holland in the 1980s can also be seen at the Telecommunications Museum in Pleumeur Bodou, near Lannion in Bretagne. The same museum also has on display one of the original Foy-Bréguet telegraphs.

An outstanding exhibit on the French optical telegraphs can be found in the Postal Museum of Paris. Other exhibits can be found in the Postal Museum of Nantes, and in the small museum dedicated to Claude Chappe in his birthplace, Brûlon. At the museum in Brûlon, the original eyewitness statements to the experiment from 1791 can be seen. At the Postal Museum in Nantes several original documents, letters, and manuscripts from the Chappe era have been preserved. Among them are notes from Claude Chappe from 1793 on the selection of the stations for the first line from Paris to Lille, and the letter from Abraham Chappe to the Telegraph Administration from 1844, detailing a proposal for a final revision of the signaling codes.

(Coll. Kon. Kommerskollegium)

Chapter Three
Abraham N. Edelcrantz

A Man Named Clewberg

The designer and builder of the Swedish optical telegraph network was born on 29 July 1754 in the city of Åbo, named Abraham Niclas Clewberg.[1] Like Claude Chappe, Clewberg came from a relatively well-to-do family and seemed destined to become a scholar. His father, Carl Abraham Clewberg (1712–1765) was professor of ancient languages at the Royal Academy of Åbo. In 1752 he married 16-year-old Agatha Charlotta Fahlenius (1736–1817), 24 years his junior. As far as we know, Abraham Niclas had just one sibling, a sister named Sara Charlotta, who was born just after his father's death in 1766.

A.D. 1754

Abraham Clewberg was a bright student. On 18 July 1772, two weeks before his eighteenth birthday, he completed a doctoral thesis in optics. But Clewberg also had an interest in the arts, and to round out his education he wrote a second doctoral thesis in 1773, in literature. The young Doctor in Science and Literature then started working as a teacher and librarian.

A.D. 1772

In his spare time, Clewberg wrote poetry. He became a member of *Utile Dulce*, a society dedicated to the study of everything that was "Useful and Beautiful." There he met Johan Henrik Kellgren (1751–1795), also a student at Åbo at the time, who would soon acquire fame as a Swedish poet. They became lifelong friends. When the Swedish king Gustaf III (1746–1792) visited Åbo in 1775, the 21-year-old Abraham Clewberg was asked to recite some of his poetry. He apparently made such an

A.D. 1775

---

1. The notes to this chapter start at p. 256.

Figure 3.1 King Gustaf III (left) and A. N. Edelcrantz (right).
(Coll. Statens Konstmuseer (left), Tekniska Museets Arkiv (right))

impression that he received an invitation to visit the court in Stockholm. Soon afterwards Clewberg was hired in his capacity as a librarian, and asked to reorganize the private library of the king.

For some years Clewberg alternated between working as a librarian in Stockholm and teaching at the Royal Academy in Åbo. He taught both courses on electricity and on literature.

A.D. 1783 In April 1783 Abraham Clewberg decided to move to Stockholm permanently, and quickly started acquiring a series of prestigious titles. He first received an appointment at the court as Secretary of Protocol. In 1786 he gained membership in the Swedish Academy, partly in recognition of a poem, *Ode to the Swedish people,* he had written to celebrate the
A.D. 1787 opening of the Swedish Parliament that year.[2] In 1787 he was promoted further to Private Secretary of King Gustaf III.

Two years later, at the age of 35, Clewberg was raised to the peerage. As one of the marks of this honor he was given a new name: Edelcrantz.[3]

THE THEATER

One of Edelcrantz's assignments from 1783 was as the assistant director, and later director, of the Swedish Royal Theaters. As a perk benefit of that job, he obtained an apartment in the Opera House in central Stock-
A.D. 1790 holm, directly opposite the Royal Palace.[4] He lived there from 1790 until his death.

The king had a strong interest in the arts, particularly in the Royal Theaters, so Edelcrantz's appointment must have been significant. The

Figure 3.2 Gustaf IV Adolph (left) and His Uncle Carl (right).
(Coll. Kon. Kommerskollegium. Photos: Svenska Porträttarkivet.)

king actively invited scholars, poets, artists, and actors to the Swedish court. Among them were Louis-Jean Desprez, a French architect and artist of fame at the time, who worked on the decoration of the Royal Theater. The king often attempted to set strict rules for those who worked on his projects. Mediating disputes with the artists, who naturally still demanded their creative freedom, was a task that fell to Edelcrantz.

From 1790 until 1791 Edelcrantz traveled through Europe, at the king's request, to study the European theaters and to persuade more actors to come to Sweden. Shortly after his return, perhaps as a reward for a job well done, Edelcrantz received the estate *Stora Skuggan*, located on royal A.D. 1792 hunting grounds just outside Stockholm, for his personal use for one century. He built the land in classical English style, with a park, a villa, and an octagonal two-story greenhouse that has since been converted into a house. The villa and the greenhouse are believed to have been designed by Desprez. Edelcrantz used the house as his summer residence, and named it *The Shadow*.

It seemed that things couldn't go better for Edelcrantz. But the tide soon changed.

Difficult Times
On 16 March 1792 the man who had brought Edelcrantz to Stockholm and nurtured his career, King Gustaf III, became the victim of a plot and was shot by a young officer during a masquerade at the Opera House. He died two weeks later.[5]

Figure 3.3 Count Reuterholm (left) and J. A. Ehrenström (right).
(Coll. Nationalmuseum (left), Statens Konstmuseer (right))

As in the rest of Europe, the end of the eighteenth century was an uneasy period in Sweden. The monarchy came under attack, and those protected by it started losing their privileges. Gustaf III was succeeded by his 12-year-old son, Gustaf IV Adolph, but because of his age, a regency was formed under his uncle, Count Carl (Figure 3.2). The real power, meanwhile, was seized by Carl's friend and advisor Count Gustaf Adolph Reuterholm (Figure 3.3). This period, called the "Reuterholm Regime" (1792–1796), was characterized by a vicious persecution of the former friends of Gustaf III. Many of Edelcrantz's friends were thrown in prison or forced to leave the country.

One of Edelcrantz's friends from his early period in Stockholm was Johan Albert Ehrenström. Both Edelcrantz and Ehrenström had been employed as Secretary to King Gustaf III, and had both been fairly close to him. A survival instinct in Edelcrantz made him keep a low profile and take small steps to earn the confidence of the new rulers. Ehrenström was less careful. Since the assassination, he had maintained a correspondence with another former aide of King Gustaf III, General Gustaf Mauritz Armfelt, who was now employed as the Swedish ambassador in Naples. The correspondence was intercepted by the Reuterholm regime. Both Armfelt and Ehrenström were curtly accused of treason and sentenced to death.

The execution of Ehrenström was to be performed at Normalms Torg, today named Gustaf Adolph's Torg, next to the Royal Opera House where Edelcrantz had his apartment. Passing the Opera House on the way to his execution, Ehrenström spotted Edelcrantz watching the proceedings from his apartment. This is how he described what happened.[6]

When I arrived at Normalms Torg I saw how my friend Edelcrantz hurried to draw the curtains at the window of the room in which I had spent so many pleasant evenings with him and with the great [author Johan Henrik] Kellgren.

Johan Ehrenström (1762–1847) was reprieved from execution at the block, and could record the events in his memoirs. When he later reminded Edelcrantz of this experience, his friend reportedly blushed and whispered "Those were difficult times."

The First Experiments

In September 1794 the first news came from France about the telegraph developed by Claude Chappe. Intrigued by this idea, Edelcrantz immediately started to work on his own version of an optical telegraph. Within a few months, he was ready for a demonstration. It was held on King Gustaf IV Adolph's fourteenth birthday, 1 November 1794.

Edelcrantz's first telegraph design consisted of a single support beam with two rotating indicators. Each of the indicators could be set in one of four distinct positions, allowing sixteen combinations. As Edelcrantz later explained in his treatise, he had compressed the alphabet to sixteen symbols so that each sign could represent one letter from this set.[7] Edelcrantz also explained that the number of signals could be increased to 64 by allowing the indicator arms to be set in eight instead of four distinct positions, at the risk of making it harder to distinguish between the signs.

Edelcrantz constructed three telegraph stations. One was on the roof of the royal castle in the center of Stockholm. The second station was about 5 km (3 miles) away on the outskirts of Stockholm in Traneberg, opposite the island of Stora Hässingen. The third was 7 km (4 miles) further down on a tower near the so-called China Castle, a summer house on the grounds of the Royal Palace in Drottningholm, just outside Stockholm. The tower, Götiska Tornet, designed by Desprez in 1791, was the highest point in the area.

A report published on 5 November 1794 in the Swedish Newspaper *Inrikes Tidningar* (Domestic Events), described the experiment as follows:

Experiments with a Swedish Telegraph

In the honorable presence of the Royal family, on October 30, 31 and November 1, experiments were conducted with a machine that is intended for the fast exchange of messages between distant places, a similar purpose as the French Telegraph, about which the newspapers have given occasional news. The machine is invented by Chancellor Edelcrantz, one of the eighteen members of the Swedish Academy. It consists of a long standing beam with two arms of 6 ells long, each movable on an axis, the upper arm at 3 ells and the lower arm at 6 ells distance from the top of the beam. These arms indicate, through their position relative to each other and relative to the beam, 16 fixed symbols and 33 with movements [the number 33 is most likely an error by the reporter], out of which the former, characterized by concatenation of the numbers 1, 2, 3, 4, actually are used to indicate letters from the alphabet, which can be reduced to this number.

The movements of the machine are observed with ordinary telescopes, and can, when the air is clear, be seen at a distance of several tens of kilometers. The correspondence took place between the roof of the royal Castle in Stockholm and the China Castle in Drottningholm. But, since these two places cannot be seen from each other, there was an intermediate station, where the signals were repeated, situated on a mountain opposite to Stora Hässingen.

After the machines were erected, tested and adjusted at these 3 locations, the real experiment was conducted on October 31, when His Royal Majesty the Regent Himself posed questions which were answered by the Count etc. Jacob DelaGardie, using the telegraph from the Castle of Stockholm, after they had been sent by the Chancellor Edelcrantz using the telegraph at China Castle and repeated at the intermediate station by Mr. Öfverbom, Premier Engineer at the Royal Surveyor Office. For 8 questions and equally many answers, ciphering and deciphering, one hour and 26 minutes were required including the adjustment of the machines.

For the last question a new cipher was used, randomly chosen among 128 distinct, and about which the correspondent in Stockholm was not previously informed. Each signal requires approximately 4 seconds, which makes 16 signals per minute, and one minute for a distance of 160 km if the stations are 10 km apart. Thus, if the sending of a message at the first station requires 3 minutes, it can be read after 4 minutes at a distance of 160 km, after 5 at 320 km and after 6 at a distance of 480 km, etc. It should, however, be possible to increase this speed when the persons involved gain more experience than can be gained after some days of practice and for which Mr. Chappe in Paris used a full year.

On November 1, the king's birthday, the telegraph sent the following quatrain from Stockholm to Drottningholm. It was delivered in 7 minutes and humbly presented to the king by Count Jacob DelaGardie.

> This greeting from the Swedish nation
> That loves and honors their King
> Today to His Heart will bring
> A blessing to this new creation

The inventor of the Swedish telegraph has developed another version of his machine, for which a model is being built by which more than 1,000 distinct characters can be sent at greater speed and with smaller chance of error.

We can guess who wrote the poem that made up the first message transmitted. As indicated by the closing sentence of the report, though, even at the time of the first experiment Edelcrantz was already thinking about new designs that would allow for more signal combinations. The ten-shutter design that he later adopted, allowing 2^{10} = 1,024 combinations, may have already occurred to him at this time. First, however, he experimented with a variation of his semaphore telegraph design, this time allowing for eight positions per indicator, rotating the indicators not in the middle, but from their endpoints. Simultaneously, he increased the number of indicators from two to five, giving a maximum of 8^5 = 32,768 possible combinations.

The young king was pleased with the experiment. There would be no long struggle for Edelcrantz to gain official approval for further experiments.

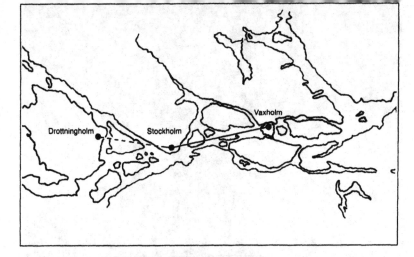

Figure 3.4 The Experimental Line to Drottningholm (1794) and the First Network Line Stockholm-Vaxholm (1795).

On 7 November, less than one week after the first demonstration, the king requested that his special Council of Advisors study the construction of an optical telegraph network in Sweden, with connections to Denmark and to Finland. In the same letter, the young king nominated Edelcrantz as a new member of the same prestigious council, virtually sealing the outcome of the study.

The Shutter Telegraph

After a series of experiments that is documented in Edelcrantz's treatise on telegraphs (see p. 132), Edelcrantz had decided to abandon the Chappe-like design of a semaphore telegraph with articulated arms, and switched permanently to a ten-shutter system. In his own words:[8]

> ... I was soon induced to give preference to the following [shutter] design with its smaller size, greater speed, and ease in its movements, increased clarity and visibility, in addition to several other factors, such as its possible use at night.

The shutter telegraph consisted of a matrix of three by three shutters, with a tenth, extra large, shutter mounted on top. The positions of a single column of three shutters could now be represented with an octal encoding. Per column, each shutter was assigned a number. From top to bottom, the shutters were numbered 1, 2, and 4. Summing the numbers of the shutters that were closed produced a column code between zero and seven. The code for a complete telegraph signal consisted of three of these octal numbers, one for each column, which could be prefixed by the letter A if the tenth shutter was also closed. The code A636 then encoded the

Figure 3.5 Model of a Nine-Shutter Telegraph, ca. 1808.
(Coll. Telemuseum, Stockholm)

position where the top two shutters in the middle column, the bottom two shutters in the first and last column, and the tenth shutter were all closed, and thus visible to the next station.

To set the shutter signals quickly, Edelcrantz designed a sophisticated control mechanism, which is illustrated in Figure 3.6. The operator could set a telegraph code on the panel and then slide it over to grab onto the wires that connected to the shutters. By pushing down on a footpedal, the right wires were pulled, and the signal was displayed. While waiting for the signal to be copied by the next station, the operator could already prepare the next signal, by using the mirror half of the control panel. As soon as a signal had been confirmed, the footpedal was released, the control panel moved to the opposite side, and by pushing down on the pedal again the next signal was set without delay. Meanwhile the telegraph

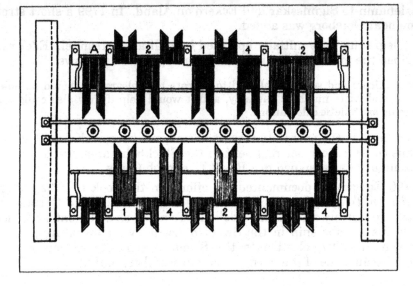

Figure 3.6 Control Panel of Ten-Shutter Telegraph, Top View.
(Source: [Risberg 1938], p. 49)

signal unavoidably passed through an all-zero position, as an extra warning to the remote station that the signal had changed.

The design from 1794 was used in a number of small variations. In some systems the function of the footpedal was performed by a crank that was rotated to pull down the shutter wires. In others, there were some changes in the way in which counterweights were attached to the shutters. In the most common version, the counterweights were attached directly to the shutters. In others the weights were suspended from longer strings. In the early models, the frame of the telegraph was a complete grid that enclosed all shutters. In the later models the outer frame was deleted, and only an inner frame remained, consisting of one or two posts with side-bars to hold the shutters. The smaller frames were probably cheaper, and easier to construct. The simplest construction, with two posts, is illustrated in Figure 3.9. When a single post was used, as shown in Figure 3.7, the shutters in the middle column had an additional opening at the top, which allowed them to clear the post when moved into the horizontal position.

THE FIRST NETWORK LINK

On 30 January 1795, barely three months after the first test, Edelcrantz A.D. 1795 obtained permission to build a first telegraph line from the Katarina Church in the center of Stockholm to the fortress of Vaxholm. The line went into operation on 28 July 1795. Between 1795 and 1797 two more telegraph lines were built: from Stockholm to Fredriksborg and from

Grisslehamn to Signilsskär and Eckerö on Åland. In 1799 a short stretch of line near Göteborg was added.

The telegraphs were initially operated by military personnel. Edelcrantz described the minimal requirements for an operator as follows:

> The officers and soldiers selected to operate the telegraphs should be able to read and write numbers passably, and it would help if they also could make simple arithmetic calculations.

The training of the operators took one week, one hour each day. One non-commissioned officer per regiment in the Stockholm area and one soldier per company was assigned to a Royal Telegraph Corps.

A.D. 1796 In 1796 Edelcrantz documented his efforts in the book that he called *A Treatise on Telegraphs*. The book was soon translated into German and French, and firmly established Edelcrantz's name as an inventor. In addition to his membership in the Swedish Academy (of literature), he now also won, in 1797, election to the Swedish Academy of Sciences. He quickly became one of the most prominent members of that body.

An Inter-Networking Experiment

Meanwhile, France was still at war with Austria and Britain. Sweden's policy was initially to remain neutral in the European conflict. When, around 1800, the British blockade of France began to damage Swedish foreign trade, King Gustaf IV Adolph decided to enter into a pact with Russia, which was soon joined by Prussia, Denmark, and Norway (then part of Denmark).

A.D. 1800

Britain, of course, was ready to enforce its blockades, so a war with the Scandinavian countries seemed likely. The king decided that an early-warning telegraph network had to be constructed along the southwest coast of Sweden, and on 19 February 1801 he gave orders for Edelcrantz personally to make the preparations. Edelcrantz left the next day. He first went to Helsingborg, the point on the Swedish coast that is closest to Denmark.

A.D. 1801

The cities of Helsingborg in Sweden and Helsingör in Denmark are separated by a narrow strait, called the Öresund. Along the shore of the Öresund, Edelcrantz selected six sites for the new line of telegraphs: Kullen, Svedberget, Pålsjö, the Kärnan fortress in Helsingborg, Glumslöv, and Kirsebergs Backar at Bulltofta, close to Malmö. Provisions were made to allow for telegraphic communications between the commanders of the Swedish fleet at sea and the shore.

A possible attack or invasion by the British was expected at the Öresund, but it was not clear which of the two countries would be the target of the first assault. Edelcrantz proposed to establish a telegraph link across the Öresund between Sweden and Denmark: the first-ever international network connection.

In a letter to Governor Toll in Helsingborg, dated 14 March 1801, Edelcrantz reported that all preparations had been made, and he asked the

Figure 3.7 Seal of the Royal Telegraph Institution and its
Approval by King Karl XIII (1748–1818).[9]
(Coll. Telemuseum, Stockholm)

governor to issue the necessary orders for the construction of the telegraphs. He also asked the governor to have the military select four sober men, who could write numbers, for each of the six telegraph stations. This order was to be given immediately so that the men could assist during the transportation and erection of the telegraphs. The letter also details Edelcrantz's proposal for inter-networking with the Danes. He had already spotted a suitable site for a telegraph on the Danish side of the Öresund, on Kronborg Castle near Helsingör. He wrote:

> This connection makes it possible to maintain a continuous contact between the commanders; the Danes will get the reports from Kullen at the same time as we do. From your own window, governor, the Kärnan Tower should be visible and you should therefore be able to send your orders from your home directly to Kullen, Landskrona, Malmö and the other stations.

Farther north, the telegraph line near Göteborg was also being extended at this time, and required Edelcrantz's presence. In the company of King Gustaf IV Adolph, Edelcrantz went to Göteborg, leaving the further preparations for the southern line to Governor Toll. The British, meanwhile, had decided to send a fleet under Admiral Nelson to attack Copenhagen. The fleet was first observed from Kullen on 21 March 1801.

With Edelcrantz in Göteborg, and the threat of a British attack greatly increased, the initiative to establish the crucial telegraph link between Denmark and Sweden moved to the Danes. Edelcrantz's counterpart in Denmark was Captain Lorenz Fisker who, inspired by the Swedish ten-shutter telegraph, had designed a variation for use in a Danish optical telegraph network.[10] In early 1801 the Danes had established a telegraph line based on the Fisker system along the east coast of Själland. The telegraph from this line at Kronborg castle, however, was directed to the south and could not be read easily from Helsingborg, as had been proposed by Edelcrantz.

By order of the Danish crown-prince Fredrik, Fisker wrote to Governor Toll on 29 March 1801 and suggested that the existing telegraph at Kronborg be used by Swedish observers from an observation point either to the north or to the south of Helsingborg, where it could be read more easily. He proposed that a high flagpole would be placed at the spot selected, so that a flag could be used to acknowledge the receipt of messages sent from the Danish side. A ball would be hoisted at a similar pole in Kronborg when messages were to be sent to the Swedes. Since the telegraphs on the Swedish side had not been constructed yet, the inter-network link could only be operated in one direction. Fisker enclosed a full description of his telegraph in his letter to Toll. He also included a code list of the 18 most relevant signals, all of which concerned the expected movements of the British fleet.

On 2 April 1801, the British fleet attacked Copenhagen. As planned, the events were reported via the telegraph to Sweden, but Sweden failed to come to Denmark's aid. The Danish fleet was defeated. The Danes signed a treaty with the British, and, understandably, declined further exchanges of intelligence with the Swedes. The first international network link was abandoned after just four days of service.

When Edelcrantz returned to Helsingborg a few days later, part of the motivation for the construction of the southern line had disappeared. Edelcrantz, nevertheless, reported to Governor Toll on 28 April that he had erected the telegraph on the Kärnan tower in Helsingborg. The other stations were never constructed. Sweden signed a treaty with Britain, and a relatively quiet period followed.

The Diplomat

The telegraphs on the Swedish network were used only intermittently in the next few years. Edelcrantz temporarily shifted his attention to other pursuits. During the next ten years Edelcrantz pursued just about every avenue that opened up to him, while somewhat neglecting his interests in the Royal Theater and the further development of the telegraph network.

From December 1801 until May 1804 Edelcrantz made a second trip through Europe at the request of King Gustaf IV Adolph, visiting Germany, Holland, Belgium, France, and England. His mission was to collect information about new industrial processes, especially on the production of alcohol, which was, at the time, an important source of income to the Swedish state.

Edelcrantz managed his task skillfully. He made contacts everywhere, using charm, wit, and intelligence. He reported his findings in letters sent back to Sweden, often using secret messages added to a regular, innocent text by using a special invisible ink which could be read only by heating the paper on which it was written. He brought back close to one thousand books from his journey.

Edelcrantz's ingenuity opened doors virtually everywhere he went. While he was visiting Berlin, for instance, Edelcrantz invented an improved boiler and was promptly admitted as a member of the Royal Academy of Sciences in Prussia. The appointment made it possible for him to visit many places that would otherwise have been inaccessible, and he used the easy access to study the organization and technology of Prussian agriculture and industry in detail.

Similarly, while visiting Paris in 1802, he is said to have invented a new A.D. 1802 lamp, and he was admitted as a member of the *Societé d'Encouragement de l'Industrie Nationale*. When he was shown Chappe's competing optical telegraph design, Edelcrantz is said to have remarked:

> There is nothing in this device that I would want to copy.

Chappe and Edelcrantz never met, and never corresponded about their designs. While in Paris, Edelcrantz did meet another inventor of a competing telegraph design—a meeting that would have important consequences for him. That person was Sir Richard Lovell Edgeworth, the Irish inventor of the so-called *Tellograph*, about which we will learn more later.[11]

Both Edelcrantz and Edgeworth became honorary members of the *Societé d'Encouragement de l'Industrie Nationale*, in both cases in recognition for their work on optical telegraphs. The acquaintance led to a number of social calls on Edgeworth and his family, who had accompanied him to Paris. Among the people Edelcrantz met there was Edgeworth's daughter, Maria.

On 3 December 1802 Maria Edgeworth was in the middle of writing a long letter to her aunt, and confidante, Mrs. Ruxton. This is, in part, what she wrote:[12]

> Here I am at the brink of the last page, and I have said nothing of the Apollo, the Invalides, or Les Sourds et Muets. What shall I do? I cannot speak of everything at once, and when I speak to you so many things crowd upon my mind.—
>
> Here, my dear aunt, I was interrupted in a manner that will surprise you as much as it surprised me, by the coming in of Monsieur Edelcrantz, a Swedish gentleman, whom we have mentioned to you, of superior understanding and mild manners: he came to offer me his hand and heart!!

Edelcrantz had fallen in love. It could, by all means, be the beginning of something good. But, the letter continued:

> My heart, you may suppose, cannot return his attachment, for I have seen but very little of him, and have not had time to have formed any judgement, except that I think nothing could tempt me to leave my own dear friends and my own country to live in Sweden.
>
> My dearest aunt, I write to you the first moment, as next to my father and mother no person in the world feels so much interest in all that concerns me. I need not tell you that my father—"Such in this moment as in all the past,"— is kindness itself; kindness far superior to what I deserve, but I am grateful for it.

Maria Edgeworth (1767–1849) was 35 years old when she wrote this. Edelcrantz (1754–1821) was 48. The age difference was not much of an issue with Maria's father. Sir Edgeworth had written about Edelcrantz's marriage proposal to his sister-in-law, also on 3 December, in the most positive terms. In that letter he reveals that Edelcrantz had first approached him, and that it had been only at his encouragement that Edelcrantz had then approached Maria.

But, Maria could not be persuaded by Edelcrantz's charm. On 8 December she wrote about the proposal once more, this time in a letter to her cousin, Miss Sophy Ruxton.

> I take it for granted, my dear friend, that you have by this time seen a letter I wrote a few days ago to my aunt. To you, as to her, every thought of my mind is open. I persist in refusing to leave my country and my friends to live at the Court of Stockholm, and he tells me (of course) that there is nothing he would not sacrifice for me except his duty; he has been all his life in the service of the king of Sweden, has places under him, and is actually employed in collecting information for a large political establishment. He thinks himself bound in

Figure 3.8 Maria Edgeworth.
(Source: [Edgeworth 1895])

honor to finish what he has begun. He says he should not fear the ridicule or blame that would be thrown upon him by his countrymen for quitting his country at his age, but that he should despise himself if he abandoned his duty for any passion. This is all very reasonable, but reasonable for him only, not for me; and I have never felt anything for him but esteem and gratitude.

There seems to have been no further contact between them, not even so much as a letter or a visit. Maria Edgeworth established herself as a successful Irish novelist, producing a wealth of books that were printed and reprinted many times. Her first major work, called *Castle Rackrent*, had been published in 1800, just before she met Edelcrantz. Her stepmother, Sir Edgeworth's fourth wife, later suggested that one of her later novels, *Leonora*, was written specifically for Edelcrantz. She described how the affair had affected Maria:[13]

> And even after her [Maria's] return to Edgeworthstown, it was long before she recovered the elasticity of her mind. She exerted all her powers of self-command, and turned her attention to everything which her father suggested for her to write. But *Leonora*, which she began immediately after our return home, was written in the hope of pleasing the Chevalier Edelcrantz; it was written in a style which he liked, and the idea of what he would think of it was, I believe, present to her in every page she wrote. She never heard that he had even read it. From the time they parted at Paris there was no sort of communication between them, and beyond the chance which brought us sometimes into company with travelers who had been in Sweden, or the casual mention of M. Edelcrantz in the newspapers or scientific journals, we never heard more of one who had been of such supreme interest to her, and to us all at Paris, and of whom Maria continued to have all her life the most romantic recollection.

Neither Maria Edgeworth nor Edelcrantz ever married.

The visits to the Edgeworths during his brief courtship had some unpleasant consequences for Edelcrantz. Since the treaty of Amiens of March 1802, France and Britain were temporarily at peace, but the two countries were still on unfriendly terms. Edelcrantz was suspected of being involved in a plot against the French and was promptly asked to leave the country as a *persona non grata*. For a short time Edelcrantz went to prison. Only a personal intervention by the Swedish ambassador to France could help release him and avoid his forceful expulsion from France. A short while later Edelcrantz decided to leave on his own accord. He went to England.

STEAM ENGINES

A.D. 1803 In London, in 1803, Edelcrantz invented a new safety valve for steam engines, for which he was awarded a silver medal and yet another coveted membership in an esteemed organization, this time the *Society for the Encouragement of Arts, Manufactures, and Commerce*. He met James Watt, who invited him to visit his steam engine factory in Birmingham. While in Birmingham, Edelcrantz promptly decided to buy four steam engines to bring back to Sweden. He persuaded Samuel Owen, Watt's collaborator in Birmingham, to come to Sweden to install the steam engines for him. Owen would later decide to stay in Sweden and start a new company. He became an important figure in Swedish industrialization.

A.D. 1804 Excited about the potential of steam engines, on his return to Sweden in 1804 Edelcrantz proposed to build a steam-driven mill in central Stockholm. He had to overcome many more obstacles in this venture than he had in the construction of the optical telegraph lines. It took him a year to obtain the necessary permissions for the construction of the mill. At the spot where City Hall now stands, Edelcrantz built his Fire-Mill. After two

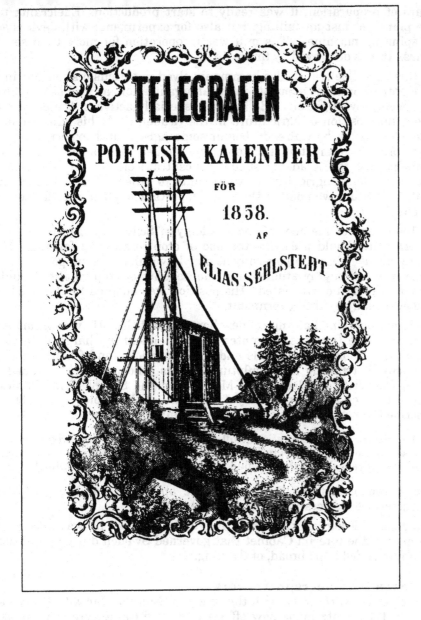

Figure 3.9 Cover of a Book by Sehlstedt.
(Source: [Sehlstedt 1858])

years of preparation, it was ready to start production. Edelcrantz used the plant not just for milling, but also for experiments with devices such as spinning machines. The mill was in operation for more than seventy years. It was destroyed by fire in 1878.

At this time Edelcrantz also became involved in serious discussions in the Academy of Sciences about its internal organization, as well as in many of its special investigations. He became especially active in the discussions about the position of agriculture in the Academy. At his summer house *The Shadow* he had already begun some agricultural experiments, and therefore his interest in the topic was piqued. He opposed those who thought that the Academy should concentrate on the fundamental sciences and leave agricultural experiments to others. Instead, he argued that agriculture was one of the most important applied sciences to serve Sweden's interest.

In 1805 another member of the Academy of Sciences suggested that the government should prescribe the use of crop rotation in farming. Edelcrantz argued that the government should withhold its support until the issue was thoroughly studied and the benefits of crop rotation could be demonstrated and calculated. His position was adopted by the Academy, and eventually by the government.

Edelcrantz obtained a range of new honors and titles. He was promoted to Director of the Theaters, appointed Superintendent in Charge of the Royal Furniture, Household Utensils and Art Collections, and Chairman of the Academy of Painting and Sculpture and its schools, which included the Royal Collection of Mechanical Models and the School of Mechanics, a predecessor of the current Royal Institute of Technology. In 1806 he described the state of this academy in his annual speech:

> The School of Mechanics is in full inactivity. It misses its director who has been absent for two years, one of the teachers has been on leave, another almost always ill and the new building for the school remains unfinished.

The statement reflects the no-nonsense approach that is said to have characterized Edelcrantz as an administrator.

A.D. 1807 The peak of Edelcrantz's career came in 1807, when he was appointed a member of the interim Cabinet that governed Sweden during an absence, for an extended trip abroad, of the king.

The Swedish Telegraph Network
In the period 1807–1809, with the renewed threat of war with France and Russia, Edelcrantz made new efforts to extend the telegraph network in Sweden. In 1809 the Swedish king, and Edelcrantz's protector, was exiled. But again, Edelcrantz managed to survive the upheaval.

A.D. 1808 In the spring of 1808 a decision was made to create a Royal Telegraph Institution, with Edelcrantz as its first director. Edelcrantz secured a position as assistant director of the Telegraph Institution for his nephew Carl Christian Limnell on 7 October 1808. Edelcrantz had taken his

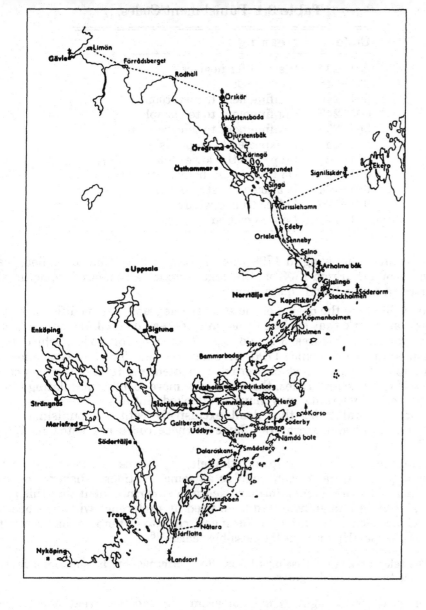

Figure 3.10 Optical Telegraph Network, 1808–1809.
(Source: [Risberg 1938], p. 91)

Table 3.1 Punishment Codes.

Code	Meaning
001–244	Warned for neglect
001–245	Hard labor
001–246	Confinement to own room
001–247	Confinement to telegraph
001–250	Confinement to telegraph at . . .
001–251	Is expected to be punished
001–721	Step onto the lower telegraph arm
001–723	Do you see anybody on the arm at . . .
001–724	Is allowed to step down
001–725	Is free from custody
001–727	I am in custody

nephew under his wing in 1798 when his sister Sara Charlotta died, just 32 years of age. From 1809 on, Christian Limnell also shared Edelcrantz's apartment at the Royal Opera House.

Around this time the design of the shutter telegraph was modified and the outer framework that enclosed the shutters was deleted, as can be seen, for instance, in Figures 3.7 and 3.9. The signaling codes, which had remained unchanged since 1796, were also revised. The new code allowed for up to 5,120 signals, which were documented in a total of thirteen code tables.[14] In these new codes, there was also more room for regulating some things that Edelcrantz may have overlooked initially. There were, for instance, several codes that dealt exclusively with the punishment of negligent telegraph operators. Some of these codes are listed in Table 3.1.[15]

The curious command to step onto the telegraph arms as a form of punishment appears to have been popular at some locations. Risberg reports that he had learned from a former telegraph superintendent that this particular form of punishment had been used by preference when the operators at the telegraph station in Hissingen, close to Götenborg, had committed an offense. He hints at the possible reason:[16]

> The telegraphing [at Hissingen] was often performed by the superintendent's, at the time, young daughters.

Fortunately, the daughters did not seem to mind this treatment much. Risberg continues:

> When they were asked a couple of years ago how it felt to stand on the telegraph arm, they remembered the experience well, but noted that "it was just fun."

After the new codes of 1808 were adopted, the motto of the Telegraph Corps became signal 636, which meant *Passa väl upp*, or "Be on guard."

Figure 3.11 Button from a Telegraph Operator's Uniform.
(Coll. Televerket Archive, Stockholm)

The signal appeared prominently in the seal of the Telegraph Institution, and on the buttons of the telegraph operator's uniforms, to serve as a reminder of the telegraph operator's duty.[17]

In November 1809 the Swedish network consisted of approximately 50 A.D. 1809 stations spread out over a distance of some 200 km (124 miles), and provided employment for 172 people.[18] It included lines from Stockholm to the city of Gävle in the north, Landsort in the south and Eckerö on Åland in the east. The telegraphs were used to signal the arrival of ships, but they also served an important early warning task for enemy attacks.

In March 1808 the Russian cavalry made such an attack, invading Åland over the ice, in the process destroying the telegraphs at Signilsskär and Eckerö. Two months later, the population revolted and expelled the Russian troops. By the end of the summer the telegraphs were back in operation. The next winter, the Russian troops invaded Åland again and this time the Swedish had to retreat over the ice to the mainland. Although surrounded by the Russians, the telegraph operator at Signilsskär stayed at his post and signaled to the retreating troops where the enemy was hiding, to prevent them from being ambushed.

After the war with Russia ended in September 1809, the telegraphs on the east coast of Sweden ceased to be of value. They were dismantled and placed in storage. In 1810 plans were renewed to establish a telegraph A.D. 1810 line on the south coast. Edelcrantz was asked to establish a telegraph line between Karlskrona and Helsingborg. The preparations were almost complete when, on 15 May 1811, the Swedish crown decided to stop the project for lack of funds. In August of that year, the position of Telegraph Inspector was created, with Carl Wilhelm Venus (1770–1851) receiving the first appointment. As one of his first acts, Venus proposed to establish a new telegraph line from Stockholm via Arholma to Söderarm. But, this

Figure 3.12 Sketch of Edelcrantz by Sergel.
(Coll. Nationalmuseum, Stockholm)

proposal too was unsuccessful. Temporarily, the Swedish telegraph network disappeared almost completely.

More Titles

The lapse of interest in optical telegraphs did not diminish Edelcrantz's popularity in Sweden. Edelcrantz had participated actively during the 1809–1810 sessions of Parliament in discussions about government support for agriculture, and had made a favorable impression on the new crown-prince, Karl Johan. Edelcrantz was soon asked to draft plans for a new Academy of Agriculture. Concurrently with the design of a new steam engine, the invention of a spinning machine, and the construction of a linen-spinning mill, he started making plans for the new Academy.

The Academy of Agriculture was established in December 1811 and started its work in 1813 with the crown-prince as president and Edelcrantz as its director. Edelcrantz's plan for the Academy emphasized experimental research. In 1814 some land next to *The Shadow* was A.D. 1814 donated to the Academy to be used for agricultural experiments. The School of Mechanics, which included the royal collection of mechanical models and its workshop, was also transferred to the new Academy.

In 1813 Edelcrantz had received another appointment, this time as President of the Government Office of Commerce. This appointment made him the prime administrator of Swedish agriculture and commerce. In 1815 Edelcrantz was raised to the rank of Baronet (*Friherre*) in recogni- A.D. 1815 tion of his public service.

Edelcrantz's Death

Edelcrantz was as intrigued by the phenomenon of death as he had been with all the other endeavors throughout his life. In his final days, with his friends collected around him, he made a point of commenting in detail on his feelings about the approaching inevitable. His last observation, on 15 March 1821, was:[19]   A.D. 1821

> Death has arrived ...

Edelcrantz was buried 7 April 1821 in the Klara Kyrka in Stockholm. Since he had no heir, the sign of arms that he had received from the king when he was raised to peerage (a laurel wreath with a lyre) was destroyed at the grave.

Although recipient of many honors, Edelcrantz did not die a rich man. It seems that money was never of great importance to him. He always had to work hard to raise funds to realize his projects. His belongings, including his summer house, were left to his nephew Christian Limnell. His library was willed to the Academy in Åbo, and his private letters were donated to the Royal Library in Stockholm.

Not until fifteen years after Edelcrantz's death was the optical telegraph network revitalized one last time, under the threat of new military attacks.

Reconstruction

After Sweden's resounding defeat in the war of 1809, the optical telegraph had, for all practical purposes, disappeared. Of the more than 100 optical telegraph operators working in the Stockholm Archipelago on 1 November 1809, only four remained on the payroll of the Telegraph Institution on 1 January 1810.[20]

In 1811 Carl Wilhelm Venus was appointed the new Telegraph Inspector, a first indication that the shutdown of the telegraph network was not intended to be permanent. Still, it lasted until 1827 before the restoration of the telegraph network around Stockholm was reconsidered. For a short time the Telegraph Institution was integrated with the Royal Engineering Corps, and thus given a military status.

A.D. 1834 On 18 March 1834 the Telegraph Institution was made part of the Topographical Corps, headed by Carl Fredrik Akrell (1779–1868). One of the first assignments Akrell received was to investigate the changes that had to be made in the Telegraph Institution after the lapse of about 25 years. Akrell proposed a comparison of the original shutter system with more recent semaphore systems that had been developed in the other European countries. It was decided to compare Edelcrantz's system with one that had been developed by Colonel Pasley in England in 1822.[21] Pasley's system, also called the "Universal Telegraph," had been in operation for some time on a trial basis in Karlskrona, so Akrell was familiar with it.

The king approved Akrell's proposal and the first tests were performed in August 1834 between Karlskrona and Drottningskär. More tests, including night transmissions, were done in 1835 between the Katarina church tower in Stockholm and Fredriksborg.

Akrell submitted his report on 21 October 1835. He concluded that the shutter telegraph was easier to operate, was faster, provided a larger code space, and in the long term would prove to be more cost-effective. On the other hand, Pasley's system was considerably easier to construct. Akrell recommended the adoption of Edelcrantz's original design for the permanent stations, and Pasley's design for mobile stations.

A.D. 1836 By 1836 the optical telegraph network had been completely restored. On 18 June 1836, the lines from Stockholm to Vaxholm and from Stockholm via Dalarö to Sandhamn were back in operation. In 1837 the first telegraph line to Vaxholm, which had up to that point only been used as a side-branch on the line along the east coast, was extended to Furusund, about 70 km (43 miles) northeast of Stockholm. In 1838 the line to Sandhamn was extended to Landsort.

The last addition to the optical telegraph network was made in 1854, when the line to Furusund was extended to Arholma and Söderarm.

The Switch To Electrical Telegraph

The electrical telegraph started making headlines in the late 1830's. The first electrical telegraphs were installed in England and in the United States in 1837,[22] in France in 1846,[23] and in Germany in 1848.[24] But the

Figure 3.13 Uniform for Shutter-Telegraph Operators
with King Carl XIV Johan's Signature, Indicating Approval.
(Coll. Televerket Archive, Stockholm)

function of the optical telegraphs in the Stockholm Archipelago was much harder to challenge than in other countries. Here it was not a simple matter of stringing lines on poles through the landscape.

A.D. 1852 At last, in April 1852 Akrell submitted a proposal to the Swedish minister of defense to establish an experimental electro-magnetic telegraph line between Stockholm and Dalarö. Most likely Akrell did not initiate the study but followed up on a request, perhaps even reluctantly. He wrote:

> Since electro-magnetic telegraphs now exist and are used for correspondence in the whole civilized world, Sweden must, without doubt, sooner or later also connect to the rest of Europe using these rapid-writing machines, the more as Denmark already has taken the initiative and provided the necessary intermediate link. This long-term objective should be remembered also in the discussion about a small experimental line. It seems to me that such a line should be established in such a direction and between such end stations that it can serve as the starting point, or connecting link, in a longer line, and that in the meantime it can provide an integral system in itself. To fund such an experiment only for the purpose of testing is not necessary. We already have in our possession machines of the model most commonly used in Europe and their use on a distance of 10 ells or 10 miles is all the same when going from idea to practice. What we have not yet tested is the preparation of the electrical cable. This must be acquired from abroad and should later be possible to manufacture domestically to provide for future needs.

Of course, it was not clear that stringing lines across the landscape was even feasible. As Dr. Jules Guyot had pointed out so eloquently in France, it would be very easy, and perhaps tempting, for an adversary to destroy the cables. The report foresees the problem:

> The gentlemen von Heland and Fahnehjelm consider an experimental line necessary to investigate whether the population of Stockholm would let an open air cable be without destroying it, and want to conclude that this experience would be sufficient evidence that also other areas would see the cable undestroyed and thus avoid the larger cost to put the cable underground. However, absence or presence of singular mischiefs in one place cannot be used to conclude anything about the situation elsewhere. Mischievous persons can be found anywhere but to try to find out where the most of them are to be expected will always be in vain.
>
> In the Royal Garden, open to us all, also to the least well-bred in the population of the capital, there is no destruction of the constructions, plantations, etc. Open flower-beds at the beautiful Rosendal Castle are left unharmed as is the Garden Associations building where people are crowding on the small walk ways during occasions when public amusements are organized. On the other hand, in the Royal Garden in Copenhagen, every flower-bed and lawn is fenced to protect it from public abuse. None of these examples provide evidence but give us hope that in Sweden, as in other countries, a telegraph line could be established through the country without having to dig it into the ground, an undertaking which in most cases should be avoided, and anyway is not very efficient as a protective measure. . . .

Akrell is almost apologetic for even raising the issue:

Figure 3.14 Inside the Reconstructed Station in Furusund.
(Coll. Telemuseum, Stockholm)

The intention behind these remarks is not to dispute the usefulness of establishing an experimental electrical telegraph line. I consider such an undertaking not only useful but necessary to make the electrical telegraph more widely known and get support for a larger effort in the public opinion, without which a future development of a complete electrical telegraph network would be hard to achieve. However, this experimental line should be established in such a direction and between such end stations that it will be easily accessible and of interest to use by as many individuals as possible, and also forms a starting point for a larger network. . . .

Next, after raising some doubts about the wisdom of the proposed trajectory for the first experimental line, Akrell makes it clear that, in his opinion, the outcome of the experiment is hardly an issue. He knows that the days of the optical telegraph are numbered:

> In whatever direction the line is established, the central office in Stockholm should be independent of that of the existing optical telegraph network at Mosebacke. It should, in my opinion, be located in the Post office or in a government building, if a suitable office space can be found in any of these places. If not, some of the crown houses on Riddarholmen could probably be used so that all cables could converge in an expanded network in the future. . . .

Based on this proposal, Carl Akrell received permission to build an experimental line between Stockholm and Södertalje. On 29 October 1852 he submitted his next report. Again, the issue of sabotage came up, but it seemed to be under control now. The report begins:

> Humble memorandum containing a proposal for an electrical telegraph line Stockholm-Södertalje, 29 October 1852, by Carl Akrell
>
> During the local investigations on which this proposal is based, the Captain of the Navy Mechanical Corps Fahnehjelm has served as an assistant, who during travels abroad has had the opportunity to learn more about electrical telegraph systems in England, France and northern Germany. In comparison between the different machines and methods used in these countries, we have reason to consider those now in use between Hamburg and Cuxhaven to be the most appropriate for use in Sweden, due to simplicity and low cost. Such a telegraph is also imported from Hamburg together with several other machines necessary for the planned experiments, such as galvanometer, lightning conductor, insulation made of gutta-percha, etc. The price of the materials necessary to import is calculated from information received by mail conversation with the manager of the Hamburg Telegraph line.
>
> Two different methods can be used when wiring between the telegraphs: One is to insulate the wire with gutta-percha and put it underground, the other is to wire it between poles in the open air, uninsulated. The former method is expensive, partly due to the preparation of the wire, partly due to the trouble to dig ditches in the kind of terrain we have in Sweden. It also introduces inconveniences. The insulation from the ground is easily broken and can also be cut by mischievous persons, resulting in a damage which is hard to detect and repair. The latter method does not introduce these difficulties. Zinc-plated wire can be used without coating and the cost is thus considerably lower. The open wire could also be cut by mischievous persons, although not as easily and the damage is easy to detect. And as the charge of electricity in the wire caused by lightning can be dealt with using lightning-insulators, all reason seems to support the use of open air wire on poles.
>
> The starting point of the telegraph line can and should be determined considering convenience of the public only, when sending and receiving messages. In Stockholm, the post office is the most suitable since it is located in the middle of the city, close to the Royal Castle, the expeditions, the government offices, the police, the harbor, etc, which is why this location is assumed in the sequel. In Södertalje, the end-station should be close to the channel, the road and the guesthouse, and in this respect also there the post office is the most suitable. . .

Next Akrell submits a detailed budget for the construction and management of an experimental line. He comments on ways to recover some of the expenses, first by closing some of the optical telegraphs, but also by opening up the use of the telegraph to the general public—something that had rarely been tried before:

> By charging a small fee for the use of the telegraphs, a possibly not insubstantial compensation could be received for the annual operating cost. According to one tariff issued this year in Halle for telegraph messages, a message containing at most 20 words and sent over 100 km distance costs 1 Rdr 5 s and 20–50 words 2 Rdr 16 s. Such a high tariff should not be adopted here initially but it could as a test be set to 12–16 s for 20 words and less and 24–32 s for 20–50 words and an additional 8 s for every 10th word exceeding 50.

> An additional income could be generated and also a large number of visitors attracted by selling tickets for visitors that wish to see the telegraph and learn about its principles and operation. This is done in Hamburg and several other German locations.

As a result of the experiments, the Swedish Electrical Telegraph Institution was soon instituted, again headed by Akrell. Then, in 1856, the A.D. 1856 administration of the optical telegraph was combined with that of the new Electrical Telegraph Institution, as a first step towards its disappearance. But, over the next five years little else happened. The problem of a more rapid switch-over was, to a large extent, a financial one. The annual report of the Telegraph Institution from 1863 explained, A.D. 1863

> Since the purpose of the telegraph institutions is to convey messages from one place to another as fast and safely as possible, and this purpose can only incompletely be reached using optical telegraphs due to the signaling often being hindered by fog or haze and furthermore can not be conducted during the dark hours, the question of replacing the optical telegraphs erected on the east coast of the country, outside the entrance to the capital, was raised as early as 1857, but as the calculation of all the involved costs made by the Telegraph Board on Royal Command resulted in such a high cost that funds for the realization of the entire plan could not be raised, it was decided only to establish an electrical telegraph line from Stockholm to Dalarö and as a consequence [only] three optical telegraphs were closed in 1858.

For almost ten years electrical and optical telegraph stations were used side by side, the optical telegraphs reaching where the electrical cables could not lead, such as some remote Swedish islands. In 1864 there were A.D. 1864 174 electro-magnetic telegraphs, with 250 operators, but also 24 optical telegraphs with 66 operators (49 on the east coast, and another 17 at the west coast, near Götenborg). Three years later there were still 18 optical telegraphs in service, employing 42 people.

In the annual report of the Telegraph Institution from 1867 the following A.D. 1867 comments can be found:

> The lack of electrical telegraph lines to several important places, like Arholma, Sandhamn and Marstrand, which for the moment are connected to the rest of the telegraph network only by optical telegraphs, is becoming increasingly

serious. The optical telegraphs are often out of operation due to natural hindrances, such as rain or snow, storm, haze, etc. Due to such reasons, signaling has not been possible for the following number of hours of normal duty hours during 1867 at the different stations: Arholma 213, Sandhamn 252, Landsort 360 and on the west coast up to 404 hours of the normal duty hours. The large degree of inconvenience and endangerment for sea travelers caused by this is obvious. Consequently, requests have been made to the Telegraph Board to act in favor of the establishment of electrical telegraph connections to Arholma and Sandhamn, and regarding the latter, the Royal Majesty has approved the inclusion of an electrical connection to Sandhamn in the budget for construction work on the telegraph lines next year and that the necessary local investigations can be started this fall using a crown vessel, at the expense of the Telegraph Board.·

A.D. 1881 The last three optical telegraphs were closed in 1881, later than in any other European country.[25] The annual report of the Swedish Telegraph Board from that year reflected on the event:

> With the closing of these stations, the last part of the optical telegraph institution in Sweden has been discontinued. Regarding the introduction of the same, it should be mentioned that the first optical telegraph institution in Sweden was of Swedish origin and erected in 1794, but then only for messages between Stockholm and Drottningholm, whereafter, during the wars of Sweden 1808 and 1809, such telegraphs were erected in the Archipelago of Stockholm to Gavle, Landsort and Sandhamn. These telegraphs, which shortly thereafter and due to several reasons, decayed, were reerected in 1836 so that correspondence could be conducted not only in military and official matters, but also on the account of the public. . . .

> As replacement for the, in several aspects incomplete, optical telegraph system, new inventions have made it possible for the transport of immaterial communications to benefit from the great advantages of the electrical telegraph and, especially for military purposes, the heliograph and the electrical light given access to new methods for optical messages to replace the now abandoned signaling system.

As in the United States, the era of the optical telegraphs was followed by a brief period of enchantment with heliographic devices. In the end, of course, the electrical telegraphs won decisively.

Bibliographic Notes
An extensive study of the Swedish optical telegraph network was made by Allan Cyrus in 1912, [Cyrus 1912]. A second important study was performed in 1938 by N. J. A. Risberg, [Risberg 1938]. Both works are in Swedish and have not appeared in English translations. Many details about the size of the telegraph network in each year can be found in the annual reports published by the Royal Telegraph Institution, of course, also in Swedish. An overview in German can be found in [Herbarth 1978]. The network is also described, though in less detail, in [Wilson 1976], and in our own [Holzmann and Pehrson 1994].

The Telemuseum in Stockholm has a permanent exhibition on optical telegraphs. The only complete station of the Swedish network that still exists

Figure 3.15 The Shutter Telegraph in Furusund.
(Photo: Gerard J. Holzmann, 1991)

can be found in Furusund. It is described in [Malmgren 1964], [Risberg 1938], and [Cyrus 1912]. The post was in operation from 1837 until 1866, and restored to its original state in 1964. It is opened to the public one day each year. Locally, however, Furusund derives more fame from more recent visitors.[26] The writer August Strindberg (1846–1912) is said to have spent some time in the town during occasional summer visits. Curiously, Strindberg had been an (electrical) telegraph operator at Sandhamn, in 1873, before he became an author. There is no record that he ever stayed at the telegraph house in Furusund.

Chapter Four
A Treatise on Telegraphs

This chapter contains what we believe is the first English translation of a remarkable document written in 1796 by Abraham Niclas Edelcrantz. It describes Edelcrantz's design for the optical telegraph that was used to build the Swedish network in the late eighteenth century.

Well before electrical telegraphs were adopted, almost every country in Europe had at least a few optical telegraph lines in use. Because most of these lines were used only for governmental and military communications, it is hard to find accurate descriptions of their construction and usage. In this regard, Edelcrantz's description is an exceptional find. It spells out in detail how optical telegraphs should, or should not, be constructed, and how the telegraphs of his design were meant to be operated.

Edelcrantz's communication protocols include features that have only recently been rediscovered in modern data communications. They include, for instance, methods for error control, flow control, rate control, compaction, and encryption. This document is a rare instance of the careful, well-documented study of a twentieth century topic by an eighteenth century scholar.

NOTES ON THE TRANSLATION

A first translation from Swedish was made at our request in 1990 by a professional translator from the Language Center in New York. This chapter contains an annotated and revised version of this translation. Our attempt has been to create an accurate and readable text that preserves some of the eloquence and atmosphere of the original document.

In the original the paragraphs were numbered and not titled. We have added the titles, using the table of contents as a guideline. The numbering of sections in the treatise is preserved in this text, with only one exception. In the original document §44 is missing. From the table of contents it is clear, though, that this is the result of a clerical error. The final two sections from the treatise, §45 and §46, are therefore numbered §44 and §45 here. In several other cases we have made small sacrifices to modern rules of typography, especially when not doing so would have impeded the readability of the translation.

All illustrations in this chapter are reproduced from Edelcrantz's treatise with their original figure numbers in place. The copper engravings were scanned in on a 300 dpi scanner. Some blemishes, dust spots and scratches were removed with our own digital photo-editing software. The figures were then reproduced on a 200 dpi digital printer and halftoned for this book. We have placed each figure as close as possible to the first place of reference. In the original publication all illustrations were collected at the end of the book, the usual practice at the time.

Edelcrantz's sometimes elaborate footnotes to his text have been placed at the end of the book, for consistency. Some of the most wonderful observations can be found there. See, for instance, footnotes 19, 29, 71, and 75.

All added page references, editorial remarks, and other annotations are placed in a distinct font, enclosed in square brackets *[like this]*, both in this chapter and in the notes, which can be found starting at p. 257. Page references that appear inside annotations refer to the pages of the book you are holding now.

AFHANDLING

OM

TELEGRAPHER

Och.

Förfök

Til en ny Inrättning däraf;

AF

A. N. EDELCRANTZ

CANTZLIRÅD, KONUNGENS HAND-SECRETERARE,
ARCHIVARIE AF KONGL. MAJ:TS ORDEN, EN
BLAND DE XVIII AF SVENSKA
ACADEMIEN.

Med Kopparftycken.

STOCKHOLM,
Trvckt hos JOHAN PEHR LINDH,
1796.

131

TREATISE ON TELEGRAPHS
And Experiments
With a New Construction Thereof

by

A. N. EDELCRANTZ
STOCKHOLM, 1796

§1 *[About Signals in General]*   There are two ways to send messages rapidly over long distances. The first uses individual signals, each with a separate predefined meaning; the second uses sequences of signals, which are sent in arbitrary combinations to build sentences from words and letters. The use of individual signals dates from the oldest times. They were used in two different ways, based on either visible or audible effects. The visible signals included beacons made with fire or smoke,[1] torch signals,[2] flags, banners, warning signs, and more recently fire rockets, etc. The audible signals included drum signals, trumpets, and later cannon shots, etc. All such signals, however, can convey only predefined messages, orders, questions, events, etc. They do not have the same perfection in expressing ideas, in all their possible variations, that is made possible by ordinary speech or writing, and which has also been achieved in recent times with the machines that are known as "telegraphs." No matter what meaning a predefined signal is able to convey or how quickly it can be sent, its use is limited since the smallest change in the message conveyed will make the signal unusable,[3] and would require the definition of a new signal, so that, to be sufficient, the number of distinct signals would need to be almost infinite. The flag and light signals ordinarily used at sea, although lately much improved *[see p. 12]*, are similarly limited since their use cannot be extended far beyond that of the predefined signals. They are not nearly as perfect as real telegraphs. The difference in the ability to express ideas between these methods and the telegraph is comparable to the difference between hieroglyphics and ordinary writing.[4]

§2 *[History of the Telegraph from Ancient Times]*   Real telegraphy, or after the meaning of the word,[5] the art of writing at a distance (by composing letters and words), was known even in ancient times. Polybius and Julius Africanus *[see p. 27]* record its use by the Greeks and Romans, using kettles with burning twigs or straw in oil, indicating letters in such a way that one to eight fires in the first series encoded the first eight letters of the alphabet, and similarly, fires in the next two series were used to encode the remaining sixteen letters. One, two, or three separate fires lit at a distance were used to indicate the number of the series intended. A similar, less cumbersome, method was invented by Democleitus *[see p. 26]* and improved upon by Polybius. The alphabet was divided into five groups of letters, with five letters in each group, except for the last group which contained only four letters. Two sets of torches were placed perpendicular to the direction of transmission; the number of torches on one side indicated the group number, and on the other side the position of the letter within that group.[6] These devices were simple but slow and inaccurate, especially at a time when for lack of magnifying telescopes the distances covered must have been quite small, and their usage must have been limited to nighttime.

A device which seems to be similar to these Greek inventions is the so-called *Stegano-graphia Trithemiana*. The inventor, *[Johannes]* Trithemius, a Benedictine monk who lived at the end of the fifteenth century *[1462–1516]*, claimed to be able to send messages over any distance using fire. The true nature of his art was never revealed.[7] Therefore, the first experiments with telegraphy after the Greeks,[8] are the ones described by Athan Kircherus *[1602–1680]*. According to him,[9] letters made of thick paper or other opaque materials, either glued to mirrors held in the sun or placed in front of a light source, would create shadows which, when the rays were focused by a convex lens onto a flat surface, could express words or sentences. One can easily see how difficult this would be to accomplish and that it would be feasible only at small distances, although Porta *[see pp. 8, 40]* claimed that in a similar manner he was able to write on the moon,[10] and Corn. Agrippa *[a sixteenth century writer]* tells that Pythagoras, when traveling through Egypt, similarly wrote to his friends with letters reflected on the moon and read in Constantinople.[11]

Also notable is an idea from an unknown person that is contained in a letter to Schottus *[1608–1666, see p. 32]*. He proposes to establish communication between Mainz and Rome by erecting 5 poles on a hill at such a distance from each other that they can easily be distinguished with a telescope from five to six *[Swedish]* miles away.[12] A pulley is attached to the top of each pole to hoist a stick, a sheaf of straw, or other objects to the top. If the alphabet is divided into five groups of letters, an object is first raised to indicate the group number. After the first object is lowered, another one is raised to indicate the number of the letter within the group. The art is the same as that of the Greeks but adapted to daytime use. The inventor, however, seems to be the first to have suggested the use of telescopes. Someone named Kessler *[see p. 34]*, who lived at the beginning of the last century suggested using letters cut from the bottom of barrels, using them to spell out words that would be readable at great distances.[13]

Amontons *[see p. 39]*, a French physicist, who lost his hearing as a child, is said to have considered a visual sign language using some kind of machine, the range of which could be extended by the use of telescopes,[14] but how it was designed is not known to me. At the end of the last century, Rob. Hooke *[1635–1703]* submitted an idea to the English Academy of Science to use a system with movable figures, hung from a wooden framework in the air, for constructing sentences that could be read at great distances *[see pp. 35, 52, 184]*. At night the same figures would be illuminated by torches, however, this idea as well as several of those mentioned above were never put into practice.

Fig. 1.

More recently, someone called Dom Gauthey *[see p. 42]* reported a way of transmitting messages rapidly by shouting into long tubes.[15] His method is inspired by experiments with the 1,000 fathoms *[ca. 1.8 km]* long tubes of the steam-engine works at Chaillot in Paris. He believes that, in this manner, sound could be transmitted even farther and that the tubes could be extended to a length of 6,000 ells *[ca. 3.6 km]*. Thus, 150 such tubes, and 150 persons, could be used to transmit a message over a distance of 50 *[Swedish]* miles *[ca. 535 km]* in 40 to 50 minutes.[16] Guyot describes a method of spelling out a message with cutout letters, a method similar to Kessler's.[17]

Another method similar to the above, but simpler, is described by Paulian *[Aime Henri Paulian, 1722–1801]* in his article on the *Telegraph* in *Dictionaire de Physique*. It uses a transparent figure consisting of one vertical and three horizontal lines, see Figure 1, cut out in a black board, 20 feet square. The lines are 14 feet long and 3 feet wide. The figure has ten sections which are viewed against the sky in the daytime and against a fire or some other light at night, and each section can be made visible or obscured with shutters.[18]

It is also said that the well-known reporter *[Henry]* Linguet when incarcerated at the Bastille in 1782, offered to reveal such an art in return for his freedom *[see p. 204]*, but although he was set free shortly thereafter it has never been reported that his idea was put in practice or what it entailed, but it was thought to have something to do with electricity.[19]

Mr. Bergstrasser in Hanau is said to have described several methods in his *Synthematographie*, using fires, rockets, smoke, different levels of sound produced by drums, trumpets, cannon-shots, and so on, and combinations of these signals,[20] but none of these have been tried or put into practice *[see pp. 42, 182–184]*.

Shortly after Mr. Chappe's invention, which was next in time and which will be discussed below, Mr. Burja presented a dissertation on ancient telegraphy to the Berlin Academy on 25 September 1794, and he also described two of his own inventions. The first consists of a large tube with a slot in the bottom for inserting cutout letters. The letters are made visible to the viewer by holding the tube in front of a light. Mr. Burja stated that these letters could be visible also in daylight. The second invention,

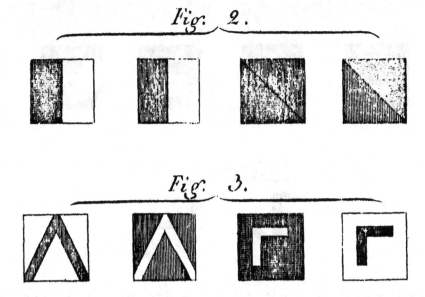

Fig. 2.

Fig. 3.

similar to that of the Greeks but simplified,[21] consists of four torches, positioned in two rows, forming signals that correspond to the alphabet. In daytime, flags instead of torches are used in the same positions.[22]

The renowned Mr. Achard in Berlin *[see p. 184]*, is said to have invented a composite variable signal element constructed from a triangle, a parallelogram, and a circle, movable around a common axis to produce composite figures which can be changed in many ways.[23]

Among the more complete descriptions on the subject that have appeared, the work on *Telegraphy* published in 1795 by Mr. Bockmann in Carlsruhe stands out. In his treatise, which also contains historical references, the principles of all telegraphic methods are divided into three categories: those based on sound, light, and electricity, the three natural phenomena with the greatest propagation speed.

All of the methods mentioned earlier belong to the first two types. The author has considered the general use of electricity *[see p. 205]*, but he admits that *light* is the best method of all, although its application at times may need to be combined with those of the others.

Mr. Bockmann divides telegraphic signals into four kinds. First,[24] surfaces or planes displaying two well separated colors *[Figure 2]*. Second,[25] colored surfaces displaying painted figures of a different color *[Figure 3]*. Third,[26] transparent figures on a dark background *[Figure 4]*. Fourth,[27] dark figures on a transparent or light background *[Figure 5]*. He also adds several observations on the use of telegraphy.[28] I do not know, however, if any large scale testing has been done.

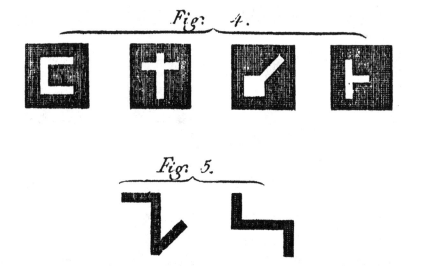

Fig: 4.

Fig: 5.

§3 *[Qualities Needed by this Machine]* A good telegraph system requires two important features: (*a*) Perfection of the design of the machine and its signals; (*b*) Perfection of its movements and controls. The first feature requires: (1) A sufficient number of signals for expressing letters and the more common words and sentences; (2) Clarity of these signals, so that each one can be seen individually and can be easily distinguished from the others; (3) A simple *[method of]* encoding that is easy to memorize and understand. The second feature requires: (1) A minimal effort in the operation of the machine, with minimal friction; (2) Rapid movements, allowing for a fast changing of signals; (3) The certainty that errors and ambiguities can be avoided.

§4 *[The French Invention]* The credit for having been the first to combine these features in a working telegraph belongs to Mr. Chappe in Paris.[29] He not only suggested but also realized the transmission of messages on a large scale, over any distance, including anything that can be expressed by words almost as perfectly as can be done by ordinary writing, but at a speed exceeding that of sound. This art, perhaps intended more for public than for private use, should gain considerable attention at a time as eventful as the present, when the fate of countries and of millions of people sometimes depends on quick decisions, and when the importance of news only increases with the speed at which it can be disseminated, so that people can anticipate or prevent its consequences.

It was especially welcome in a nation that, once it had chosen for a new form of government, could see with pleasure the efforts of human genius to remove one of the deficiencies that was attributed to its former government: tardiness.

136

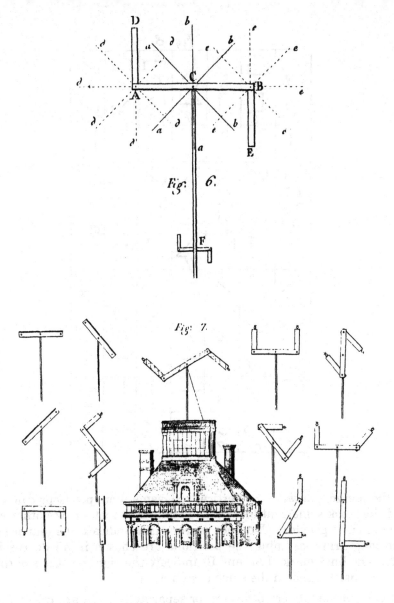

§5 *[The French Invention II]* The French telegraph, according to the written and verbal reports,[30] consists of a long arm AB, Figure 6, movable
around its midpoint C, which is attached to a vertical rod CF which sup-
ports the arm and raises it high enough to make it visible from a distance.
Two other rods, AD and BE, are attached to each side of the arm AB.
They are about half the size and they also move around their endpoints,
where they are attached to AB. By varying the angles of the three arms

Fig. 8.

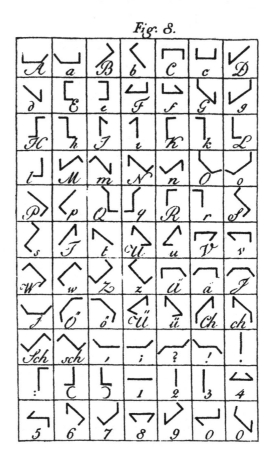

with the horizon, or with the vertical rod, semaphore positions can be produced that look somewhat like the old runic alphabet, or like other alphabets of ancient peoples. The lines marked *aCb* indicate the four positions of the long arm, assuming the positions are chosen in 45 degree increments. The lines marked A*d* and B*e* indicate the eight positions of the two shorter arms,[31] based on the same assumption.

A total of 256 semaphore positions, or separate signals, are possible using combinations of angles for the three arms.[32] As far as I know, there have not yet been any reliable reports about the mechanical design of this machine, how it is set and how messages are encoded into semaphore signals *[cf. Figure 8]*, all of which can be done in a variety of ways depending on the inventiveness of the user.[33]

There are probably three similar, but smaller arms at the base of the telegraph, inside the observatory, attached to the upper arms in such a way

that each signal set at F *[Figure 6]* produces a signal higher up. It is not known, and opinions differ, whether the telegraph works with strings across pulleys, with springs, or with a type of gear that copies the position of the smaller arms at F to the larger arms on top, etc. *[see p. 79]*. In any case, it can be supposed that the arms AD and BE have some kind of counterweight at A and B opposite the point of rotation, which makes the effect of their weight negligible in all positions.

§6 *[The First Swedish Telegraph]* As soon as this machine and its signifi-cance was reported in the newspapers,[34] efforts were made all over Europe to either find out how it worked or to devise new methods to accomplish the same purpose.

In September 1794 I began experiments in this area which led me to several telegraphic devices, some of which were similar and some of which were completely different from the French system, a description of which

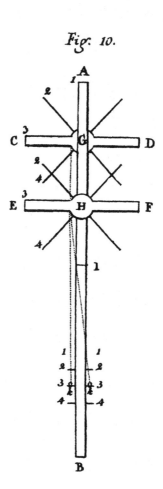

Fig. 10.

had still not been made available.[35] Since then I have continued these experiments, in order to perfect the design and operation of a telegraph that, after weighing all factors, I believed would combine most benefits.

The first design I used was similar to the one in Paris. AB, in Figure 10, is a vertical rod, to which two others are attached, CD and EF, movable on axles at G and H in such a manner that GA, GC, GH, EH are all equal. A wire runs from each arm CD and EF across pulleys at G and H to a ring which can be attached to iron pins 1, 2, 3, 4, at k, k. The two arms can be moved with these strings from their vertical position, which is their position at rest, to a horizontal position, or to two inclining ones 45 degrees above or below the latter. These four positions are indicated by the numbers 1, 2, 3, 4 at the top of the figure and are produced by hooking the rings on either side onto the corresponding pins. Thereby 4 × 4 = 16

140

Fig. 11.

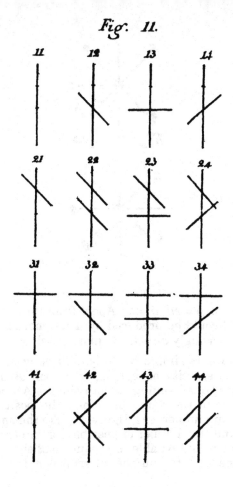

combinations can be produced, Figure 11, as also shown in the following table, where the first number indicates the position of the upper arm and the second number that of the lower arm. The letters of the alphabet, reduced to 16, are found below them:

11	12	13	14
a	b	c,k	d,t

21	22	23	24
e,d	g	h	i

31	32	33	34
l	m	n	o

41	42	43	44
p	r	s	u

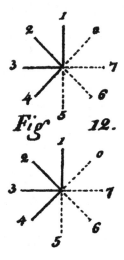

Fig. 12.

The letter $f = ph$, å = o, ö = eu, $q = k$. Apart from these 16 signals, 48 new ones for a total of 64 could be produced by using more rotations, although it would then be increasingly difficult to distinguish between them.

Although this machine is simple in design, there were difficulties in its operation due to the scarcity of signals, so I soon abandoned it. If the movable arms, instead of extending on both sides of AB, were only half the size, then, according to the same principle, the positions of each arm would become eight in number, see Figure 12, like the smaller arms in the French telegraph, and the number of possible combinations would become 64. Three such arms would be able to produce 512 signals, 4 = 4,096, and 5 = 32,768, or in general, if the number of arms is n, the number of signals would be 8^n.

If the telegraphs were constructed according to this principle, each short arm would have a counterweight so that it could be balanced in all positions. The movement, which was 45 degrees in each step, could then be accomplished either by using a string across a pulley attached to the axle, or a gear with a corresponding lever. The positions of the arms could be expressed by the numbers from zero to seven, which, if we assume that three arms would be used, would produce a coding table similar to the one that is attached to this treatise [see p. 149], which could easily be used for such a machine.[36]

Instead of a perpendicular support, the structure would benefit from being horizontal, see Figure 13, but when a telegraph with several short arms is being set up, each arm must have its own support, otherwise two of the positions would be identical and the number of changes would be only seven. This is shown in Figure 14, where the positions of the five arms encode signal number 36,204.

142

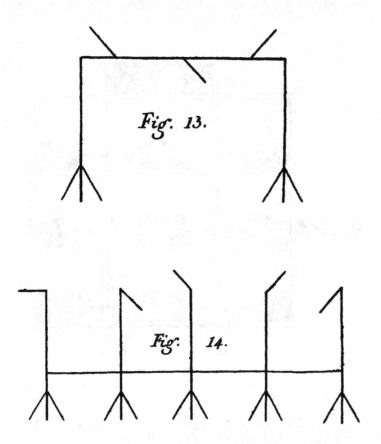

Fig. 13.

Fig. 14.

The principle of this design is simple, there is an abundance of signals and ease in producing them. On the other hand, I was soon induced to give preference to the following design with its smaller size, greater speed, and ease in its movements, increased clarity and visibility, in addition to several other factors, such as its possible use at night.

§7 [*The Second Telegraph, the Actual Object of this Study*]   Points *a, b, c, d, e, f,* in Figure 15, represent a framework, similar to a grid, where ten shutters labeled *l* are placed at equal distances in three vertical columns, the middle of which contains four shutters and the others three each. Each of these shutters, which should be made as light and thin as possible from wire, copper, or iron plates, is attached to an axle *o–n*, the ends of which are inserted into corresponding holes in the sides of the grid. An arm *m–s* is attached perpendicular to the direction of axle *o–n*, but at an angle of 45 degrees to the plane of the shutters. A brass wire leads from

143

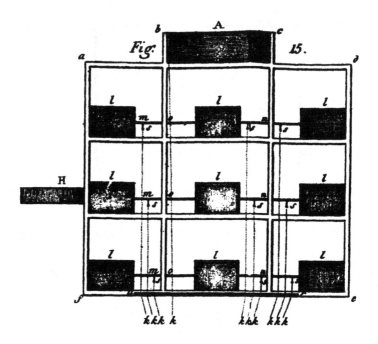

the endpoint *s* to the bottom of the grid. With this wire, the shutter can be placed either horizontally or vertically, as desired.

Figure 15 shows all the shutters in their vertical position, and Figure 16, which gives a side-view, shows the shutters in their horizontal position. When the shutters, which are fairly thin, are viewed from some distance and parallel with the horizon, it is easily apparent that in the position shown in Figure 16 they are almost unnoticeable, but they become visible when they are pulled into a vertical position by wire *s–k*. The machine assumes the first position by itself, since the shutters on the one side at *l* in Figure 16 are pulled down by a weight,[37] *q*, attached to wire *l–q*, and come to rest on hook *l–p*.[38] They are stopped by the wire-hook *l–p* in Figure 16, which is normally behind the shutter but is shown in front of it in the figure for the sake of clarity.

In order for the wires not to interfere with each other, the arms *m–s* within each column are placed at varying distances from their shutters, and they go down through small holes in board *u–r [Figure 15]*, or *u, u, u* in Figure 17, which shows its plan. By routing these wires through board *w–w* and attaching them to ten rings labeled *t*, one for each finger, it becomes possible on smaller machines to make shutters visible or invisible at will, using the movements of the hands alone.[39]

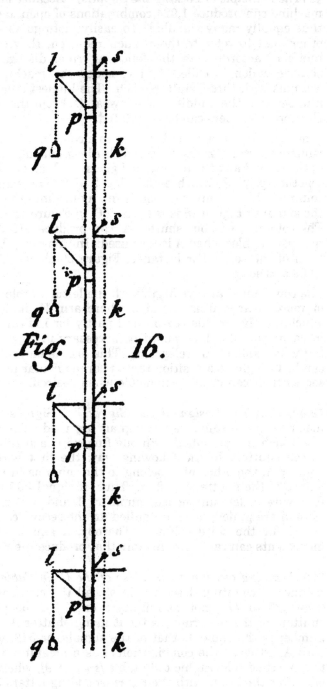

Fig. *16.*

§8 *[The Principle of Locking the Signals]* Because of this construction, the machine can produce 1,024 combinations of open and closed shutters, and thus equally many signals.[40] To easily distinguish the signals from each other, and to refer to them when required, they can be represented by numbers according to the following rule: disregarding the uppermost shutter which is called A, I consider the machine to consist of three columns with three shutters each. The highest shutter in each column is numbered 1, the middle 2, the lowest 4. From these values for the single shutters, all others can be calculated.

When the first and second shutter in a column are made visible, I call it 3, which equals 1 + 2; the first and third combined gives 5, which equals 1 + 4; the second and third combined gives 6, which equals 2 + 4; and all three together gives 7, which equals 1 + 2 + 4. The same rule is used for all columns. If no shutter is visible in any column, that means 0. Therefore, the signal in Figure 18 is read as 356; in Figure 19 it reads 170, and so on. The columns, without shutter A, can produce 512 different signals. The number doubles when A is also used. In this case, the letter A is placed in front of the code. For instance, Figure 20 shows A706, Figure 21 shows A003 and so on.

The count must always begin with the leftmost column of the telegraph,[41] or more clearly, from the side where arm H, in Figure 15, is situated; which, partly for this reason and partly for indicating the middle square in each column (which might be necessary in foggy weather), is attached to the left side of the telegraph. This arm is movable on hinges so that it can be brought to a position that is perpendicular to the shutters, and consequently it can be made invisible when desired.

§9 *[Mechanical Design of the Signals]* Signals are produced on the machine in the same way as signals are read. The ten wires $u-t$ (Figure 17), which can be pulled with one finger in each ring (see §7), correspond to the shutters in the following way: the first wire on the left goes to shutter A, the other nine belong to the columns in the same order as the values of the shutters: 1, 2, 4. Thus, if signal 305 is to be produced, the first wire is left untouched, numbers 1 and 2 of the wires for the first column are pulled; none are pulled for the second column; and 1 and 4 are pulled for the third column. Thereby, a simple combination of finger movements can raise the shutters that produce the required signal.

§10 *[Meaning of Signals and Use of the Code Table]* According to the manner of counting described in §8, all the combinations of three digits from 000 to 777, not containing 8 or 9, can be produced by the nine shutters of the telegraph, without using shutter A. It is clear that their number is the same as that of the signals, or 512, which can be doubled with A. Each of the combinations has a meaning which can be found in the attached telegraphic code table *[see p. 149]*, where the numbers follow one after the other with their corresponding letters or syllables in alphabetical order.

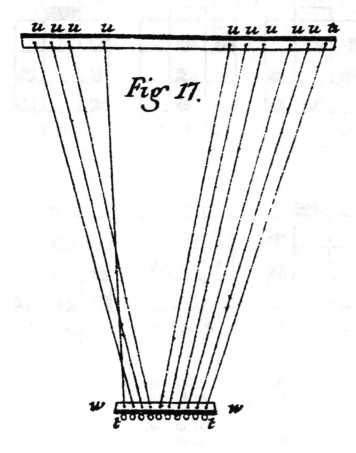

Fig 17.

To design the table I tried, by means of fairly difficult calculations, to include the most common syllables, in addition to single letters, and some commonly used words. The application of the table is easily understood.[42] There are two rows of numbers: the ones in front of the syllables are from 000 to 777, the others reversed from 777 to 000. The first number is used in telegraphic correspondence during the day, the other is used at night, as explained further below. The sum of the two numbers is always 777. Single shutters are used to encode the nine numerals,[43] and consequently these shutters have a different value when used alone than when they are used in combinations. Shutter A represents a zero if used as follows:

$$001 = 1 \qquad A001 = 10$$
$$002 = 2 \qquad A002 = 20$$
$$004 = 3 \qquad A004 = 30$$
$$010 = 4 \qquad A010 = 40$$

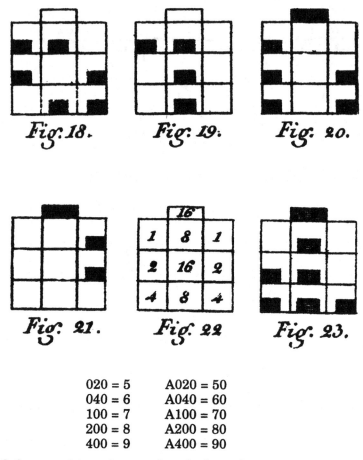

Fig. 18.   Fig. 19.   Fig. 20.

Fig. 21.   Fig. 22   Fig. 23.

020 = 5	A020 = 50
040 = 6	A040 = 60
100 = 7	A100 = 70
200 = 8	A200 = 80
400 = 9	A400 = 90

To avoid the repetition of zeros, hundreds and thousands are encoded as separate signals in the table.[44]

Certain easy to remember signals are preferred for the expression of common words that are used in most communications, and these are indicated with italics in the table, since they provide a meaning that is independent of the other codes, such as 272, 525, 757, etc. There are some unassigned numbers at the end of the table, to which one may give any desired meaning, suited for the subject being communicated.[45] There will also be a special table for the signals that result from the code combinations with A. That table will be more comprehensive, since its signals will express whole words, phrases, and sentences, but it will also be more useful,[46] since it helps to reduce the length of messages [a compaction method].

§11 [Ways of Changing the Codes]   When secrecy is required, all of the meanings may be changed by altering the codes; the possibilities are almost limitless. The limits of this treatise do not permit a more detailed

148

Telegraphisk Chiffre-Tabell.

000	100	200	300	400	500	600	700
000 · · · 777	100 · 7 · 677	200 · 8 · 577	300 · kan · 477	400 · 9 · 377	500 R · · 277	600 · fu,fv · 177	700 Talflut 077
001 · 1 · · 776	101 · dr · 676	201 · gu · 576	301 · kar · 476	401 · mit · 376	501 · ra · 276	601 · fvar · 176	701 · vår · 076
002 · 2 · · 775	102 · dt · 675	202 · gui · 575	302 · ke · 475	402 · mo · 375	502 · ran · 275	602 · fvenfk · 175	702 · vå · 075
003 A · · 774	103 · du · 674	203 · gå · 574	303 · ki · 474	403 · mod · 374	503 · rd · 274	603 · fy · 174	703 · vg · 074
004 · 3 · · 773	104 · dy · 673	204 · går · 573	304 · kl · 473	404 · mof · 373	504 · re · 273	604 · få · 173	704 · väl · 073
005 · ab · 772	105 · då · 672	205 · gå · 572	305 · kla · 472	405 · mt · 372	505 · regn · 272	605 · få · 172	705 · vän · 072
006 · ad · 771	106 · dä · 671	206 · gö · 571	306 · kn · 471	406 · mu · 371	506 · ren · 271	606 · fåt · 171	706 · vär · 071
007 ordflut 770	107 · där · 670	207 · gör · 570	307 · kna · 470	407 · mur · 370	507 · ri · 270	607 · fö · 170	707 repeter. 070
010 · 4 · · 767	110 · dö · 667	210 H · · 567	310 · ko · 467	410 · my · 367	510 · riked. 267	610 T · · 167	710 X · · 067
011 · af · 766	111 · ha · 666	211 · ha · 566	311 · kom · 466	411 · mycke 366	511 · ra · 266	611 · ta · 166	711 Y · · 066
012 · ak · 765	112 E · · 665	212 · haf · 565	312 · kon · 465	412 · må · 365	512 · ro · 265	612 · tan · 165	712 Z · · 065
013 · al · 764	113 · ed · 664	213 · hal · 564	313 · kor · 464	413 · mål · 364	513 · rt · 264	613 · te · 164	713 Å · · 064
014 · alt · 763	114 · efter 663	214 · hamn · 563	314 · kr · 463	414 · män · 363	514 · ru · 263	614 · telegr. 163	714 · Ål · 063
015 · am · 762	115 · el · 662	215 · han · 562	315 · kra · 462	415 · mä · 362	515 · ruun · 262	615 · ten · 162	715 · Än · 062
016 · an · 761	116 · eller 661	216 · hand · 561	316 · ku · 461	416 · mä · 361	516 · ry · 261	616 · ter · 161	716 · äng · 061
017 · and · 760	117 · eld · 660	217 · har · 560	317 · kv · 460	417 · mär · 360	517 · ryss · 260	617 · ti · 160	717 · är · 060
020 · 5 · · 757	120 · em · 657	220 · ho · 557	320 · kva · 457	420 · mö · 357	520 · rå · 257	620 · tid · 157	720 · åt · 057
021 · ap · 756	121 · en · 656	221 · hel · 556	321 · ky · 456	421 · mör · 356	521 · råd · 256	621 · till · 156	721 · åter · 056
022 · ar · 755	122 · er · 655	222 · hjelp · 555	322 · kå · 455	422 N · · 355	522 · rä · 255	622 · tim · 155	722 Tal.ned 055
023 · arm · 754	123 · es · 654	223 · hem · 554	323 · kä · 454	423 · na · 354	523 · räk · 254	623 · tin · 154	723 Ä · · 054
024 · as · 753	124 · et · 653	224 · her · 553	324 · kö · 453	424 · namh 353	524 · rät · 253	624 · to · 153	724 · äkt · 053
025 · at · 752	125 F · · 652	225 · het · 552	325 L · · 452	425 · natt · 352	525 · vänta 252	625 · tor · 152	725 · äg · 052
026 B · 751	126 · fa · 651	226 · hi · 551	326 · la · 451	426 · nd,nt 351	526 · rö · 251	626 · tr · 151	726 · äll · 051
027 · ba · 750	127 · Tal.up. 650	227 · Tal.up. 550	327 · lag · 450	427 · ne · 350	527 · rök · 250	627 · tu · 150	727 ändre 050
030 · bak · 747	130 · faller 647	230 · hin · 547	330 · land · 447	430 · nej · 347	530 S · · 247	630 · tull · 147	730 · äm · 047
031 · bar · 746	131 · fan · 646	231 · hit · 546	331 · le · 446	431 · ner · 346	531 · fa · 246	631 · tufend 146	731 · än · 046
032 · be · 745	132 · far · 645	232 · ho · 545	332 · lek · 445	432 · ng · 345	532 · fak · 245	632 · tv · 145	732 · äng · 045
033 · beg · 744	133 · fat · 644	233 · hop · 544	333 · lem · 444	433 · ni · 344	533 · fal · 244	633 · ty · 144	733 · änk · 044
034 · berg · 743	134 · fe · 643	234 · hos · 543	334 · lev · 443	434 · nog · 343	534 · fam · 243	634 · tyfk · 143	734 · är · 043
035 · bl · 742	135 · fel · 642	235 · hu · 542	335 · let · 442	435 · nor · 342	535 · fan · 242	635 · tå · 142	735 · ät · 042
036 · bi · 741	136 · fi · 641	236 · hundra 541	336 · li · 441	436 · ns · 341	536 · fe · 241	636 · tä · 141	736 · ätt · 041
037 · bland 740	137 fienden 640	237 · hur · 540	337 · lif · 440	437 · nu · 340	537 · feg · 240	637 · tö · 140	737 Ö · · 040
040 · 6 · · 737	140 · fin · 637	240 · hus · 537	340 · lig · 437	440 · ny · 337	540 · fen · 237	640 U · · 137	740 · öd · 037
041 · bo · 736	141 · fl · 636	241 · hy · 536	341 · lik · 436	441 · nyfs · 336	541 · fer · 236	641 · uk · 136	741 · öf · 036
042 · bon · 735	142 · flagg 635	242 · hå · 535	342 · ljus · 435	442 · nä · 335	542 · fi · 235	642 · ull · 135	742 · öfver 035
043 · bor · 734	143 · fo · 634	243 · häl · 534	343 · lo · 434	443 · nä · 334	543 Chiffer 234	643 · un · 134	743 · ök · 034
044 · br · 733	144 · folk · 633	244 · här · 533	344 · lt · 433	444 · när · 333	544 · fk · 233	644 · up · 133	744 · ögd · 033
045 · bref · 732	145 · for · 632	245 · hä · 532	345 · lu · 432	445 · näft · 332	545 · fkull · 232	645 · ur · 132	745 · ök · 032
046 · bu · 731	146 · fr · 631	246 · hän · 531	346 · ly · 431	446 · nö · 331	546 · fkepp 231	646 · us · 131	746 · öm · 031
047 · by · 730	147 · fram · 630	247 · fram · 530	347 · lå · 430	447 · nöd · 330	547 · fkicka 230	647 · ut · 130	747 · ör · 030
050 · bå · 727	150 · frå · 627	250 · hö · 527	350 · låg · 427	450 O · · 327	550 · fkog · 227	650 V · · 127	750 · öt · 027
051 · bårt · 726	151 · ft, vt 626	251 · hög · 526	351 · lkug 426	451 · och · 326	551 · fkrif · 226	651 · va · 126	751 · ött · 026
052 · bä · 725	152 · full · 625	252 · höger 525	352 · löger 425	452 · od · 325	552 · fl · 225	652 · val · 125	752 025
053 · bö · 724	153 · fy · 624	253 · hör · 524	353 · läg · 424	453 · om · 324	553 · flg · 224	653 · vakt 124	753 024
054 · C · 723	154 · få · 623	254 I · · 523	354 · läng 423	454 · on · 323	554 · fm · 223	654 · val · 123	754 023
055 D · 722	155 · får · 622	255 · ja · 522	355 · lär · 422	455 · opp · 322	555 · flt · 222	655 · van · 122	755 upm.ned 022
056 · da · 721	156 · fä · 621	256 · jag · 521	356 · låt · 421	456 · or · 321	556 · fjä · 221	656 · var · 121	756 021
057 · dal · 720	157 · fält · 620	257 · if · 520	357 · lö · 420	457 · ord · 320	557 upm.up. 220	657 · vax · 120	757 fer ej 020
060 · dan · 717	160 · fö · 617	260 · ig · 517	360 · lön · 417	460 · oss · 317	560 · fjön 217	660 · ve · 117	760 017
061 · dansk 716	161 · för · 616	261 · ik · 516	361 · lös · 416	461 · ott · 316	561 · fl · 216	661 · vem · 116	761 016
062 · de · 715	162 G · · 615	262 · il · 515	362 M · · 415	462 P · · 315	562 · flut · 215	662 · ven · 115	762 015
063 · del · 714	163 · ga · 614	263 · illa · 514	363 · må · 414	463 · par · 314	563 · fm · 214	663 · venfter 114	763 014
064 · dem · 713	164 · gar · 613	264 · in · 513	364 · man · 413	464 · par · 313	564 · fn · 213	664 · ver · 113	764 013
065 · den · 712	165 · ge · 612	265 · ing · 512	365 · mat · 412	465 · pe · 312	565 · fo · 212	665 · vi · 112	765 012
066 · der · 711	166 · gen · 611	266 · intet · 511	366 · me · 411	466 · pen · 311	566 · fot · 211	666 · vid · 111	766 011
067 · det · 710	167 · ger · 610	267 · is · 510	367 · med · 410	467 · per · 310	567 · fom · 210	667 · vig · 110	767 010
070 · (.) · 707	170 · ju · 507	270 · ju · 507	370 mellan 407	470 · pi · 307	570 · for · 207	670 · vil · 107	770 långf. 007
071 · di · 706	171 · gl · 606	271 · jå · 506	371 · men · 406	471 · pl · 306	571 · fp · 206	671 · vin · 106	771 006
072 · dig · 705	172 · gn · 605	272 · galit 505	372 · mer · 405	472 · po · 305	572 · fpr · 205	672 · vind 105	772 005
073 · din · 704	173 · go · 604	273 · jäm · 504	373 · mi · 404	473 · por · 304	573 · ft · 204	673 · vit · 104	773 004
074 · dit · 703	174 · god · 603	274 K · · 503	374 · mig · 403	474 · poft · 303	574 · ftad · 203	674 · vr · 103	774 003
075 · do · 702	175 · gr · 602	275 · kk · 502	375 · mil · 402	475 · pr · 302	575 · 202	675 · vu · 102	775 002
076 · dom · 701	176 · gra · 601	276 · ka · 501	376 · min · 401	476 · pu · 301	576 · ftor · 201	676 · vå · 101	776 001
077 · fort · 700	177 · gt, kt 600	277 · kal · 500	377 · miss · 400	477 · på · 300	577 · ftr · 200	677 · väld · 100	777 · · 000
700	600	500	400	300	200	100	000

STOCKHOLM, Tryckt hos Johan Pehr Lindh, 1795.

investigation. Several already known kinds of cryptography could be applied to this use. However, because of the construction of this machine and the way the signals are produced, the method I use, which can be applied without significant changes to all telegraphs, is the following [an encryption method].

ABCD, in Figure 24, is a square of paper or parchment, divided into as many smaller squares as required by the number of syllables or signals.[47] There are holes in the paper, equidistant from each other, in each square. Above them the letters or syllables which constitute the code table are written in alphabetical order. EFGH is another square, divided into equal squares, adjacent to each other, and equal in size to four of those on the first paper, or consisting of four squares equal to the table or grid ABCD.

Numeric codes corresponding to the syllables written on the grid ABCD are entered in the same order in each of these squares, so that when the grid is placed on a square such as EJMN, the number corresponding to the code table will show in the round opening below each syllable. It will be the same if the grid ABCD is placed on any of the three other squares JFKN, NKHL, or LNMG; however, if it is placed in any other position, such as ROPQ, it becomes apparent that each syllable would end up above a different number than before and that in consequence the meaning of the signals or the code changes.

The number of the possible permutations, when the edge d of the grid remains parallel to EF, is as great as the number of codes in each of the squares, because that is how many times, for instance, the upper corner A of the grid can be moved without returning to its original position. Since the other three edges of the grid e, f, g, can also be at the top, parallel to EF, and the grid can then be moved in the same manner, a similar number of new and separate changes in the code are again possible for each such basic position. Consequently, if the number of squares on the paper or grid is n, the number of code changes in these four basic positions is $4n$. Furthermore, if the grid is turned over and the same letters or syllables are written on its back in reverse alphabetical order, or from right to left, as in STUX, an equal number of new code changes are possible, using the same principle by turning the edges of the reverse square, h, i, k, l, making the total number $8n$.

The code table in Figure 11, like the telegraph in §6, consists of only 16 digits, consequently $8n$ is 128; however, for the machine described in §7, with 512 signals, I use a code table with 484 signals, therefore $8n$, or the number of code changes, is here 3,872. If signals that are combined with A are used, the square would become 1,024 and the number of code changes 8,192.

§12 [Ways of Changing the Codes II] In order to easily identify or discover which of these codes are being used in a certain message, two circumstances must be taken into consideration: first, the basic position of the grid in relation to EF and the eight edges d, e, f, g, h, i, k, l, and

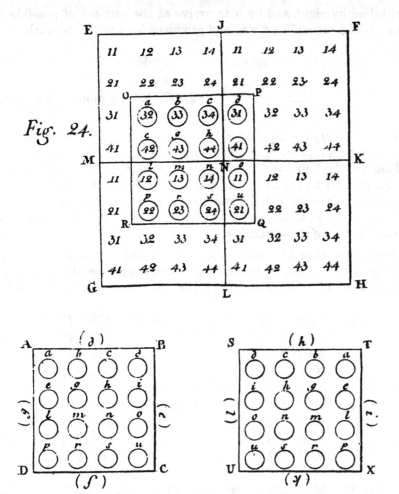

Fig. 24.

second, the placement of the grid in each basic position. The former is indicated, not by the letters, but by the numbers that correspond to them in the ordinary table. The latter is indicated with the number that, in the given position corresponds to a prearranged syllable or word [i.e., an arbitrary grid element], which is called the *key* to the code and is its secret. When the upper edge and the placement of the grid are given, all the rest can be determined.[48]

§13 *[Ways of Changing the Codes III]* The number of code changes can be increased considerably in the following manner. If the grid is divided into four equal squares, each one of them could have four separate positions by turning their four edges. This would result in 4 × 4 × 4 × 4 combinations, or 256 new changes of the grid in each basic position. This number should

151

be multiplied by eight and by n to arrive at the number of possible code changes, in this case $256 \times 8 \times n$, and produces for a telegraph with

16	signals	32,768	
484	—	991,232	
1,024	—	2,097,152	possible code changes.[49]

§14 *[Ways of Changing the Codes IV]*   Each and every one of these code changes can be found using the following principle. If the position on the grid of each of the four squares is represented by 0, 1, 2, 3, all the possible combinations can be represented by a series of numbers, containing the combination of these four digits numbered from 0000 to 3333. The place-ment of the four squares on the grid would, by prearrangement, correspond to one of these numbers.

This series consists of 256 terms *[4 × 4 × 4 × 4]* and, as $256 \times 4 = 1,024$, all the changes of four basic positions can be indicated by signals from the telegraph, or on one surface of the grid, as shown by the following table.

d	0000–0333	corresponds to	000–077
	1000–1333	—	100–177
	2000–2333	—	200–277
	3000–3333	—	300–377
e	0000–0333	corresponds to	400–477
	1000–1333	—	500–577
	2000–2333	—	600–677
	3000–3333	—	700–777
f	0000–0333	corresponds to	A000–A077
	1000–1333	—	A100–A177
	2000–2333	—	A200–A277
	3000–3333	—	A300–A377
g	0000–0333	corresponds to	A400–A477
	1000–1333	—	A500–A577
	2000–2333	—	A600–A677
	3000–3333	—	A700–A777

With another prearranged signal, all these numbers can also apply to the reverse side of the grid and the positions of h, i, k, l.

It is easy to transform the *[other]* formula for the positioning of the grid into a telegraphic signal by using the following table.

a		b		a		b
00	=	00		30	=	14
01	=	01		31	=	15
02	=	02		32	=	16
03	=	03		33	=	17
10	=	04		100	=	20
11	=	05		200	=	40
12	=	06		300	=	60
13	=	07		1000	=	100
20	=	10		2000	=	200
21	=	11		3000	=	300
22	=	12				
23	=	13				

Column a contains the numbers that encode the positions of the grid, and column b contains the telegraph signals. Therefore, if 2033, 3320 are the positions given, it is easy to find the corresponding signals in the table:

a		b		a		b
2000	=	200		3000	=	300
33	=	17		300	=	60
				20	=	10
2033	=	217		3320	=	370

And if 107, 376 are given signals, the corresponding positions of the grid can be found in the same manner:

a		b		a		b
100	=	1000		300	=	3000
7	=	13		60	=	300
				16	=	32
107	=	1013		376	=	3332

It might be noted here also that the basic positions d, e, f, g for the front and h, i, k, l for the back side of the grid correspond to 000, A400, A00, A400. It follows that these numbers should be added to or taken away from the code signal, according to the circumstances [i.e., coding or decoding]. Therefore, if the signal for the position is g0123, the code signal is 33 + A400 = A433, and if the code signal is A376, the position is f3332.

§15 [Speech and Attention Signals] All telegraphic communication begins with a signal indicating a wish to transmit [see pp. 229, 231], or a *speech signal*, which should be displayed until the recipient gives the corresponding *attention signal* [a synchronization method]. Two speech signals 722 and 227, that can be used between two adjacent stations, are included in the table, where *up* and *down* refer to the position in relation to the sun. Otherwise, and when several stations are communicating, unless their

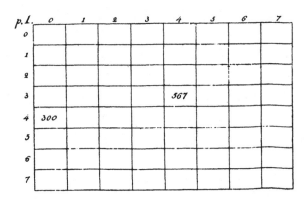

Figure 43a (Numbered out of sequence in the original.)

---

number exceeds seven, the easiest speech signal to remember is one that contains two digits separated by zero, where the first digit indicates who is communicating and the last with whom. Thus when the sixth station wants to communicate with the third its speech signal is 603.

If the number of stations is greater than seven, the speech signals could be increased in number with the help of shutter A, but such cases should be rare, since the intermediate stations at long distances are not communicating, but only repeating. When necessary, it is most easily accomplished in the following manner: the first five shutters indicate who is communicating, and the following five with whom. If we give them the values assigned in Figure 22, speech and attention signals for 31 stations can be expressed. For instance, the signal in Figure 23 means that the 30th station wants to communicate with the 28th. Two attention signals are also given in the table, corresponding to the speech signals 722 and 227; that is 557 and 755. When other speech signals are composed for several stations, their codes in the table, subtracted from A777, are used as attention signals. Therefore, attention signal 174 responds to speech signal A603, and 102 to A675, and so on *[see p. 214]*.

§16 *[The Way to Transmit Signals]* A communication between two telegraphs can be established either directly or with the help of intermediate stations, depending on the distance. Suppose that among the stations A, B, C, situated one after the other, A wants to communicate with the closest station B. First the message is composed, using numbers from the table, using as few signals as possible. Then the speech signal for the station is raised and maintained until B notices it and responds with its attention signal. When that happens A lowers the speech signal and sends the first signal of the message itself. B lowers its attention signal and repeats the new signal from A, showing that it has understood it correctly, and so on with all the other signals.[50]

154

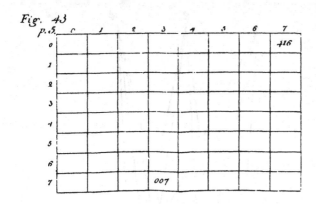

Figure 43b

Again, if A wants to communicate with C through the intermediate station B, A raises its speech signal to C, which is repeated from B to C, which responds with its attention signal to A. This is repeated back by B, and A begins the transmission which is repeated signal by signal first by B and then by C. The same thing is done if there are more intermediate stations.

If an incorrect signal should be transmitted by mistake, it can be corrected before the next signal is transmitted, by sending 272, which according to the table means *error*, and then the correct signal *[an error control method]*. In this way the correction will follow the error through all stations. During a communication there are often other fixed signals, besides the signals from the table and the attention signals, which can be useful, though not necessary, to learn by heart. With some practice their particular function will be learned.[51] If a signal cannot immediately reach the station for which it is intended, because of fog or other factors, the station where it is stopped will answer with its attention signal, and the message stops there until circumstances will allow it to reach its destination *[a flow control method]*. It might happen that the station transmitting the message cannot see well, whereas the station sending the attention signal does. In such cases, and in general when the clarity of the air is in doubt, it is best to transmit the attention signal with the help of a flag *[an out-of-band control signal]*, which because of its greater surface can be discerned even when the telegraph signals cannot.

§17 *[Table for Transcribing Signals]* Tables such as shown in Figure 43 divided by eight horizontal and as many vertical lines, are used for recording telegraphic messages. If the signals are written in the squares formed by the lines, their location can be expressed with a telegraphic code consisting of three numbers, of which the first indicates the page, the second the row, and the third the column.[52] Therefore, the signal 567 is referred

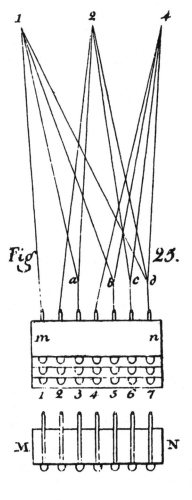

to by its location in the table as 134, 300 as 140, 416 as 507, 007 as 573, etc. This can be useful if at the end of a transmission, for reasons of obscurity in one direction, a station has not been able to repeat a signal, and wants to see it repeated because it was ambiguous, or if the transmission is interrupted for any reason and it should be resumed from a certain place [a selective repeat method].

§18 [Adjustment of the Shutters in Several Ways for Machines of Various Sizes] The way of operating the strings on small machines, described in §9, is probably easiest for those who already know the principles combining signals and strings. However, partly to be able to utilize untrained people, partly to overcome the resistance necessarily caused by friction and the weight of the larger machines, I have thought of various other mechanisms for operating the machines.

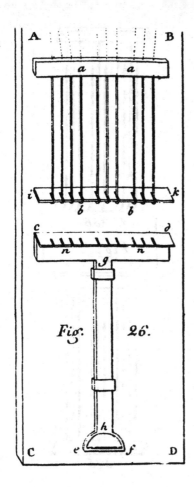

Fig. 26.

The first method, on smaller machines, is that when a combination of strings for forming the signals 3, 5, 6, and 7 is made, only one finger will be required for transmitting one signal from each column. 1, 2, and 4 in Figure 25 show single strings descending from the shutters; other strings connect them with each other in the same way as the signals are made by adding the shutters together. Therefore, 1 and 2 are connected with a single string at a which makes 3; 1 and 4 at b with another making 5; 2 and 4 at c with one making 6; and finally 1, 2, and 4 at d with the last string making 7.

The seven strings formed in this way are attached with as many strings, each with a hook e of brass or iron. These seven strings run parallel and vertically through slits in the board $m-n$, which is shown reversed in MN, and are thus pulled together to form the corresponding signals. Label $f-f$

157

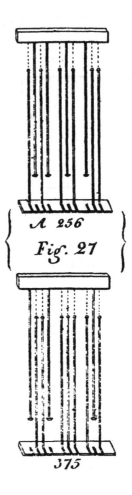

A 256

Fig. 27

375

points to seven hooks belonging to the signals from the second column, and *g–g* to those from the third *[letters e, f, and g are missing in Figure 25]*. The combinations of strings in each column are in different planes, above each other, and therefore the hooks are placed on three different boards. Thus, they do not interfere with each other. This arrangement is the easiest of all, as far as operation is concerned, since we do not have to know how the shutters are added together and untrained people can be used. However, there will be great difficulties with friction, confusion among the strings, and changes caused by dryness or humidity, unless they could easily be made of metal for their entire length.

§19 *[Adjustment of the Shutters II]*   To simplify the operation of larger machines,[53] I have used the following method: *a–a* in Figure 26 is a strip attached to a perpendicular board ABCD, placed right below the shutters.

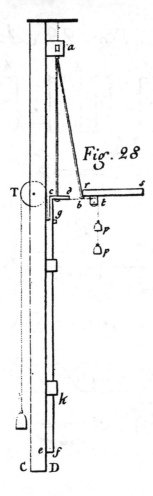

Fig. 28

At a–a the strings from the shutters are looped over ten small pulleys. Attached to their ends, just below a–a, are ten strong iron or brass rods a–b, about an ell in length, and provided with buttons b–b at the end. Iron hook $cdef$ has ten notches labeled n, one for each rod. The hook g–h is raised by a weight on a string, running over a pulley to ABCD, attached at g behind the hook, and it is lowered with foot pedal e–f. When the hook is raised, it is behind the iron rods i–k.

One can push, with the fingers, the rods needed to form a signal into the notches c–d on the hook, while stepping on e–f. When c–d is now lowered, it will catch on the buttons b of the protruding rods and will raise the corresponding shutters. Figure 27 shows the rods pulled down by the hook c–d. To avoid catching more rods than desired on the hook when it is lowered, and so that all the rods, when raised, separate from it, there is

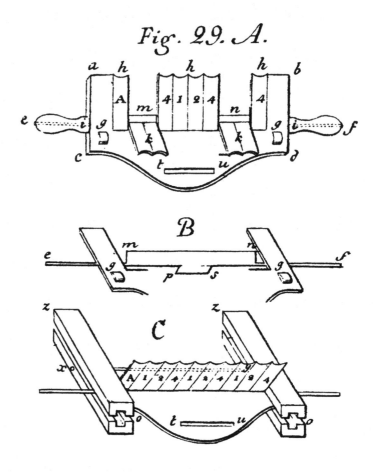

Fig. 29. A.

a small weight *p* on each rod which pulls it, in a leaning position, a certain distance away from the hook, as shown in Figure 28, where this whole arrangement is drawn in profile, and *p* is the weight, which looped over the pulley T pulls up the hook after the pedal has been pushed down, and *t* indicates the ten small pulleys over which the strings from the weights are looped and which are attached below to the board *r–s*.

§20 *[Adjustment of the Shutters III]*   To increase the speed of each signal, which would otherwise require a certain amount of time for its composition and transmission, and especially to make it clearly visible, the two first-mentioned operations can be shortened by the following arrangement: *abcd* (Figure 29 detail A) is a flat frame made of iron or brass, in which ten keys *h, h, k, k* are attached to a common axle *i, i,* in such a way that they can move, and that each of them can be placed either

160

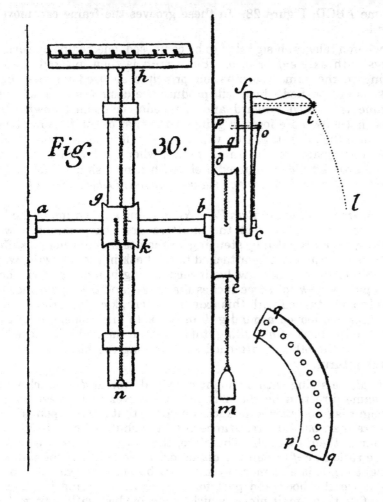

horizontally, as h, h or vertically leaning backwards at an angle of 110 to 120 degrees, as k, k. These keys, with a concave notch on one end, correspond to the rods in such a manner that when the frame $abcd$ is pushed horizontally against the hook with the rods, as many of the rods are pushed into the hook as there are keys placed in the horizontal position.

Attached to the axle e–f, detail B in Figure 29, inside the frame and under the keys h, h, is a flat brass plate m–n, which can be turned upward using the handles e and f, and this movement raises the keys when the frame is pulled back. To ease the movement of the frame and make it even and perpendicular to the wires, small pulleys g, g are attached, which fit into the grooves o, o, made from two pieces of metal o–z, Figure 29 detail C, which are attached to the sides of the board r–s and are perpendicular to

161

the frame ABCD, Figure 28. In these grooves the frame can move back and forth.

Thus, when a telegraph signal is to be composed, one begins by turning up the keys with axle $e-f$ or $m-n$. Plate $m-n$ is then lowered again, and according to the same coordination principle as used for the shutters, those keys are pushed which will produce the desired signal, after which the frame is pushed forward and the pedal is pushed down. In this manner, not only more force is gained than that of the fingers alone, but there is also the advantage that while one signal is being transmitted, the next can be prepared on the frame, so that when the hook has been raised, it can be lowered almost immediately with a new signal, and at least a third of the time needed for each signal is saved *[double buffering]*.

§21 *[Adjustment of the Shutters IV]* When using a telegraph of the largest dimensions, especially when the shutters are heavy and the wind is strong, the force extended by stepping on the pedal might not be sufficient. In that case, a crank can be attached to the hook in the following way: abc (Figure 30) is an iron axle, twelve inches in length, moving in the holes a, b. Two pulleys $g-k$ (of three inches diameter) and $d-e$ (nine inches) are attached to and turned with this axle by the crank $c-f$ and the handle $f-i$. Two strings are looped around $g-k$ in opposite directions, one of them is attached to the hook at h, pulling it down when the crank is turned in the direction $i-l$; the other is attached at n, pulling the hook back up, when the crank returns.

There is also a string with a weight m looped around $d-e$ which is moved in the same direction by the arm $f-i$ and serves to increase its power. This weight is proportioned in such a manner that it corresponds to somewhat more than 1/3 of the resistance of all the shutters, or it is able to pull down four of them by itself. Therefore, the force is not only increased in the same ratio as $c-f$ to half the diameter of $g-k$ (without the influence of the weight m), it is also more evenly distributed, with part of it used for pulling down the hook and part for raising it. A spring is attached to crank $c-f$, with a small pin o, which when pushed with a finger passes through the crank into matching small holes in plate $p-q$, thereby anchoring the crank, so that signals can be maintained without use of the hands.

§22 *[Adjustment of the Shutters V]* The largest telegraphs can be operated in this manner: one hand manages the movements of the frame, the other those of the crank. The first movements consist, when viewed separately, of five different operations: turning the axle up and down, pushing the keys down to form the signal, and moving the frame back and forth. These five could be changed to one by using the crank in the following manner: in the frame $abcd$, Figure 29 detail A, there is a slit $t-u$ into which is fitted the upper end of a board $a-b$, shown from the side in Figure 31. This board can move around the axle q; two weights $n-p$ are attached to the lower end of this board by which it is pulled in two opposite directions $d-c$ or $e-f$. Therefore, the upper end of the board pushes

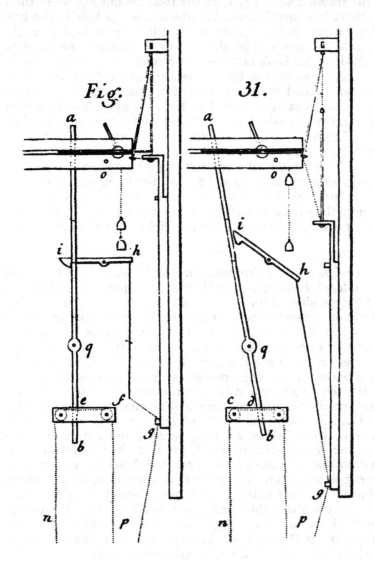

Fig. 31.

the frame towards or away from the strings.

The weight p is larger than n, and thus the natural position of the board is d–c, with the frame away from the strings. A wire chain is attached to the lower end of the hook g, its length being such that when the hook is within two inches of its greatest height the weight p on the same string is lifted; then n immediately begins to affect the frame on which the keys have been pushed: it moves towards the strings and the signal is formed.

So that the frame does not release the rods too quickly when the hook is lowered, there is a small hook at h which enters a hole in the board $a-b$ when it is pushed forward and prevents it from returning in the same position, until by means of another wire $g-h$, also attached at g, the first hook is lifted, as the hook is lowered a couple of inches and the weight p goes into action. Instead of the handles $e-i$ and $i-f$ (Figure 29 detail A), which are not needed in this construction, another plate $p-s$, bent at an angle of 150 degrees, is attached to the axle and plate $m-n$ (detail B). When the frame is pushed forward, this plate runs across a horizontal wire $x-y$ (Figure 29 detail C) without hindrance, the end of which is shown at o (Figure 31), but when the frame is pulled back by the board to position $e-f$ it encounters the same string o by means of which the plate $m-n$ (Figure 29 detail B) is raised and all the horizontal keys are pushed up again. Thus, for the person operating the telegraph there remains nothing more than the composition of the signal on the frame with the left hand, and turning the crank with the right, which could be done by a child.

§23 *[The Design of the Telegraph, Size and Color of the Shutters]*   To make the telegraph shutters and their movements most visible to the eye and most independent of the position of the sun and the clarity of the air, I have, partly for optical reasons and partly based on experiments, found it suitable first of all to paint the shutters black *[see p. 81]*, as matte and non-reflective as possible, and second to raise the machine so that it is visible to the viewer above the horizon so that the sky creates the background for the shutters. This may sometimes be difficult to realize when building the telegraphs, but it is so important that without it hardly any kind of telegraph, except those intended for nighttime use, could be generally and continuously usable. An elevated position for the telegraph is advantageous first of all because fog, smoke, and the many vapors that cover the ground to a certain height, are less likely to interfere with the line of vision and are often just below it.[54] A second reason is that so-called mirages, which are the result of refraction, especially above lakes where the air is filled with rising vapors displaying a distant horizon which is elevated above the normal one, are less likely to interfere with the view.[55] Third, and most important, the visibility of the telegraph, which depends on the contrast between its color and the background against which it is seen, is then generally the greatest.

If the outer contours of an object must be clearly discerned or, which is the same, must be clearly distinguished from their surroundings, they must differ as much as possible from the latter either in color or in brightness.[56]

If the color which has the greatest ability to reflect light is placed next to the one with the least, the difference between them, or the clearness of the contours will be the greatest. White reflects the most light and black the least,[57] consequently black objects on a white field, or white objects on a black field are the most easily visible.[58] Therefore a board painted white, placed behind the black shutters of the telegraph would have been the most useful, had I not, for several reasons, found it better to use the sky or the blue air instead of a white field. It is true that the brightness of the whitest object facing the sun is more than double that of the brightness of the air,[59] but first of all the brightness of that object is reduced when the angle of the sun's rays is changed,[60] and second, the brightness of the air at the horizon, where the telegraph is viewed, is much greater.[61] Third, this ratio changes even more on cloudy days, when often the brightness of the air is greater than that of paper. Fourth, the air at the horizon is clear in the morning before, and in the evening after the sun can be seen, when opaque objects can hardly be discerned at ground level. Fifth, when fog occurs, which is one of the telegraph's most common obstacles, it is more abundant at ground level and darker when all the light from the sky hits the layer that is just above the horizon. Consequently, dark objects are more easily discerned above than below the horizon.

All these factors have caused me to try to elevate the telegraph always above the horizon, and also to provide the shutters with as matte a surface as possible,[62] to avoid that they could, with the sun in a certain position, act as mirrors and lose their black color.

§24 *[The Design of the Telegraph II]* Furthermore, I have found through experience that it is necessary to separate the shutters by a distance somewhat larger than the shutters themselves, since the signals would be more difficult to see if they each filled one square of the grid than when they hardly fill one-third of it, as in the current design. The reason for this is the tremor of the optic nerves, especially in bright light, causing pictures that are close to each other on the retina to mix and become blurred. The effect of this tremor is increased by the well-known shimmering of the air, especially when it is filled with vapors caused by the sun. This shimmering is most marked at the horizon, where objects seem to flow into each other and are mixed together in waves, depending on the weather conditions. This state of mixing, which is greater horizontally than vertically, and its resulting blurriness, requires that the horizontal distance between the shutters be greater than the vertical one. It follows further that when the direction of the air flow is perpendicular to that of the stations, this blurriness is greatest, while it is reduced or completely eliminated when it is parallel to the stations.

Furthermore, the shutters should have a rectangular shape, rather than circular or square. The reason both for the rectangular shape of the shutters and the required distance between them lies in two phenomena that experience has taught us: first, that a black dot in a white field is visible at a shorter distance than a line of the same thickness, and a shorter line is visible at a shorter distance than a longer one of the same width; second, two lines close together look like one, unless the distance between them is at least 1/4 larger than their width, at the smallest possible visual angle.[63] During the early experiments, I painted the grid itself black, both in order to indicate the position of the columns and shutters and to increase the size of the latter by the width of the grid that supported them. However, several later experiments have taught me that it is more suitable to paint it white or red, the same as the arm, because a dark object between two other dark objects reduces the light area between them, and thus reduces their visibility. Furthermore, at great distances and in shimmering air, one might sometimes mistake part of the grid for a shutter;[64] which is avoided with the help of a separate color.

§25 *[The Design of the Telegraph III]*   Based on the reasoning in the preceding section, the vertical and horizontal diameters of the shutters and their relative distance should correspond to the numbers 4, 6, 5, 8, in order to be clearly visible even in moderately unclear air, and without increasing the dimensions of the telegraph more than necessary.

The necessary, absolute size of the shutters depends on the distances and the visual angle at which they should be visible. If we assume with Courtivron that the smallest possible visual angle for opaque objects is about 40 seconds,[65] the diameter of the object ought to be about 1/5200 of the distance in order to be visible.[66] Therefore, an object with a diameter of one ell would not be visible to the naked eye at a distance over 5,200 ells, or a little less than 1/4 *[Swedish]* miles.

A distance of one mile would require each shutter's vertical diameter to be 31/2 ells, and the entire grid 20 ells on one side and 30 on the other; for a distance of three miles the grid should be 60 ells high and 90 ells wide to be visible by the naked eye, a size that in practice would be difficult if not impossible to achieve.

§26 *[The Design of the Telegraph IV]*   To increase the visual angle, telescopes are used to view the signals. Since their power makes it possible to decrease the size and the cost of the machines, and vice versa, a minimum combined cost of the telegraphs and telescopes should be sought where the distance is known. According to the previous section, no more than an increase of one ell in the vertical diameter of each shutter and a telescope of 10× magnifying power should be necessary to make the signals visible at a distance of three *[Swedish]* miles. However, for the sake of clarity and security of observations, both the dimensions of the machine and the power of the telescope should be increased considerably above those sizes.

§27 *[The Design of the Telegraph V]*   Thus, depending on the distance and the power of the telescope, the absolute size of the shutters could be determined in each case, according to the principle that a visual angle of 40 seconds is sufficient for an object to be seen by the naked eye with the following equation: $a/5200 = lt$ or $l = ta/5200$, where a is the distance, l the actual diameter of the shutter, and t the magnifying power of the telescope. However, experience shows that, due to imperfections of the telescope and other obstacles which will be mentioned below, due to the unclarity of the air, a *clear view* at a greater distance requires a larger visual angle, which I feel should be six times 40 seconds, or 4 minutes for each shutter's vertical diameter, which gives $6ta/5200$. This increase in the visual angle can be gained through the telescope's power alone, through an increase in the size of the shutters, or both. The last two solutions seem to me the most favorable since they produce a brighter image.[67] During my experiments I found the following dimensions of the shutters more than sufficient, when seen at a corresponding distance with telescopes of 32× magnifying power:[68]

9 inch	1/2 [Swedish] mile = 9,000 ell
18	1
36	2
54	3

§28 [The Design of the Telegraph VI] When there is a chain of telegraphs, care should be taken in their placement. If there are only two, or when several stations are in a straight line, the angle of the telegraph should be perpendicular to the station. The size of each telegraph is determined by the farthest of the neighboring stations. When, as often happens, the stations are not in a straight line, the situation becomes different and the telegraph would be set at an angle to either one or both of the neighboring stations. The size of this angle, as well as the minimal width of the telegraph, should be calculated so as not to favor the visual angle of one station at the expense of the other.

In general, once the size of the telegraph is determined, it will be placed correctly when the difference between the visual angles on both sides is maximal [sic], because both these angles should be as large and as equal to each other as possible. To be precise, special notice should be taken of the larger mass of air between the farthest distances, which would require a larger visual angle to allow for the reduction in clarity caused by the foregoing, through opacity of the air and other obstacles to the light.

§29 [Telescopes] It would seem redundant to require a visual angle five to six times greater than the calculations indicate, but one is mistaken to think that the distance at which one can see clearly with a telescope would be proportional to its magnifying power. With a telescope that magnifies 1200× one should then be able to read writing at 1200× the distance it can be read with the naked eye. This is far from the truth. Short's great telescope, which before Herschel's was one of the best in the world, magnifies 1200×, but with it one cannot read writing at a distance greater than 200× that of the naked eye.[69] Therefore, one should divide by six the magnifying power of that telescope to arrive at its correct effect on the visibility of small, opaque objects. But, with others it is different and there are probably no theories as yet for determining the divisor in all individual cases, so one has to be content with consulting experience. What is generally known with some degree of accuracy is that this divisor is smaller for small magnifications than it is for larger ones. In my experiments I have almost never observed a smaller divisor than four or five.

Since telescopes need only be designed to be aimed at a certain fixed object, they do not require an expensive stand. In this regard, their length, which will often reduce their cost, is not a drawback either. The so-called celestial oculars which combine magnification with greater clarity, seem to be the most suitable, even though they turn the objects upside down. With a little practice the reading can be accomplished, with great assistance from the positioning arm of the telegraph. The angle of view does not have to be more than one degree and to screen out peripheral light it is helpful to increase the length of the tube outside the objective with a pipe that is blackened on the inside.

Because of the above, it should be easy to determine the kind of telescope that combines the greatest advantages for the purpose of telegraphy. With respect to the need for a small angle of view, a combination according to Galileo's method, using a concave ocular that shows the objects upside down, could be used to advantage. And to increase the light even more, a similar construction for use by both eyes, or a so-called binocular telescope, according to Rheita, would also be useful, since experience has taught us that two eyes give more light and receive a stronger impression than one. The clarity does not double, though, for when one eye is closed the other pupil will open more.[70] Such efforts to increase the effect of the telescope are only useful in those instances where fairly long distances are necessary. For normal distances, an average telescope is more than sufficient.

§30 *[Clocks]*   Besides telescopes, it is said that the telegraphs in France also require accurate clocks, but with the shutter telegraph the measurement of time would only be needed as a reminder of certain pre-agreed times for the transmission and reception of messages *[see p. 188]*.

Drawing conclusions from the length of time that a signal lasts, seems unreliable at best, and is otherwise without use for a machine that has a surplus of signals.

§31 *[Operation]*   With the construction described in §20–21, one person will suffice to operate even the largest telegraph, especially at the terminal stations. The telescope, which should be available at every station, should be placed close by, so that the operator can observe and operate the shutters; however, for the sake of greater accuracy, and especially at the intermediate stations, where observations need to be made with two telescopes and in two opposite directions, two people should be at hand to relieve each other in the observations while the machine is idle. This does not require any more understanding than possessed naturally by most people. Almost the only skill required is the ability to write numbers and to add the numbers 1, 2, and 4. During the experiments that I carried out for the past 1½ years, children could easily be employed. They could be trained in a few hours.[71]

That is why I thought that, especially for the largest machines, I should sacrifice some of the simplicity of design and construction for the greatest simplicity and ease of operation. When one is often forced to utilize less trained people, it is important not to burden their memories or their understanding with too many different facts.[72]

§32 *[Distance between Stations]* Where there is a long chain of telegraphs, it would be advantageous to reduce the number of telegraphs and increase the speed of transmission, by placing the stations farther from each other. Since the earth is round, horizontal objects at a greater distance disappear from view, even though their visual angle might still be discernible. The refraction of light, which is the greatest at the horizon, alleviates this disadvantage somewhat and elevates the objects.

Taking both of these circumstances into consideration, one could consider that the greatest distance at which two telegraphs would be discernible to each other would be five Swedish miles, if their greatest possible height over the horizon were one hundred ells.[73] Such great distances, however, would entail high costs in the required size and power of both the telegraphs and the telescopes, so for this reason alone they must be reduced, even if other circumstances would not require it. The air, although clear and transparent to a certain altitude above the ground,[74] is still more or less mixed with vapors, smoke, and other heterogeneous particles close to the ground.

This is the reason why the distance between the stations needs to be reduced below that allowed by the curvature of the earth and the power of the telescopes. The increased size of an object might increase the visual angle, but both large and small objects disappear in fog and smoke. The use of the telegraphs would be too limited by the number of hazy days and periods of haziness throughout the day, if the distances were not adjusted so that this inconvenience would be less of a hindrance.[75] It seems to me that 90,000 to 100,000 feet are distances that should not be exceeded, except when absolutely necessary; and where locations do not require otherwise, such as by lakes, the distance between normal stations should not exceed 70,000 feet or about two Swedish or five French miles.[76]

§33 *[Observatory]* The observatory, where the telescopes and the controls are placed, should be situated, on the larger machines, right below the grid. This room ought to be painted black and be provided with fairly small windows or openings, no larger, if possible, than required for the diameter of the telescope, so that no unnecessary daylight might tire the eye.[77] The pupil opens more in a dark room, allowing more light to enter from the same object. For the same reason it is advisable that the operator wear around his head a black thick veil or cloth, which will hinder the effect of light from foreign objects on all sides.

§34 *[The Speed of the Telegraph]* The speed of the telegraph is measured in three ways: first the number of stations which is on average traversed per message, which I will designate S, the value of which for the Swedish telegraph is two. Second, the number of letters expressed by each signal is designated B. According to the attached code table *[see p. 149]*, it averages two, but when combined with the codes that use the A shutter it will become more. Third, the time required for the composition of each signal T, is about ten seconds for the larger machines or six signals per minute.[78] Thus the speed of the telegraph is directly proportional to S and B and inversely proportional to T. Specifically, it is BS/T.[79]

The time required to transmit a message to a given location is equal to the product of the time to form each signal and the sum of the number of signals and stations. If the time for each signal is t, the number of signals is N, and the number of stations is n, the amount of time required for each message is then $t (N + n)$.[80]

§35 *[Obstacles to Telegraphy]* The greatest obstacle to the use of the telegraph is precipitation of rain or snow, as well as smoke and fog. Among the seasons, summer and fall are generally less suitable than winter and spring. The reason for the difficulties often lies in the nature of the various climates and the locations. Flat upland areas usually have cleaner air than those that are uneven, swampy, or wooded. It has been mentioned previously that coal smoke in England *[see p. 196]* and vapors with smoke along great rivers make the air unclean. During the summer, wood smoke creates problems in Sweden. Strong storms make operating the machine difficult and also reduce the transparency of the air somewhat. Bright sunshine causes the pupil to contract and the optic nerves to vibrate strongly,[81] making them slack and uncertain. It also, together with the heat that rises from the ground, produces a haze which makes observations difficult during the summer. The shimmering or wave-like motions of the air, caused by bright sunshine,[82] vapors or other factors, which occur in almost all seasons especially in the middle of the day, make the observation of small, closely-spaced objects difficult.

Most suitable are overcast days when the air is also somewhat clear,[83] since direct sunshine mostly creates problems. The cooler the air is in the summer, the better. Experience has shown that air that is high in humidity, such as before and after rainfall, is fairly clear and transparent.[84] In general, mornings and evenings are the most suitable parts of the day.

§36 *[Use of the Telegraph at Night with Lights]* To make this telegraph usable even at night I have made the following device: a light is attached behind each of the 10 shutters, far enough away that they do not interfere with the movement of the shutter, and somewhat above the shutter's center. When the machine is idle these ten ten lights are visible, but if a signal is composed in the usual manner all those that correspond to the vertically raised shutters disappear *[Figure 32]*. Therefore, the remainder of the first ten form the special signal which can be found in the second column of each row in the table and which corresponds to the remainder after subtraction from the previous signal 777. Thus, the code for daytime use is found before,[85] and that for nighttime use behind each syllable.

At shorter distances, and with small machines, this is easily accomplished, but there are a few problems with its performance and usage at

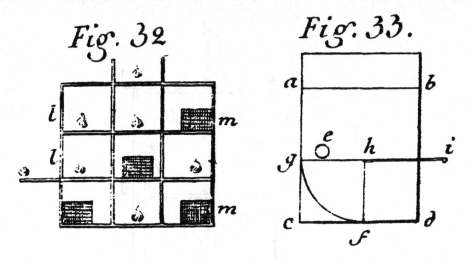

Fig. 32   Fig. 33.

larger distances.[86] I have therefore considered the following device of more use: *abcd* (Figure 33) is a tin lantern in which there are no other openings for the light than two round holes *e* on opposite sides, covered with thin glass, between which is placed a good light in such a way that it can throw its light in two directions. Quadrants *ghf*, made of tin, on both sides of the lantern, are movable around the axle *h* so that a string in the arm *i* can pull them in front of the holes *e*, but they fall back by their own weight when the string is released. Ten such lanterns are attached to the vertical stand ADBC (Figure 34) in the same order as the shutters in daytime. The strings from each are joined at the base of the machine to a control, according to the same principles as the shutters. Since there is less weight and friction to overcome in this case, no other mechanism is needed than the fingers, regardless of the distance.

This device has the advantage over the day-telegraph that it does not need to be, or rather should not be, above the horizon, but can be placed low and is easier to use and construct. It is free from several problems that plague the day-telegraph and, when combined with it, can double the usage and benefits of telegraphy.

§37 [*The Use of Lights in the Daytime*] It is known that stars are visible from the bottom of deep mines in the middle of the day. It remains to be seen if the lights could be visible even in daytime with the help of fairly long telescopes, whereby nothing more than the device previously described would be needed, which in many respects would be a great advantage. The stars in the sky can be observed in the middle of the day, even close to the sun, with the recently invented equatorial telescopes of Short and Ramsden. Therefore, it is even more likely that lamplight against a dark background, where all outside light has been eliminated, would become visible. In that case, the circumstances in regard to telescopes would differ from what was described in §27. The ones that

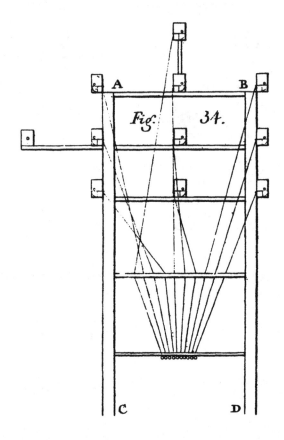

magnify the most would be the most suitable without noticeably decreasing the impression of the lights on the eye.[87]

§38 *[General Advantages of the Telegraph]*   Opinions are divided about the usefulness of these machines. Some people reject them because the lack of clarity of the air prevents their use,[88] but the capability to look through fog and darkness will probably never be invented and also shipping is a useful science even though contrary winds and storms often occur.

Others feel that the cost is so significant that it outweighs its usefulness.[89] However, besides the advantage to a government in being able to dispatch its orders within 15 minutes across the entire country, and in the same short time being able to find out what is happening in the most distant locations, you cannot make a comparison between the cost on the one hand and the usefulness on the other, when you take into consideration the fact that in times of war or otherwise, when important events take place that might affect the whole country, many thousands of people depend on the speedy transmission of information in order to take the appropriate measures.

Keep in mind also how much the reduction in couriers will save both in time and money.[90] The use of such machines during the current war in France has given incontrovertible proof of that.

§39 *[General Advantages of the Telegraph II]* This machine is actually useful in two ways: first of all, when it is only a question of the speed of communication between two places; second, when such communication cannot be accomplished in any other way. A letter between Sweden and Finland normally takes four to five days, but if this route were divided into telegraphic stations, it would take three to four minutes. If the delivery of the mail were to be interrupted by seasonal obstacles, the uncertainty of the sea, contrary winds or a storm,[91] communication could remain open either with the usual speed of the mail, if telegraphs were situated where the main obstacles are to be found, as by the Åland Sea, or with the greatest possible speed if they were erected all the way.

From both sides of lakes, which for several reasons might be difficult to cross, from forts under siege, or from beacons, coastlines, or ports to ships at sea, the telegraph might be the only means of transmitting messages. On certain occasions at sea, it seems that this machine could easily replace the currently used flag or light signals, which take more time to change, are less clearly discernible and less perfect when it comes to conveying messages.[92]

If a succession of telegraphs were installed for longer distances and in more directions, fugitives would find it harder to escape and would be more easily recaptured. Such an installation would also benefit the individual, whose correspondence regarding business transactions, the insuring of ships, etc., would more than offset the cost.[93] Between neighbors, out in the country, especially around lakes, it would provide both a useful and an enjoyable communication for a modest expense.[94]

§40 *[Contributions to Science of the Telegraph]* Science would most probably benefit from these installations if they were more common. Each telegraph is a real astronomical observatory which, with the addition of some instruments and some training of those who run it, might enrich science with new discoveries. The theory of the effects of air refraction could be expanded with daily findings; meteorology in particular, this least developed and perhaps most difficult of all the sciences, could receive remarkable information, when one considers the influence on the clarity of the air of cold and heat, humidity, storms and weather changes, fog and precipitation, and other phenomena. A daily comparison of the relationship of the barometer, the thermometer, the hygrometer, the anemometer,[95] and the air electrometer, to the diaphanometer[96] and cyanometer suggested by Mr. Saussure,[97] could perhaps in time lead to unexpected results.

§41 *[Use of the Telegraph by People of Different Nations for Communication and Understanding]*   By increasing the number of shutters of the telegraph and the number of signal combinations, so that the signals can express ideas instead of syllables and letters, it would be possible to express one or several meanings with one signal, not predetermined as they are at sea, but containing all the turns and variations in ideas and expressions occasioned by each new circumstance. One might even be able to create a kind of universal language, whereby people of all nations could communicate without knowing each other's language.[98]

§42 *[History of the Swedish Telegraph]*   The experiments with the Swedish telegraph in general were performed between Drottningholm and Stockholm on October 30 and 1 November 1794,[99] and on 30 August and 18 October 1795. *[see p. 101]*. The King, the Regent, and the entire Royal family were present at all of these.[100] Furthermore, many other experiments were performed in the same period of time between the stations around the capital.[101] These stations consist of first the Katharina Church, which is the main station in Stockholm and from which one can communicate with Drottningholm, Carlberg, and with the fortresses Fredricsborg and Vaxholm.[102]

Three telegraphs were erected this spring and are now in operation on both sides of the Åland Sea, at the post office in Grisslehamn and on Signilsskär, at a distance of 31/4 *[Swedish]* miles from each other and at the post office at Eckerö, 11/2 *[Swedish]* miles from Signilsskär.[103] Communications will probably be extended from these, on the one side from Grisslehamn to Stockholm via Fredricsborg, with four to five intermediate stations, and on the other side from Eckerö to Finland or Åbo, with six or seven intermediate stations.[104]

§43 *[Description of the Telegraph Installed in London]*   After this treatise was completed, I received an engraving from London, depicting the telegraph that was installed on the Admiralty building on February 1796 *[see also p. 191]*, together with the following description, see Figures 35–43.

When the telegraph looks like it does at A *[Figure 36]*, with all the shutters open, it is not in operation; when the shutters are closed as at C *[Figure 35]*, it is beginning operation and indicates that the next telegraph station should pay attention and respond. When it looks like it does at C, with all shutters closed, the opening of the first shutter indicates the letter *a*, the second *b*, the third *c*, the fourth *d*, the fifth *e*, the sixth *f*, which together is called the first course. In the second course the telegraph at first looks like it does at A, with all shutters open, their closing will then indicate the letters *g*, *h*, *i*, *k*, *l*, *m*, in the order shown by the figure. In the third course the telegraph looks like it does at B: the opening of the closed shutters and the closing of the open shutters indicates the letters *n*, *o*, *p*, *q*, *r*, *s*, as shown by the figure. The fourth course begins with the position shown at D, after which the opening or closing of one shutter indicates the letters *t*, *u*, *v*, *w*, *x*, *y*, *z*.

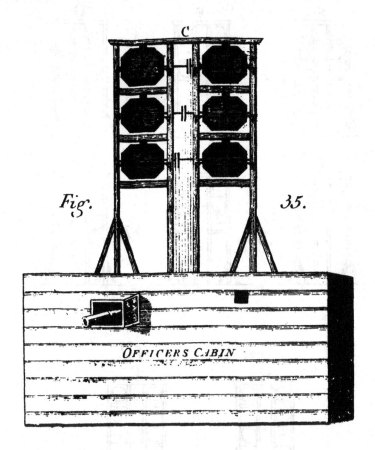

Fig. 35.

OFFICERS CABIN

Special positions of the telegraph, E, F, G, etc., indicate to which port, fleet, or admiral the orders are being sent, as well as the direction a fleet should take, and so on.

§44 *[Description of the Telegraph in London II]* It is easily seen that this device, which as far as the shutters are concerned is similar to the one I have described in this treatise, and which I reported and realized as early as in 1794, is otherwise quite different.[105] All other telegraphs usually require at least one signal per letter. This system seems to require two separate signals in order to express every letter in the alphabet, and in consequence appears twice as slow as ordinary telegraphs, but six times as slow as those telegraphs where one signal can indicate syllables of three or four letters.

The basic number of signals on this machine is sixty-four, but if you use combinations of signals there is no limit to their number on this, or on any

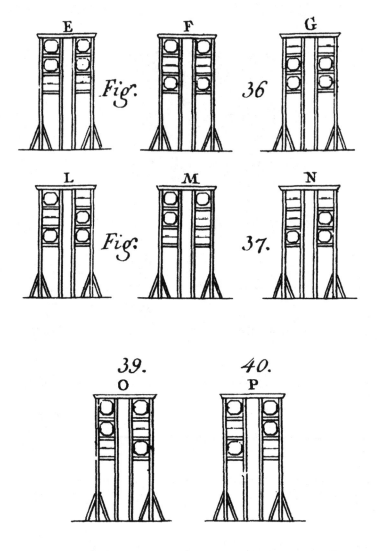

other, telegraph. Since the positions here are not expressed as numbers, one has to memorize their meaning, or consult a table after observing each signal, which might cause problems and lead to mistakes. This machine, the external or internal construction of which I know nothing about, does not seem to be build in such a manner that the shutters can show against the sky. Since the shutters are also fairly close to each other, it must encounter great problems from the shimmering of the air, both when the air is clear and when it is not.

Recent newspaper reports stated that the telegraph has been taken down, because it could be used at most twenty-five days per year. I do not know

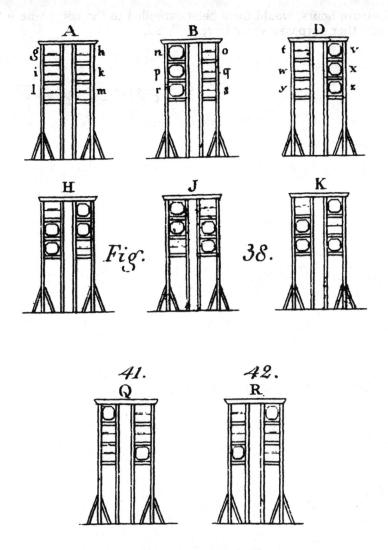

Fig. 38.

whether it has been replaced with another design.

§45 *[Conclusion]* Much should probably have been added to this treatise in order to explain more clearly the mechanical composition of the various parts of the telegraph, its position and structure in various locations and for various purposes, the handling of incidents that may occur during a transmission, the ways of saving time and so on,[106] the training of the people who will be working with it etc.[107]

But, most of this can be learned by each and every one with some practice,[108] and furthermore, the limits of this small effort, which is the fruit of leisure hours, would have been extended to the point where time needed for other purposes would have suffered.

Chapter Five
Other Countries

After Chappe's and Edelcrantz's first successful experiments, the government of practically every country in Europe was flooded with proposals from serious and not-so-serious inventors for similar, improved, or simply different telegraph designs.

Edelcrantz noted in his treatise:[1]

> It often happens, with regard to new inventions, that one part of the general public finds them useless and another part considers them to be impossible. When it becomes clear that the possibility and the usefulness can no longer be denied, most agree that the whole thing was fairly easy to discover and that they knew about it all along.

He forgot to mention another mechanism that would prevent the authorities in one country from directly adopting an improvement that came from another, particularly when the two countries were enemies. An example of this appears in the first letter on the French semaphore telegraph that was published in the British journal *Gentleman's Magazine* in September 1794.[2] Almost apologetically, the letter concludes with a quote from Ovidius: *Fas est ab hoste doceri* [It is right to learn, even from an enemy].

A similar sentiment was expressed by Napoleon Bonaparte when he was shown a German improvement of a telegraphic device. He is reported to have rejected the contraption with the curt remark: *C'est une idée Germanique* [It's a German idea].

In the first few years after Chappe's telegraph began operating, the effort in most of the surrounding countries was to come up with a better, but mostly a different, design that could be adopted with pride. Since

---

1. The notes to this chapter start at p. 270.

Chappe's system was one of the first, it is understandable that indeed better devices would be developed. One of the flaws of Chappe's telegraph design was the difficulty in assigning symbolic codes to semaphore positions. The signs could only be set, read, and recorded as pictograms. Edelcrantz solved that problem elegantly by switching to the system of three rows of shutters, symbolically represented by three numbers.

Germany, England, and America later adopted a variation of Chappe's semaphore that similarly allowed a numeric encoding of semaphore positions.[3] It seems that each improved version of the optical telegraph in one country drove other countries into sillier and inferior designs, with the apparent motive that if it couldn't be better, at least it could be different.

In Russia, optical telegraphs were installed relatively late. On 8 April 1839 a line of stations was completed between St. Petersburg and Warsaw. It consisted of 220 stations, employing six operators per station. This first Russian state telegraph is said to have been established by Tsar Nicolas I, and was based on Chappe's design. Using a combination of this optical telegraph and couriers, a message could be sent from St. Petersburg to Berlin in about three days. Shaffner reported in 1859 that the abandoned telegraphs of this line could still be seen, but were deteriorating rapidly. The line was therefore probably not in operation for long.

Norway, Denmark, and Finland

Norway, Denmark, and Finland, being close to Sweden, were most influenced by Edelcrantz's design, but none of these countries would adopt it without modifications.

In Norway various types of flag signaling systems were used until at least 1807. In 1808, Captain Ole Olsen constructed a new telegraphic device, that was rather close in appearance to Edelcrantz's system.[4] Instead of ten shutters, Olsen's device had six flaps, mounted in two rows of three flaps each (Figure 5.1). The shutters, or flaps, could be placed in three positions: up, down, or obscured from view in a horizontal position. Olsen's device thus allowed for $3^6 = 729$ code combinations, of which only 229 appeared in the signal books. In 1810, a substantial line of 227 optical telegraph stations was completed, connecting Halden, along the coast, via Oslo to Trondheim. The stations were built fairly close together, on average 4 to 5 km apart, to overcome the problems of fog and poor visibility. The line was in operation for only a few years. After the war had ended in 1813, the Danish-Norwegian monarchy was economically ravaged. The maintenance of the optical telegraph stations became too costly, and by the end of 1814 the line was closed down, never to be rebuilt.

In Denmark a first experiment was performed in 1794 inspired by, and based on, Chappe's design, but it was not adopted. A general study of signaling systems was performed for the Danish Admiralty between 1796 and 1798. At first, however, this led conservatively to the adoption of a variation of a flag signaling system.

The Danish naval captain Lorenz Fisker (1753–1819) submitted a new

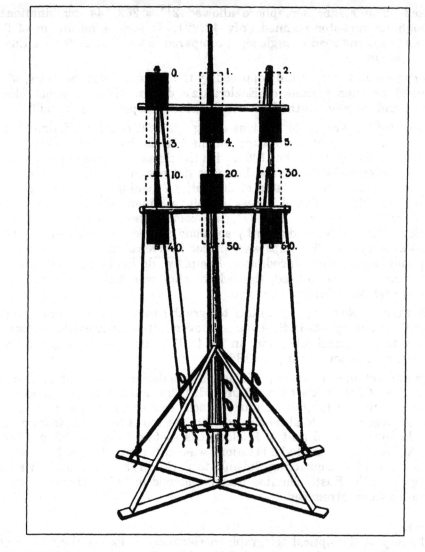

Figure 5.1 Olsen´s Six-Shutter Telegraph (Norway, 1808).
(Coll. Norsk Telemuseum, Oslo)

proposal to the Admiralty in December 1799 to build a telegraph with eighteen rotating flaps.[5] Sixteen flaps were organized in a square grid of four by four flaps, and two additional flaps were placed in a single row on top of that grid. Each flap was 3 ells long and 1.25 ells wide (ca. 2×0.75 meter), and could be rotated from a vertical to a horizontal position with strings. Unlike Edelcrantz's system, each flap was always completely exposed. The Fisker semaphore allowed $2^{18} = 262,144$ combinations, although its inventor claimed only $42,221$. It took a minimum of 22 seconds to set and read a single sign, compared to six seconds for the Edelcrantz system.

Fisker's proposal was initially opposed by the Danish Postal Services, who preferred another variant of Edelcrantz's design. It was nonetheless adopted and installed at the Batterie Quintus in Copenhagen in 1800.

In early 1801 a line of 24 stations along the east coast of Själland was built, under the threat of an attack of the British fleet. The attack came on 2 April 1801. In the fall of 1801, with the threat gone, the line was discarded. Construction on a new line was not begun until 1808. When it was finished the line consisted of 26 stations leading from Heisinger at the Northern tip of Själland, across the island Fünen, to Kiel on the mainland (now in Germany). In 1811, the complicated Fisker system was replaced with a simpler design by someone named Schumacher. In the Schumacher system, five flaps were placed in five columns, each in one of ten possible positions, encoding a five-place decimal number. Where smaller code spaces sufficed, the Schumacher was also used with four, three, or just two columns.

Other than in Norway, the optical telegraphs remained in service more than half a century. As in Sweden, they even initially survived the installation of the electrical telegraphs in 1854. The last optical telegraph line in Denmark was not closed until 1862.

In Finland yet another variant of Edelcrantz's design was adopted. It was proposed by Captain Carl Otto Ramstedt (Figure 5.2).[6] It contained two columns of five rectangular shutters each, connected in five rows to a mast. A large ball could also be raised into the top of the mast, to increase the code space beyond that of Edelcrantz's system to 2048 different signals. A line of an estimated 80 stations was built along the southern coast of Finland in 1854, connecting Helsinki to Turku in the West, and towards Leningrad in the East. The line was abandoned in 1855, when electrical telegraphs were introduced.

Germany
The history of the optical telegraph in Germany is longer than in most other countries, but also more painful. Johann Bergstrasser (1732–1788) published his first works on telegraphy in Germany in 1785,[7] and performed some early experiments in 1786.[8] He pleaded for the support of rich benefactors who could enable him to perform experiments on a larger scale. In a letter he wrote in 1795, for instance, he referred to the many ideas he had published in 1785 that had remained unused:

> Since I cannot perform any experiments, I cannot [verify and] record my ideas about the many possible improvements, modifications, and use of these signals. I am, however, completely convinced of an inexpensive construction, and of the feasibility of the scheme. Experiments cannot cost much; they can, however, only be performed in the field; such as the land of a wealthy nobleman who can

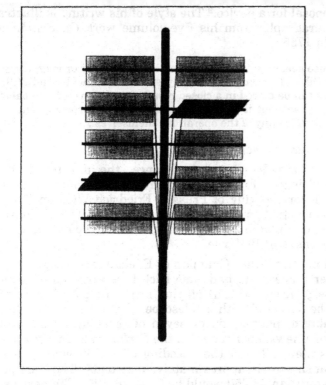

Figure 5.2 Ramstedt´s Ten-Shutter Telegraph (Finland, 1854).

spend a few thousand thaler on a useful speculation.

He would never succeed in securing such support. When the Chappes were more successful in France, Bergstrasser became increasingly frustrated. He wrote in 1796:

> What is today called a telegraph, I called a signal-post as early as in 1784, as shown in the Appendix. This Appendix [with excerpts from Bergstrasser 1785] also proves that the real telegraph was born on German soil.

And, in the same work, quoting from a letter he wrote on 19 November 1794, just after news of Chappe's success in France became known, he wrote:

> That my proposal to connect Berlin via Leipzig, Magdeburg, Hanover to Hamburg has never been executed, like the proposal of the gentlemen Chappe to connect Paris to Lille, is not the fault of my method.

It appears that Bergstrasser was heartily ignored in everything that happened later. Most of the writers who referred to Bergstrasser later complained that in his voluminous works it was impossible to discover any specific proposal for a device.[9] The style of his writing is illustrated by the following paragraphs from his five-volume work *On Synthematography*, published in 1785:

> I do not use speaking tubes, and even less electricity or magnets; also no wires or tubes, like Mr. Gauthen [usually spelled Gauthey]. And still, part of my apparatus can be placed in a closed room, anywhere in a large palace, wherever desired; . . . without it being necessary that the correspondents can see each other, or perform any of the operations themselves . . .

Bergstrasser never revealed a convincing method.

Soon after Chappe's success in France, the director of the German Academy of Sciences, Franz Karl Achard, held a demonstration of an optical telegraph for the king of Prussia, Friedrich Wilhelm II (1744–1797). For this demonstration, on 1 March 1795, Achard had constructed two semaphores, one placed on the Julius tower in Spandau, the other on a tower of the castle at Bellevue.

Achard did not use either Chappe's or Edelcrantz's design or apply any of Bergstrasser's ideas. He had gone back to a variation of Robert Hooke's dubious design from 1684, displaying large cutouts of character symbols that could be observed with a telescope. Achard used five different symbols, probably displaying six or seven of these symbols simultaneously. According to a newspaper report in the *Berlinska Tidningen* from 3 March 1795, the system allowed the encoding of 23,750 words, each of which could be transmitted in approximately 20 seconds. The least power of five that is greater than 23,750 would be $5^7 = 78,125$. The newspaper report, by the way, referred to both Chappe and Edelcrantz, so it is virtually certain that their designs were known to Achard at the time.

Also in 1795, Baron (Freiherr) Karl Buschendorff submitted a proposal to connect the main cities in Germany with, of course, another private design. A precise description of the design he proposed is not preserved. Apparently, neither Achard or Buschendorff had the charisma, the connections, or the stamina that Chappe or Edelcrantz had. Neither of their proposals was acted upon, and they did not pursue the matter after the first rejections.

Between 1796 and 1837 many other proposals were submitted, but none adopted. The main concerns working against the optical telegraph lines were the expense of their construction, and the visibility problems caused by fog. Most proposals from this time target mobile telegraphs for use by the army, instead of fixed installations, as in other countries. The optical telegraph itself seems to have had the support of the king, but it failed to trigger the interest of those who had to execute the plans.

On 12 June 1819 the king of Prussia, Friedrich Wilhelm III (1770–1840), ordered an experiment to be performed with the optical telegraph. The responsibility for the experiment was placed with a newly appointed Minister of Defense named Karl von Hake. Dieter Herbarth, in his study from 1978, describes in amusing detail how von Hake managed to delay and to

Figure 5.3 Seal of the Prussian Optical Telegraph.
(Source: [Herbarth 1978], p. 48)

frustrate virtually every attempt to carry out the experiments.[10] When the study of the optical telegraph was finally allowed to be completed on 23 May 1830, the recommendation was to employ a variation of Edelcrantz's system, using 12 instead of 10 shutters, giving four times as many combinations. On 28 June 1830 the German Cabinet ordered the construction of a short stretch of line, with three telegraph stations, between Berlin and Potsdam. Operation and maintenance were entrusted to a section of the army consisting of one officer, two under-officers, and ten enlisted men.

From this point on things started to move more quickly. Based on the experiences with the first line, a new proposal was submitted in December 1830 by *Postrat* Carl Pistor (1778–1847). Pistor proposed to construct a permanent line for general governmental use connecting Berlin to Koblenz. He recommended a minor variation of Watson's design from England.[11] Watson's semaphore was based on articulated arms, reminiscent of Chappe's design, but it allowed for easier coding and a larger code space. Pistor's design was favored by von Hake, recommended to the king on 22 September 1831, and adopted. On 16 October 1831 the cabinet appointed a commission to prepare the construction of the line from Berlin to Koblenz, based on Pistor's proposal.

On 21 July 1832 the construction of the line from Berlin to Koblenz was assigned to Major Franz August O'Etzel (1784–1850), who pursued the matter vigorously. The line was completed in June 1833. In all, 64

185

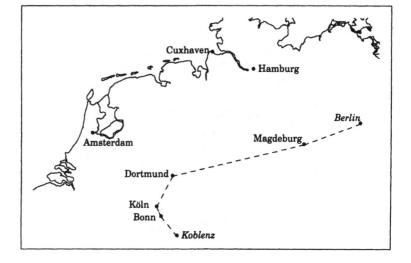

Figure 5.4 The Line from Berlin to Koblenz (1833).

telegraph stations were constructed, leading from Berlin through Potsdam and Magdeburg via Köln and Bonn to Koblenz.[12] Each station was equipped with two telescopes, with a focal length of 78 cm (approx. 30 inches), and a magnification factor of roughly 50×. The first station was built in a former astronomical observatory in the Dorotheenstrasse in Berlin. On 4 February 1835 Major O'Etzel officially became the first Telegraph Director, appointed directly by the king. At its peak the optical telegraph line in Germany employed 200 people, comparable to the number in Sweden, but fewer than in France.

No other official optical telegraph lines were built in Germany, so no telegraph network comparable to that in France or Sweden ever existed. In 1837 one Johann Ludwig Schmidt did open a separate commercial line from Hamburg to Altona and Cuxhaven, with government permission. It was in operation until 1848, but its use appears to have been restricted to giving early notification to Hamburg of the arrival of ships in Cuxhaven. The telegraph design used by Schmidt was yet another variation, though not clearly an improvement over the other designs in use at that time. It consisted of a single support column with three movable indicators mounted in the form of a cross, one indicator pointing straight up, the other two pointing left and right. Only 62 different signal combinations could be made, sufficient for the letters of the alphabet, the ten numerals, and control codes such as "start," "stop," and "there is a fire."

In 1847 Schmidt constructed a second commercial optical telegraph line, from Bremen to Bremerhaven. The line was linked to the Hamburg–Altona line via three intermediate stations, producing what is perhaps the only example of a private data network of optical telegraphs.[13]

Figure 5.5 The Reconstructed Optical Telegraph at Köln-Flittard.
(Photo: Björn Pehrson, 1991)

In 1848, the year that O'Etzel retired, the first electro-magnetic tele-graphs were installed, with strong support of O'Etzel himself.[14] Inevit-ably, on 1 June 1849 the optical telegraph line between Berlin and Kob-lenz was decommissioned. Schmidt's private lines lasted only a few years longer. The line to Hamburg was abandoned in 1850, and the line to Bre-men in 1852.

The Berlin to Koblenz line rarely carried more than one or two messages per day. The telegraph operators, nevertheless, were required to check the neighboring stations at least once per minute through their telescopes, and of course more frequently (about once every 10 seconds) when mes-sages were being transferred. In the absence of message traffic, the termi-nal station in Koblenz was required to transmit a filler message to Berlin every hour on the hour. In the absence of other traffic, this message, *Nichts Neues* (No News), would reach Berlin in roughly one minute.

Each intermediate station along the line had the choice to pass on the *Nichts Neues* token, or to insert a message of its own: a discipline reminis-cent of token-ring polling techniques used in modern computers. When the *Nichts Neues* token finally reached the end point, it indicated that no further traffic from Koblenz towards Berlin remained, and the polling pro-cess was repeated in the opposite direction, returning the virtual token back to Koblenz.

Of course, what precisely constituted a whole "hour" had to be standard-ized. Looking only at the sun, noon-time at Koblenz is inevitably about 30 minutes later than noon-time at Berlin. Therefore, once every three days the clocks at the various stations along the telegraph line were synchron-ized with the clock in Berlin, with Berlin time taking precedence. The clock message would be transmitted from Berlin at the exact moment of a full hour, and had to be forwarded with the greatest possible speed towards Koblenz, and then bounced back towards Berlin. Under ideal conditions, the clock signal could return to Berlin in about one minute, passing twice through all 65 telegraph stations.

The net speed of the telegraph for the transmission of real messages, how-ever, was unimpressive. A single 30-word message transmitted from Kob-lenz on 17 March 1848 took 1.5 hours to reach Köln. In many cases, longer messages could take several days to be completely transmitted, especially when visibility was restricted by rain or fog in the summer or by snow and shortened daylight hours in the winter.

England and Ireland
The application of optical telegraphs was more successful in England. As early as in 1767 Sir Richard Lovell Edgeworth (1744–1817), whom we met earlier in Chapter Three, reported on his telegraph experiments to the Royal Society of Ireland. His telegraph had two movable wings mounted on a single pivot.[15] But the experiments and the report went largely unno-ticed. After reports of Chappe's success reached England in 1794, Edgeworth's interest in telegraph design was rekindled, and he started

new experiments, as did many others.

In 1795 the British Admiralty still ordered the construction of 48 new signal towers that could display a small number of predefined signals, using an arrangement of balls and flags.[16] The towers were built along the south coast of England, stretching from Sheerness to Land's End. They were soon replaced with better designs.

On 19 November 1794 Edgeworth demonstrated a new telegraph design, which he called a *Tellograph*. He recalled what led him to do this in a letter to the Earl of Charlemont, written in 1795:[17]

> When I heard of the French telegraph, a new object arose for my exertions. I recalled to my mind experiments that I had tried so long ago as the year 1767, when I practiced this species of aerial communication; and thinking that it might be peculiarly useful to this country [Ireland], I constructed some machines with which I conversed, in August 1794, between Parkenham Hall, (the seat of Lord Longford), and Edgeworthstown.

A little later in the same letter, he explains:

> *Tellograph* is the name I give to my machine, to denote that it conveys words instead of letters.

The Tellograph had only a single pointer, with eight possible positions, allowing just eight separate signals to be sent. A report in the newspaper of that day described it as follows:[18]

> The Right Honorable Speaker of the House of Commons has been the first in this country to prove the expedience of using the telegraph. The last was erected on Mount Oriel, near the Speaker's at Collon, another on the hill of Skreene, in the country of Meath, fifteen miles distant . . . . Each party took their station and when the necessary signals were made they indicated to and answered each other at that distance in the space of five minutes. The whole apparatus is nothing more than a triangular stand about fourteen feet in height placed on an imminence on the top of which is fixed an index which turns on a swivel. The index has eight different situations in the circle it describes signifying the eight figures (0, 1, 2, 3, 4, 5, 6, 7). The person at the corresponding station taken fifteen miles off can thoroughly perceive by the help of a good telescope, every situation of the index and each party at each station is furnished with a glossary or a dictionary to explain the signals; thus the ideas of one may be in a few minutes communicated to the other.

The experiment was performed at the request of the Irish Speaker of the House, who was a close friend of Edgeworth. Edgeworth's letter from 1795 ends with the statement:

> Mr. Edgeworth has, at no small expense, both of time and money, brought his plan to such perfection, that he is willing to establish a correspondence between any places his Excellency shall point out, and to suffer the whole loss, if his plan shall be found deficient either in secrecy or expedition.

Despite this offer, the Speaker had to report to Edgeworth later that his

Figure 5.6 Lord George Murray.
(Source: [Holmes 1983])

plan "would not be pursued." It appears that the bottleneck was at the British Admiralty, which, consulted by the Speaker, had decided that:

> . . . [it] does not see any purpose in this country [Ireland] for which he could be warranted in incurring the expense.

The real reason for the rejection was more likely that the British Admiralty had by this time already committed to another design. In 1795 Lord George Murray (1761–1803) had proposed to the British Admiralty to build a variation of Edelcrantz design, a six-shutter telegraph, allowing $2^6 = 64$ different codes to be transmitted.[19] The design differs from Edelcrantz's telegraph in only minor details. Instead of three columns, each mounted with three rectangular shutters, Murray's design had two columns, each with three octagonal shutters. It was described in the *Encyclopaedia Britannica* of 1797 with praise, but also with some critical notes:

> This telegraph is without doubt made up of the best number of combinations possible; five boards [shutters] would be insufficient, and seven would be useless. It has been objected to it, however, that its form is too clumsy to admit of

190

Figure 5.7 Early Model of Murray's Six-Shutter Design.
(Coll. Victory Museum, England)

its being raised to any considerable height above the building on which it stands; and that it cannot be made to change its direction, and consequently cannot be seen but from one particular point.

Edelcrantz's prior design is not mentioned, but his influence seems undeniable. After describing the British design in his treatise in 1796, Edelcrantz politely referred to this "coincidence," by dryly remarking in footnote 100:[20]

Several foreigners, among them Englishmen, have also witnessed these experiments.

In September 1795 the British Admiralty accepted Murray's design and constructed a first line of 15 stations, going east from London via Chatham to Deal, with a branch north from Faversham, via Tonge, to Sheerness. The line was completed on 27 January 1796. Signals could be sent from London to Deal in about one minute.

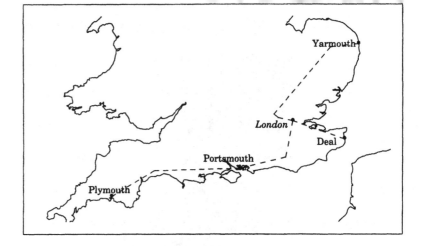

Figure 5.8 The Three Main Lines to London, ca. 1808.

George Murray received 2000 pounds for his invention. The contractor who had built the first line, George Roebuck, was appointed Superintendent of British Telegraphs at an annual salary of 300 pounds. The beginning network was extended in 1796 with 10 additional stations for a line going south from London via Beacon Hill to Portsmouth. In 1806 it was extended again, with 22 additional stations leading from Beacon Hill 200 miles southwest to Plymouth. In 1807 a line of 18 stations from London north via Hampstead to Great Yarmouth was added. By 1808 George Roebuck had a total of 65 telegraph stations under his supervision, all based on Murray's shutter design.

George Murray's design was used until about 1816. Perhaps as a result of some frustration with the limitations of Murray's system, over 100 new designs for telegraphs were submitted to the British Admiralty and the British Parliament between 1796 and 1816. Those who had to evaluate these would understandably become increasingly skeptical with each new and improved version submitted to them. The frustration this led to among the more insistent inventors from that time is clear in the following statement from one of them, Lieutenant John Macdonald:[21]

> If an angel from heaven were to offer an unexceptionable plan, he would be ordered to walk, or fly, off with it, if he had not an article to offer which is not quite fit for angels to deal in, viz. Parliamentary interest.

Macdonald's self-assigned mission was to get the Admiralty to adopt his, quite reasonable, coding tables for use with both the land-based and the naval optical semaphores. Despite almost 30 years of trying, he only seems to have succeeded in annoying the Admiralty board to the point where his letters and proposals were no longer even acknowledged—an

Figure 5.9 Working the Ropes, Murray's Design.
(Source: [Holmes 1983])

unusual move, and something that, of course, infuriated Macdonald even more. The British Admiralty had adopted the popular *Trafalgar Code* from Admiral Sir Home Popham in 1803, and it saw no reason to switch to an untried scheme developed by a lieutenant.[22]

The "man of science" at the British Admiralty at the time, who had to deal with the stream of inventions, was its secretary, Mr. Barrow. Very likely, the large majority of the proposals he rejected out of hand were truly undeserving. On 11 July 1816, however, he received the following letter from Sir Francis Ronalds, with what was probably the first proposal to replace the optical telegraph with an electro-magnetic one. It was addressed to Lord Melville, who was First Lord of the British Admiralty at the time.[23]

Mr. Ronalds presents his respectful compliments to Lord Melville and takes the liberty of soliciting his Lordship's attention to a mode of conveying telegraphic intelligence with great rapidity, accuracy, and certainty, in all states of the atmosphere, either at night or in the day, and at small expense, which has occurred to him whilst pursuing some electrical experiments. Having been at some pains to ascertain the practicality of the scheme, it appears to Mr. Ronalds and to a few gentlemen by whom it has been examined, to possess several important advantages over any species of telegraph hitherto invented, and he would be much gratified by an opportunity of demonstrating those

193

Figure 5.10 Sir Home Riggs Popham.
(Coll. National Maritime Museum, Greenwich, England)

advantages to Lord Melville by an experiment which he has no doubt would be deemed decisive, if it should be perfectly agreeable and consistent with his Lordship's engagements to honour Mr. Ronalds with a call; or he would be very happy to explain more particularly the nature of the contrivance if Lord Melville could conveniently oblige him by appointing an interview. [Signed, Upper Mall, Hammersmith, 11 July 1816.]

Mr. Barrow's answer of 5 August 1816 could have been chiseled on his grave:

Mr. Barrow presents his compliments to Mr. Ronalds, and acquaints him with reference to his note of the 3rd inst., that telegraphs of any kind are now wholly unnecessary; and that no other than the one now in use will be adopted.

At about this same time, the British Prime Minister is reported to have answered a parliamentary question on the subject as follows:[24]

Mechanical telegraphs are now so perfect that I doubt if they can be improved, they certainly answer all calls that are likely to be made on them, but if improvements are forthcoming they must not be looked for in the ingenious

194

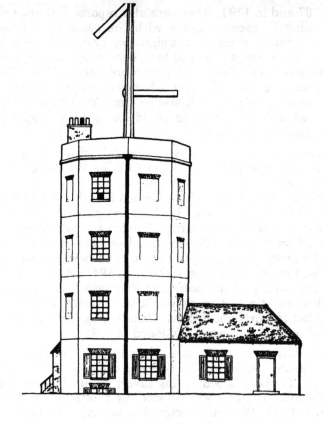

Figure 5.11 Popham's Two-Arm Semaphore.
(Source: [Holmes 1983])

electrical toy just referred to by the Hon. Member.

Sir Francis did not pursue the matter further, nor did he try to lobby other bodies. It would take another twenty years before William Cooke and Charles Wheatstone would do so, and succeed by selling the first electromagnetic telegraphs to the British Railways.

Despite Mr. Barrow's insistence that no new designs would be adopted, the British Admiralty abandoned George Murray's shutter telegraph the same year, and adopted a new design from the British Admiral Sir Home Riggs Popham (see also page 13). His semaphore was designed to be usable both on land and on ships, and consisted of just two movable semaphore arms that could be placed in one of seven positions, allowing $7^2 = 49$ different signals.

The design of a single post with rotating arms was, of course, not entirely new. We saw earlier that Sir Edgeworth had experimented with similar designs in 1767 and in 1794. There are also reports that as early as 1801, not withstanding Chappe's success with the semaphore telegraph, the French had also put in place a coast signaling system consisting of a mast with three indicator wings attached to it, each wing being placed in one of eight possible positions. This system was proposed by the Frenchman C. Depillon, as an improvement over Chappe's design. Around 1807 the Depillon semaphores had been installed from Vlissingen in the Netherlands, to Bayonne in France, and could easily have inspired the later semaphore designs in England.

Popham's design was used for only a relatively short period. In 1822 it was replaced with a design of Colonel Charles W. Pasley (1780–1861). Pasley's system also had two movable arms, but his system allowed each arm to be set in one of eight positions, much like the Depillon semaphore, producing 64 code combinations. Pasley's design was used, for instance, for the construction of a new line from London to Portsmouth. The line it replaced, based on Murray's design, had been abandoned in 1816 when the threat of war temporarily diminished. The new line from London to Portsmouth was in operation from 1822 until 1847. A start was also made with the reconstruction of the branch to Plymouth, this time starting not at Beacon Hill but at a station called Chatley Heath, close to London on the new London to Portsmouth line. Construction on the branch to Plymouth started in 1825, but was abandoned in 1831.

The last important development took place in 1827. In that year, reserve Marine Lieutenant Barnard L. Watson constructed a commercially operated line of 11 stations connecting Liverpool along the coastline westward to Holyhead. The line was apparently profitable, and was kept in operation until 1860. Watson's design was perhaps the best of all semaphore designs in the style of Chappe. It consisted of a single support column with three indicator pairs mounted at the top. Each of the three indicators could be set in one of ten positions, allowing a decimal encoding of signals. Watson defined nine code groups, each of 1,000 signals. A first signal of each series would be used to select the required signal group, or code book. Watson's design was also adopted by O'Etzel on the Berlin to Koblenz line, with some minor, mostly mechanical, variations.[25]

In 1839 Watson's system was modified to have four indicator pairs, set on two support posts, multiplying the number of usable code combinations by ten.

The weather was a limiting factor in the use of the optical telegraphs in England. Edelcrantz noted:[26]

> According to articles in recent papers, in London, where the air is almost always filled with coal smoke, less than 25 days a year are clear enough for this purpose, but it seems that the telegraphs there, as well as the French, are not visible against the sky, without which great difficulties with their use must arise.

A Parliamentary report for the period April 1839 to April 1842 gives the

Table 5.1 Outage of Semaphore Stations (Days).

Period	Admiralty	Chelsea	Putney	Portsmouth
1839–1840	133	64	42	21
1840–1841	106	70	49	28
1841–1842	84	77	51	16
Total	323	211	142	65

number of days when the British optical telegraphs between London and Portsmouth were not available due to the limited visibility (Table 5.1).[27] A note attached to the report explains that when the Admiralty station in London could not operate, messages would be taken to either Chelsea or Putney and transmitted from there to Portsmouth, alleviating somewhat the effect of the smog.

On 31 December 1847 the last of the Admiralty's optical telegraph stations were closed. Proposals for new semaphore designs nevertheless continued to be submitted to the British Army and Navy. Between 1906 and 1914 the British Army, for instance, received 27 such proposals. Some were tried briefly; most were rejected outright.

The Netherlands and Curacao

In January 1794, when Claude Chappe had already started constructing the first line of optical telegraphs from Paris to Lille, the Netherlands considered proposals for a new early warning signaling system that was to be installed along the Dutch coastline. The signaling posts in these proposals were still thought to be equipped with only beacons, cannons, and flares. But a lack of funds delayed the completion of the line. The full line of 63 stations was only completed after the invasion of the French troops, one year later. Under the influence of the French, the stations were now also given a capability to exchange a limited array of flag signals.

It is not too surprising that for coastal signaling a design different from the Chappe telegraph was used. The coastal system in France had traditionally also been based on flag signals and beacon fires. When it was replaced in 1801, the new system that was adopted (designed by C. Depillon) was still quite distinct from Chappe's design.

When the Dutch decided in 1798 to replace the flag signals, they chose an elaborate new system with movable discs and triangular vanes, designed by coast signaling director J. Van Woensel (1740–1816). It was installed along the Dutch coastline in 1798–1799.[28] With small modifications, and an interruption between 1801 and 1803, inspired by the treaty of Amiens, this line of stations remained in service until 1813. During the French occupation of the Netherlands, the Chappe telegraph lines were extended to Vlissingen (1809), linking to the Dutch line, and also directly to Amsterdam and Apeldoorn (1810). After the defeat of Napoleon's army in 1814 most stations were either destroyed or dismantled.

Figure 5.12 The Dutch Coastal Telegraph from 1799.
(Coll. Municipal Archives, The Hague, Netherlands)

In 1830 Belgium declared itself independent from the Netherlands. To oppose this move, the Netherlands made preparations for the retaking of its lost territory. Government advisor Antoine Lipkens was commissioned in 1831 to establish new optical telegraph links to facilitate the communications. Instead of the French system, a design that resembles Murray's six-shutter telegraph was chosen. Lipkens designed his telegraph with six rotating disks, each disk two meters in diameter.[29] The disks were mounted on church-towers, in two rows of three disks, slightly tilted towards each other, as also shown in Fig. 1.11 (p. 36).

Within weeks Lipkens had a first link, between the Hague and Breda, in operation. A little later, the navy base in Vlissingen was also connected. It took one minute to send a message from the Hague to Vlissingen, transferred by nineteen disc semaphore stations, roughly ten kilometers apart. The disk telegraph was in operation until 1839. Detailed instructions are preserved in the State Archives in the Hague. A model of the Lipkens telegraph, built by its author, can be found in the Modellenkamer of the Rijksmuseum in Amsterdam.

In 1993 the remains of an optical telegraph line were discovered on the Dutch island of Curacao, near Venezuela.[30] A line of four stations connected Fort Amsterdam to a lookout point on the east coast of the island. Its primary function was to report the approach of ships from the lookout point to Fort Amsterdam. An archeological excavation at the sites of the former stations revealed unusually well-preserved remains, including the remainder of one complete optical telegraph mast, of the type proposed by Antoine Lipkens in 1831, with the shutters still in place. Instead of discs of woven twigs, as originally proposed by Lipkins, however, carefully counterbalanced metal discs had been used.

Jay Haviser, who located the remains at Curacao, traced the history of this line back to plans for the installation of a first *signaling post* on sketches for the construction of Fort Nassau that date from 1825. These plans do not detail the type of telegraph to be used, and indeed the Lipkens design did not exist yet at this time. The first Lipkens-style telegraphs can be seen at Fort Amsterdam on paintings that date from 1855, but it is likely that they were installed there considerably earlier. The telegraphs still can be spotted on paintings and photographs from the fort as late as in 1910. On a photo of Fort Amsterdam taken in 1910 the original mast is joined by a second one that is placed at a slightly different angle. This new telegraph faces east, towards Fort Rif, where around this time the first electrical telegraphs had been installed.

Haviser, in his study of the optical telegraphs at Curacao, noted that someone named Carlos Heykoop was said to be signalmaster at one of the optical telegraph stations until his death in 1917. The masts of the telegraphs were chopped down in 1940, when they became an obstacle to a nearby airstrip. Optical telegraphs may therefore have been used at Curacao for almost a century, from 1825 to 1917, longer than anywhere else in the world.

Spain

By 1846, three main lines of optical telegraphs branched out from Madrid to the north, east, and south of Spain.[31] The line to the east went to Valencia, and from there up the coast beyond Barcelona, reaching to the frontier with France. A second line led from Madrid south to Toledo and from there down to Cadiz, on the south coast of Spain. A third line led straight north of Madrid to the west side of the frontier with France, near Bayonne. Messages were also carried (by courier) from the Spanish system to the French and vice versa, thus establishing a communication link from Paris to Barcelona, Madrid, and Cadiz. It is this link that Napoleon referred to in 1808, in his note to Vice-Admiral Decrès, quoted in Chapter Two. "The line to Spain" is also referred to in *The Count of Monte Cristo* from Alexander Dumas, which also features in C. S. Forester's novel *Hornblower and the Hotspur.*

There may also have been a connection with a line in Portugal, connecting Porto to Lisbon. That link, if it existed, branched off from the Madrid to Cadiz line, and reached Portugal via Badajoz.

Australia

A first line of optical telegraphs was installed in Sydney in 1827. The design was a two-arm semaphore, most likely a version of Popham's design from 1816, allowing seven positions per arm, for a total of $7^2 = 49$ combinations. The arms were placed above each other on a single support post. When in operation, each arm could assume one of the clock positions two, three, and four o'clock, or eight, nine, and ten o'clock. In rest, the arms would point down in the six o'clock position.

In 1832 the semaphores were equipped with one extra arm, expanding the number of combinations to $7^3 = 343$. In 1838, finally, Watson's design from 1827 was adopted, using three arm-pairs, each of which could be set in one of ten positions. Codes from 0 to 999 were encoded by using the top arm-pair for units, the middle for tens, and the bottom for hundreds. For codes with a numeric value of 1,000 and up extra signal flags would be used.

The telegraphs in Sydney were originally used to signal ship arrivals and departures from South Head to Fort Phillip on the west side of Sydney Cove. Another line of 24 stations was built on Tasmania, with Hobart as one of its terminals. In 1857 the first electric telegraph lines were built on Tasmania. The optical telegraphs coexisted with the electrical ones for a relatively long period. The last semaphore on Tasmania was not taken out of operation until 1880.

The codes used on these telegraphs included the usual provisions for secrecy through the use of private codes, but, curiously, during normal operations little attempt was made to hide the meaning of the signals from the general public. Masters writes, for instance:[32]

> The late Mr. R. R. Rex Sr., who died in January 1936, aged 95 or thereabouts, told the writer some years ago, that nearly everyone on the waterfront knew the Code. The old gentleman vigorously demonstrated with his arms (to the consternation of several bystanders!) the different movements of the semaphore arms, showing that he still remembered all about it.

Unlike the British system, the Australian code relied on the use of signal flags in addition to the semaphore arms. For example, a so-called *Blue Peter* flag, a blue flag with a white rectangle in its center, was used to signal to a remote station that a transmission was about to begin. It was to be acknowledged with the raising of the same flag. The same Blue Peter was also used to signal errors. By hoisting the flag "half-yard," a sender could warn the receiver that either it had copied the semaphore position incorrectly, or that the sender was about to replace its own erroneous signal.

An interesting out-of-band signal in use on these lines, was known as the *dip*. This signal was made by shaking one of the bottom arm-pairs up and down, while the other arm pairs displayed the station number that the sender wanted to communicate with. The dip was thus used to bypass the usual initialization protocol with the Blue Peter, and it may have been used to bypass intermediate stations in the chain when visibility was good. The dip may have been an invention of Australian telegraph operators in the field; its use was discouraged by the telegraph administrators.

America

There is remarkably little information to be found on optical telegraph lines in the United States. There is clear evidence that the American army used heliographs,[33] and various flag signaling systems,[34] but apart from a few isolated references and illustrations, the use of Chappe-like telegraphs with articulated arms, or shutter systems like Edelcrantz's or George Murray's, is not described in detail.

The credit for the construction of the first optical telegraph line in the United States probably belongs to Jonathan Grout.[35] Grout's line, in operation between 1801 and 1807 connected Boston to Martha's Vineyard via Hull, Scituate, Marshfield, Plymouth, Sandwhich, Wood's Hole, and Edgartown, a total distance of about 104 km. It was based on Chappe's design. Another line was constructed by John Parker in the 1820s, connecting Boston to Nantucket.[36]

Telegraphs based on Popham's design were in use in and near San Francisco between 1849 and 1853, to announce the arrival of different types of ships, such as steamers, brigs or schooners.[37] The famous "Telegraph Hill" in downtown San Francisco served as one of three stations, with the other two stations placed at the Presidio House and at Point Lobos.

In 1813 Christopher Colles published a proposal to construct an optical telegraph line from Maine to New Orleans, but he was unsuccessful. A new proposal, this time to connect New York to New Orleans, was submitted to the United States Congress in 1837, by John Parker and Samuel Reid. Samuel Reid, harbormaster of the Port of New York, had studied the French and English optical telegraphs and could promise "proven European technology."[38] The proposal, however, was not approved, and the line was never constructed (see also p. 205).

An illustration from 1838 shows a three-arm semaphore that was placed

Figure 5.13 Semaphore at Fort Thompson.
(Source: [Lewis 1970], p. 27)

at Staten Island near New York, looking much like Watson's design from 1827,[39] or Pistor's variation from 1830.[40] It was said to communicate with two other stations, one at Sandy Hook, and one at Merchant's Exchange in Manhattan. Another illustration shows the same location twelve years later (Figure 5.13).[41] The old three-arm semaphore is still visible, but without its arms. A semaphore of similar design, also with three separate arms, is placed next to it, indicating that optical telegraphs may have been used at this location throughout the period from 1838 until 1850.

Between 1840 and 1845 an optical telegraph line was in operation between Philadelphia and New York, operated by a Philadephia stock broker who was interested in quick notification of fluctuations in the stock market.[42] Around this time, however, the electrical telegraphs were beginning to score decisive victories.

Needles and Wires

The story of the electrical telegraph, and the struggle to have it adopted, is just as colorful as that of the optical telegraph. Fortunately, it is also preserved in considerably more detail. To be sure, the principle of electrical telegraphy was already known at the time of Edelcrantz and Chappe.

Often described is the letter to the *Scots' Magazine*, dated 1 February 1753, and published on 17 February 1753.[43] The letter, titled *An expeditious method for conveying intelligence*, describes an electric telegraph with 24 parallel wires: one for each different code, or character, to be transmitted. Small copper balls were placed at the receiver near the terminals of each wire. By discharging a Leyden jar, the sender could place a static electric charge on one of the wires and thus cause the corresponding ball at the receiver to become charged and attract a piece of paper with a letter-code.[44] This is how the author explained it:

> Sir: It is well known to all who are conversant in electrical experiments, that the electric power may be propagated along a small wire, from one place to another, without being sensibly abated by the length of its progress. Let, then, a set of wires, equal in number to the letters of the alphabet, be extended horizontally between two given places, parallel to one another, and each of them about an inch distant from that next to it. At every twenty yard's end, let them be fixed in glass, or jeweler's cement, to some firm body, both to prevent them from touching the earth, or any other non-electric, and from breaking by their own gravity. Let the electric gun-barrel be placed at right angles with the extremities of the wires, and about an inch below them. Also let the wires be fixed in a solid piece of glass, at six inches from the end; and let that part of them which reaches from the glass to the machine have sufficient spring and stiffness to recover its situation after having been brought in contact with the barrel. Close by the supporting glass, let a ball be suspended from every wire; and about a sixth or an eighth of an inch below the balls, place the letters of the alphabet, marked on bits of paper, or any other substance that may be light enough to rise to the electrified ball; and at the same time let it be so contrived, that each of them may reassume its proper place when dropt.
>
> All things constructed as above, and the minute previously fixed, I begin the conversation with my distant friend in this manner. Having set the electrical machine going as in ordinary experiments, suppose I am to pronounce the word *Sir*; with a piece of glass, or any other *electric per se*, I strike the wire S, so as to bring it in contact with the barrel, then *i*, then *r*, all in the same way; and my correspondent, almost in the same instant, observes these several characters rise in order to the electrified balls at his end of the wires. Thus I spell away as long as I think fit; and my correspondent, for the sake of memory, writes the characters as they rise, and may join and read them afterwards as often as he inclines. Upon a signal given, or from choice, I stop the machine; and, taking up the pen in my turn, I write down whatever my friend at the other end strikes out. . . .

This remarkable letter was signed with just the initials "C. M." The identity of the sender has never been established. Since the letter was mailed from the town of Renfrew, there is some evidence that one Charles Marshall of that town could have been the author, but there are several other contenders with the same initials who equally well could have originated the letter.[45]

Between 1746 and 1787 at least five proposals for electrical telegraphs were published, exploiting the same principles.[46] The transmission of electric charges across metal wires was first experimented with in 1746 by Father Joseph Franz in Vienna, who sent charges through a wire 5,300 feet long. The experiment was repeated by many others, for example on 18 July 1747 in London by a doctor, William Watson, who ran a metal wire from one side of the (wooden) Westminster bridge to the other.[47] According to Ignace Chappe, Doctor Watson was assisted by a large number of people, whom he identifies by name as Folkes, Cavendish, Berwis, Graham, Birch, Daval, Trembley, Ellicot, Robin, and Schort. In Chappe's words:[48]

> The experiment demonstrated that electrical matter could traverse a distance of four English miles within the blink of an eye.

A particularly interesting proposal was published anonymously in the *Journal de Paris* on 30 May 1782, and in the *Mercure de France* on 8 June 1782. The proposal reads as follows:[49]

> Let there be two gilt iron wires put underground in separate wooden tubes filled in with resin, and let each wire terminate in a knob. Between one pair of knobs, connect a letter formed of metallic [tin-foil] strips after the fashion of those electrical toys, called "spangled panes;" if now, at the other end we touch the inside of a Leyden jar to one knob, and the outside to the other, so as to discharge the jar through the wires, the letter will be at the same instant illuminated.
>
> Thus, with twenty-four such pairs, one could quickly spell all that was desired, it being only requisite to have a sufficient number of charged Leyden jars always ready. . . .

So far, the proposal is similar to C. M.'s earlier design, with the only addition of a method for insulating metal wires in underground tubes. But the writer takes it a few steps further:

> These means could be simplified by having only five pairs of wires, and attaching a character, or a letter, to each of their [31] combinations . . . ; six wires would, in the same way, yield sixty-three, and thus one could arrive at a sort of tachygraphy, or fast writing, one character (or signal) sufficing for a whole word, or phrase, as may be previously agreed upon.

Here, almost casually, three significant proposals are made. There is a proposal for a five-bit numeric code,[50] a proposal for a dictionary encoding of words and phrases based on this numeric code,[51] and the term *tachygraphy*, which was later borrowed by Claude Chappe to describe his own semaphore design.[52]

Hennig wrote in 1906 that the articles were "without any question" written by the French reporter Henri Linguet, who tried to use this invention, or a later variant of it, to buy his release from incarceration in the Bastille.[53] Edelcrantz also refers to Linguet in footnote 19 (page 259), where he considers an allegation that Chappe borrowed part of his design from Linguet. Both Hennig and Edelcrantz report that Linguet was unsuccessful in buying his freedom, and died under the guillotine in June 1794.

Bockmann, who was referred to by Edelcrantz as the source of the allegation, also made the following far-fetched claim:[54]

> But, one will ask, how did Chappe obtain this [Linguet's] secret? My answer is: from Robespierre! Because the so-called eyewitness, and Chappe's close friend,

of whom so much has been already said, admits explicitly that he had found and read a description of the whole apparatus, the calculation, and the secret alphabet N.B. N.B. among Robespierre's papers!

Ignace Chappe, Claude's older brother, addressed the allegation in his book, debunking the story by noting that Chappe had demonstrated his telegraph design as early as in 1792, while Linguet was not arrested until October 1793, and thus could not have made his offer to Robespierre until somewhere between October 1793 and the date of his execution in June 1794.[55]

Bockmann, in a more serious moment, also discussed, as early as 1794, the potential for the exploitation of electricity for telegraphic communication. He made an attempt to classify a number of ways in which the principle might be used. Most amounted to the sudden discharge of statically charged copper wires, connected to large batteries of Leyden Jars, to generate either audible or visible sparks that would encode messages. Fortunately, for his personal safety, his conclusion was that the expense of constructing the apparatus required for this type of telegraphy was, for the time being, prohibitive.

It was not until 1819 that electro-magnetism was thoroughly studied and described by Hans C. Oersted. Then, in 1831, Michael Faraday in England and Joseph Henry in the United States discovered nearly simultaneously the principle of electro-magnetic induction. The first electro-magnetic telegraphs based on this principle were constructed in 1837, again almost simultaneously by William Cooke and Charles Wheatstone in England, and by Samuel Morse and Alfred Vail in the United States In fact, the English seem to have had a slight edge on the Americans. The first patent of Cooke and Wheatstone for a "five-needle" telegraph, titled a *Method of Giving Signals and Sounding Alarums at Distant Places by Means of Electric Currents Transmitted through Metallic Circuits*, dates from 12 June 1837. The first demonstration of Morse "pendulum" telegraph took place at New York University on 3 September 1837, with Alfred Vail, a student at NYU at the time, in the audience.

The first application of the needle telegraph in 1837 was on a stretch of railway between Euston and Camden Town in England. The Morse Code and the final Morse-Vail telegraphic instrument both date from 1838. Morse presented his device in 1837 to the United States Congress, to be considered for a line between New York and New Orleans. His proposal was rejected.[56] Like Claude Chappe before him, it took Morse many years to convince the authorities of the usefulness of his device, or even of its superiority over the optical telegraph. The famous "first message," *What hath God wrought?*, sent by Morse to inaugurate a first American electrical telegraph line from Washington to Baltimore, dates from 24 May 1844. By 1851, the electrical telegraph had won decisive victories over its optical predecessor. In that year even the Stock Exchanges in London and Paris had been connected by electrical telegraphs.

Meanwhile, also the era of the electrical telegraph has almost ended.

Only a short while before the publication of this book, the descendant of the company that introduced the electrical telegraphs in the United States, the American Telephone and Telegraph Company (AT&T), decided to close down its last telegraph services, noting dryly that digital data networks had taken over all but an insignificant fraction of the traffic. *The New York Times* published the following report on 18 December 1991:[57]

> *HANGING UP* —AT&T said yesterday it had closed down the service that gave the company its last name—its 104-year-old telegraph service. The business was a victim of better and less expensive telecommunications, like electronic data processing and quite probably facsimile machines.

Even the electrical wires of the world's telecommunications networks are gradually being replaced by higher capacity optical fibers. And thus, two hundred years after Chappe and Edelcrantz, optical telecommunications is—once again—only just beginning.

Bibliographic Notes

Details on the developments described here can be found in the outstanding surveys of [Fahie 1884], [Woods 1965], [Wilson 1976], [Herbarth 1978], and [Aschoff 1984].

The history of the Norwegian, Danish, and Finnish optical telegraph systems is treated in, respectively [Ellefsen 1994], [Poulsen 1994], and [Elo 1994], as well as in [Herbarth 1978], and [Wilson 1976]. Details on the Dutch optical telegraphs can be found in [Staring 1890], [Ringnalda 1902], [Brink and Schell 1954], [Romburgh 1989], and [Romburgh 1991]. The discovery of the Lipkens telegraph at Curacao is documented in [Haviser 1994].

A description of George Murray's shutter telegraph appears in [Michaelis 1965], and [Reid 1886]. Murray's and Popham's semaphore designs are described in detail in [Wilson 1976] and [Holmes 1983].

The electrical telegraph designed by Sir Ronalds, and his unsuccessful effort to persuade the British Admiralty to consider it, is detailed in [Appleyard 1930], and in [Fahie 1884]. Descriptions of the early electrical telegraphs can be found in many works. See especially [Fahie 1884], but also [Prescott 1877], [Marland 1964], [Hubbard 1965], and [Michaelis 1965].

Chapter Six
About Invention

In the first few weeks after the completion of the optical telegraph line from Paris to Lille, the German author J. L. Bockmann wrote with undisguised excitement:[1]

> Der irrt, wer alles schon für aufgefunden hällt! Der nimmt den Horizont für Gränzen einer Welt!
>
> [Those who think that everything has already been invented, are mistaken! They let the horizon define the boundaries of their world!]

The construction of the new French and Swedish telegraphs, starting in 1794, was received as a significant event, signaling the beginning of a new era. Yet, long before 1794, the potential usefulness of a practical long-distance communication system had been known. Developing new communication systems had been the pastime of uncounted would-be inventors for centuries. They based their systems on the use of pigeons, torches, flags, helioscopes, water-clocks, flash-cards, and probably quite a few other means that have escaped reliable documentation. So, what made Chappe's and Edelcrantz's contribution so special?

It appears that Chappe and Edelcrantz were the first persons who systematically studied and solved all the problems that stood between the mere idea of optical telegraphy and its implementation: the construction of a large-scale, working system. An article in a recent edition of an encyclopedia states:[2]

> Invention is an act of creativity that results in a device, process, or technique novel enough to produce a significant change in the application of technology. The application is fundamental to invention. Credit for invention has

---

1. The notes to this chapter start at p. 271.

frequently been claimed for someone who conceived an idea, but the inventor is the person who not only had the idea but worked out the method of putting it into practice. Thus Leonardo Da Vinci conceived of flying machines and self-propelled vehicles and showed great ingenuity in working out possible designs, but he did not invent either the airplane or the automobile.

Most of Chappe's and Edelcrantz's predecessors were keenly aware of the potential importance of a practical system for long-distance communication. Polybius, for instance, was most impressed with its potential for either waging or deterring war.[3]

It is evident to all that in every matter, and especially in warfare, the power of acting at the right time contributes very much to the success of enterprises, and fire-signals are the most efficient of all the devices which aid us to do this. For they show what has recently occurred and what is still in the course of being done, and by means of them anyone who cares to do so even if he is at a distance of three, four or even more days' journey can be informed. So that it is always surprising how help can be brought by means of fire messages when the situation requires it.

Robert Hooke, writing in 1684, had a grander vision still:[4]

I could instance a hundred ways of facilitating the method of performing this design with the more dexterity and quickness and with little charge; but that, I think, will be needless at present . . . The same character may be seen in Paris, within a minute after it hath been exposed in London.

And in 1797, the authors of the *Encyclopaedia Britannica* speculated:[5]

The capitals of distant nations might be united by chains of posts, and, the settling of those disputes which at present take up months or years might then be accomplished in as many hours. An establishment of telegraphs might then be made like that of the post; and instead of being an expence, it would produce a revenue.

Almost all the early writers also noted that they considered themselves fortunate to be living at the time that they lived, with science making such remarkable progress. Polybius, for instance, wrote in *The Histories*:[6]

. . . in our time all arts and sciences have so much advanced that knowledge of most of them may be said to have been reduced to a system.

Similarly, in the preface of Franz Kessler's book from 1616, after a few brief remarks that so many discoveries from the ancients were being neglected, it says:[7]

We can, however, also proudly note that today many arts are developing that our forefathers had absolutely no knowledge of.

Similar remarks can be found in Wilkins's book from 1641. A few years later, in 1665, the British philosopher Joseph Glanvill extrapolated even further in his *Scepsis Scientifica*:[8]

Figure 6.1 The Magician Merlin and the Telegraph.
(Coll. Musée de la Poste, Paris)

And I doubt not but posterity will find many things that are now but rumours verified into practical realities. It may be, some ages hence, a voyage to the southern unknown tracts, yea, possibly the moon, will not be more strange than one to America. . . . And to confer at the distance of the Indies by sympathetic conveyances may be as usual to future times as to us in a literary correspondence.

That men should confer at a very distant removes by an extemporary intercourse is a reputed impossibility, yet there are some hints in natural operations that give us probability that 'tis feasible, and may be compast without unwarrantable assistance from daemoniack correspondence.

Glanvill's remarks were based on some misleading statements about the possibility of magnetic telegraphs, that can be traced back to Giambattista della Porta, over a century earlier.[9] But, there are times when even those who exaggerate can turn out to be right in their predictions.

Or are they? The part that was judiciously omitted from the above quotation (indicated by the dots) reads:

To them that come after us it may be as ordinary to buy a pair of wings to fly into the remotest regions as now a pair of boots to ride a journey.

Which nicely illustrates that, indeed, it is one thing to conceive of the potential of an idea, but quite another to turn it into a practical invention. In this area, Claude Chappe and Abraham Niclas Edelcrantz had little competition.

209

"No, no. It's three thumps for call waiting and five thumps for call forwarding."

Figure 6.2 Drawing by Stevenson, © 1988.
(The New Yorker Magazine, Inc.)

Four Fundamental Steps

There are many details to be considered before one can build a working telegraph system, with or without electricity. In retrospect, it is not hard to trace what the most significant steps in the development were. They can be summarized as follows.

o The first step was to build systems that could be used to signal, or rather broadcast, a small set of simple, predefined messages. Beacon fires are in this class, but so is the more sophisticated *clepsydra* telegraph of Cleoxenus and Democleitus.[10]

o The second step was to build systems that could be used to signal arbitrary messages, not just those from a predefined set, by assigning predefined codes to the letters of the alphabet. Polybius's torch telegraph was the first device of this type.[11] Very few of the designs from the next two millenia would manage to escape the limitations of this basic spelling method. Kessler's design from 1616, for instance, was still based on spelling, and so was Hooke's design from 1684.

o The third step was the adoption of a numeric code to assign values to common words and phrases, so that not every message needed to be spelled out laboriously, letter by letter. This step was hinted at by several authors, for instance by Wilkins in 1641, but it was not implemented until the middle of the eighteenth century, inspired by the new naval flag signaling methods that were first developed in France.[12] Neither Franz Kessler nor Robert Hooke developed these methods. Ignace Chappe later credited not the British or the French, but the German Bergstrasser with the introduction of systematic numeric codes for the purpose of telegraphy.[13]

o The final step was the realization that the numeric codes should include special control signals and protocol procedure rules that could be used to regulate the message exchange itself, but that did not contribute directly to its contents. To be able to use a system at all, a mechanism of some kind to solve this problem had to be adopted by all designers of telegraphs. The earliest example of a control signal is Polybius's use of an out-of-band signal to indicate the start of a message.[14] Not much progress on this issue was made until the end of the seventeenth century, when in 1684, Robert Hooke[15] proposed a first set of explicit control codes.[16] Protocol procedure rules still had to be improvised in the field by Chappe and Edelcrantz. The first explicit descriptions of these improvised rules are the instructions for telegraph operators that are reproduced in Appendices B and C.[17]

Each of the four steps was of fundamental importance, and must have seemed equally revolutionary when it was perfected. Initially, though, other complex issues, such as ciphering methods, that are less fundamental to the design of the telegraph system as such, were given more attention. This can be noted in the works of Giambattista della Porta from 1553,[18] Kessler's work from 1616, and Hooke's lecture from 1684. Also Edelcrantz gives much attention to the issue in 1796, devoting several pages to it in his treatise.[19]

Inventing Control Signals

There were 14 control signals in Edelcrantz's first code, and 16 in Chappe's first code, both dating from 1795. They are reproduced here in Tables 6.1–6.3.

The numeric values for the signs from Edelcrantz's code in the tables are as they were defined in the treatise.[20] For the purpose of this overview, the Chappe semaphore signs are encoded in three character sequences. The middle character represents the position of the regulator: V for vertical and H for horizontal. The first and the last characters represent the positions of the two indicator arms as numbers between 1 and 8. The number 1 symbolizes an indicator pointing straight up. Each increment of the number, up to 8, symbolizes an extra clockwise rotation of the indicator arm, in increments of 45 degrees.

There are only six control signals that were defined unambiguously, with almost the same meaning in both codes. Eight more control signals were defined only by Edelcrantz, but not in Chappe's first codes. The first two of these (Repeat and Wait) were later added by Chappe. Three others (two Attention signals, and the Word delimiter signal) may have been present in Chappe's code under different names. Code 727, used by Edelcrantz for switching from one encoding method to another, was not used in the

Table 6.1 Control Signals Defined in Both Codes.

Edelcrantz		Chappe	
Sign	Name	Sign	Name
227	Speech (North)	2H8	Activity (Paris)
722	Speech (South)	1H1	Activity (Lille)
272	Error	2H6	Error
757	Fog	3V7	Suspend–Fog
222	Help	4V8	Suspend–Failure
700	Close	5H5	Close

Table 6.2 Control Signals Defined Only by Edelcrantz.

Sign	Name	Note
707	Repeat	Added by Chappe in 1809
525	Wait	Added by Chappe in 1809
557	Attention (North)	Perhaps same as Chappe's Correct Reception
755	Attention (South)	idem
007	Word delimiter	Perhaps a data character in Chappe's code
727	Switch codes	Never used in Chappe's code
077	Faster	idem (for rate control)
770	Slower	idem (for rate control)

Table 6.3 Control Signals Defined Only by Chappe.

Sign	Name	Note
7H3	Correct reception	Perhaps same as Edelcrantz's Attention
1H5	Suspend–Absence	Perhaps same as Edelcrantz's Wait
4H5	*Ignaire* (Paris)	To announce night transmissions from Paris
5H6	*Ignaire* (Lille)	idem, originating at Lille
7H8	*Monitif d'Harmonie*	Deleted in 1809, Preceded *Harmonie*
7H1	*Harmonie*	Deleted in 1809, Synchronization signal
1V5	Idle	Never used in Edelcrantz's code
3V2	Adjourn for 1 hour	idem
4V7	Adjourn for 2 hour	idem
4H6	Priority (Lille)	idem (to override Activity signs)

French codes. The remaining two codes, 077 and 770, do occur in an undated code table that is preserved in the collection of the Musée Postale in Paris (see Figure 6.4). Since this code table mentions station codes for Perpignan and Narbonne it probably dates from after 1840.

Ten control codes occur in Chappe's code from 1795, but not in Edelcrantz's first code. Two of these (Correct Reception and Absence) may again have appeared there under a different name. Two other codes (*Harmonie* and *Monitif d'Harmonie*) were used in the French system for the

Table 6.4 Control Signals Added by Chappe in 1809.

Name	Usage
Priority (Paris)	To override a priority signal from Lille
Correction	For retransmitting (parts of?) a message
Repeat	For repeating the entire message
Wait	Short-term delays
Delay	Longer delays
Adjourn 3 hour	Long adjournments between transmissions
Suspend/Temp. Failure	Not requiring a visit from the inspector

synchronization of the clocks in the stations along the telegraph lines.[21] They were not defined in the Swedish code from 1795, but a comparable code was added in a later revision. The instructions of 1837 for the Swedish system (see Appendix C, p. 236, pt. 4) state that the clocks were synchronized at the start of each transmission series, thus achieving the same effect as the Harmonie signals.

The two codes for announcing night transmissions have no counterpart in any of the Swedish codes, but they also seem to have disappeared from the revision of Chappe's code that was published in 1809. They were probably deleted because night transmissions had proven to be less than useful.

The remaining four codes were soon added to the Swedish code tables. In 1808, for instance, four different Adjournment or Suspension signals had been defined (see Appendix C, 1808:7). Descriptions of priority signals for the Swedish codes are also absent from the code table of 1795, but they can be found in all surviving copies of the station instructions, starting with those from 1808 (see Appendix C, 1808:4, 1809:10, 1837:7).

The revision of Chappe's code published in 1809 was only one in a series of adjustments that were made. It was meant to be used on the line from Paris to Brussels. Many of the signals were reassigned in a seemingly arbitrary manner, which makes it hard to make direct comparisons with the original version. Seven specific control signals, however, were present in the new code, and not in the original one.

Two of these (Repeat and Wait) had been present in Edelcrantz's code from the start. One other (Correction) did not have an explicit representation in Edelcrantz's code, but was likely captured by an expanded usage of the Repeat signal, as will be discussed in more detail later. The other control codes appear to be more ad hoc; adding mostly some special cases of earlier defined signals.

Protocol Procedure Rules
The meaning of all the control signals from Edelcrantz's first code is explained in his treatise.[22] There is no comparable document that defines the meaning of the control signals from Chappe's first code, but a copy of the Operating Instructions from 1809 has been preserved.[23] These two

texts by Edelcrantz and Chappe are probably the first explicit discussions of the concept of a signaling protocol in history.

In the following, we will focus on the definitions of protocol initialization, error control, rate control, and flow control.[24] Edelcrantz and Chappe, in effect, discovered many of the principles used in modern data communications, about 150 years before the first computers were built.

INITIALIZATION

Communication, says Edelcrantz, is initiated by the sender with a specific control signal, which he called the *speech signal*. It is to be acknowledged by the receiver with another control signal, called the *attention signal*, which was possibly acknowledged with a *correct reception* signal (although this is not stated explicitly in the operating instructions).

There were two *speech* or *activity* signals in Chappe's code: one for messages originating in Paris, and one for messages originating at the station at the remote end of the line, such as Lille or Brussels. The Chappe code says explicitly that the activity signals may never be generated by the intermediate stations, which means that they were not allowed to carry on an independent conversation.

This restriction did not exist in the Swedish network. This meant that in the Swedish system it had to be determined unambiguously which two stations wanted to talk. Edelcrantz gave several methods to solve this that come close to the standard control formats that are used today in data communication protocols: he defined a variant of the speech signal that encoded both the station identity of the receiver and that of the sender. For an unambiguous acknowledgement of such a "free" speech signal, Edelcrantz had the receiver take the complement of the code received, and return it to the sender. This makes the acknowledgement serve as both a synchronizer and as an error check on the original signal. As far as we know, this technique has not been used since.

Communication, in both the French and the Swedish systems, was normally completely synchronous. A sending station was required to display a signal until it was confirmed correctly by the next station, and only then could it move on to the next. The one exception to this rule was when the connection between two stations in a chain was broken, for instance by poor visibility or due to mechanical problems with one of the telegraphs. In that case, the last station in the chain could serve as a buffer, and save up the incoming messages, to be forwarded once the obstacle was removed.

ERROR CONTROL

The error control methods initially proposed by Edelcrantz and Chappe were only rudimentary. Both methods seem to be based directly on Hooke's proposal from 1684. There was a single control signal (272 in Edelcrantz's code, 2H6 in Chappe's code) that signified an error condition. It could only be used to erase the last signal sent, rather like a backspace.

Figure 6.3 The New Chappe Telegraph Operator.
(Coll. Musée de la Poste, Paris)

The definition is not quite complete, though, at least by modern standards. It is, for instance, not specified by either Chappe or Edelcrantz what two error signals in a row would mean: the erasure of the first error signal by the second, or the erasure of the two message signals that preceded the two error signals.

RATE CONTROL

In the first code published, Edelcrantz had already adopted Hooke's suggestion to include control codes in his protocols for the dynamic adjustment of the transmission *rate* of a sender. He defines control signal 770 for slowing down a fast sender, and 077 for speeding up a tardy one.[25] In the handwritten code from the Musée Postale in Paris, referred to earlier, two similar signals can be found. The descriptions given for these two are

215

Les signaux ont passé lentement [The signals have been sent (too?) slowly] and *Les signaux ont passé rapidement* [The signals have been sent (too?) quickly].

Even today, rate control methods are considered an advanced feature of a communications protocol, not to be found in many implementations.

FLOW CONTROL

Edelcrantz defines a coherent set of signals to implement a flow control discipline. Among these is signal-code 707, which was used to request the retransmission of a signal, probably as suggested in §4.17, by following it with the signals for a three-digit number that referred to a location of a signal in the logbook of received messages. Such a *selective repeat* mechanism was reinvented almost 170 years later in data communications protocols, and is still considered a more advanced alternative to a simpler flow control strategy known as *go-back-n*.[26]

Chappe added *repeat* and *correction* signals in the 1809 revision of his code, but it is not well-documented how these signals were used. It appears that they were of a more basic type, perhaps only to indicate the retransmission of larger portions of a message at the initiative of the sender.

Both Edelcrantz and Chappe defined control signals to suspend transmissions for short or long-term reasons, reminiscent of modern day *stop-and-wait* protocols. There is no explicit mention of signals in either code that can be used to resume transmissions, but an exchange of the standard speech and attention signals could have served that purpose.

THE REVISION OF 1808

Edelcrantz's revised signaling code from 1808 contains some changes from the principles that were laid down in the original code from his treatise.[27]

The most important change was that in almost all cases message exchanges were assumed to be initiated by Stockholm only. This restricted one of the features of the original code that allowed intermediate stations to communicate at any time. In the revised code, terminal stations waited to be polled from Stockholm for news, unless they had high priority messages to transfer. Intermediate stations on a branch could still communicate, but only during periods of leave that were explicitly granted by Stockholm.

The new regulations were reinforced in an addendum to the instructions that was issued in 1809. The addendum defined some extra control signals for relaying error conditions back to Stockholm (signal 060), for interrupting low priority traffic for a more urgent message (signal 606), and for broadcasting orders from Stockholm across the entire network (signal 646).

The addendum also defined a series of ad hoc control codes that the receiver of a message could use to acknowledge receipt: five variations of what today would be called positive acknowledgements (A227, A774,

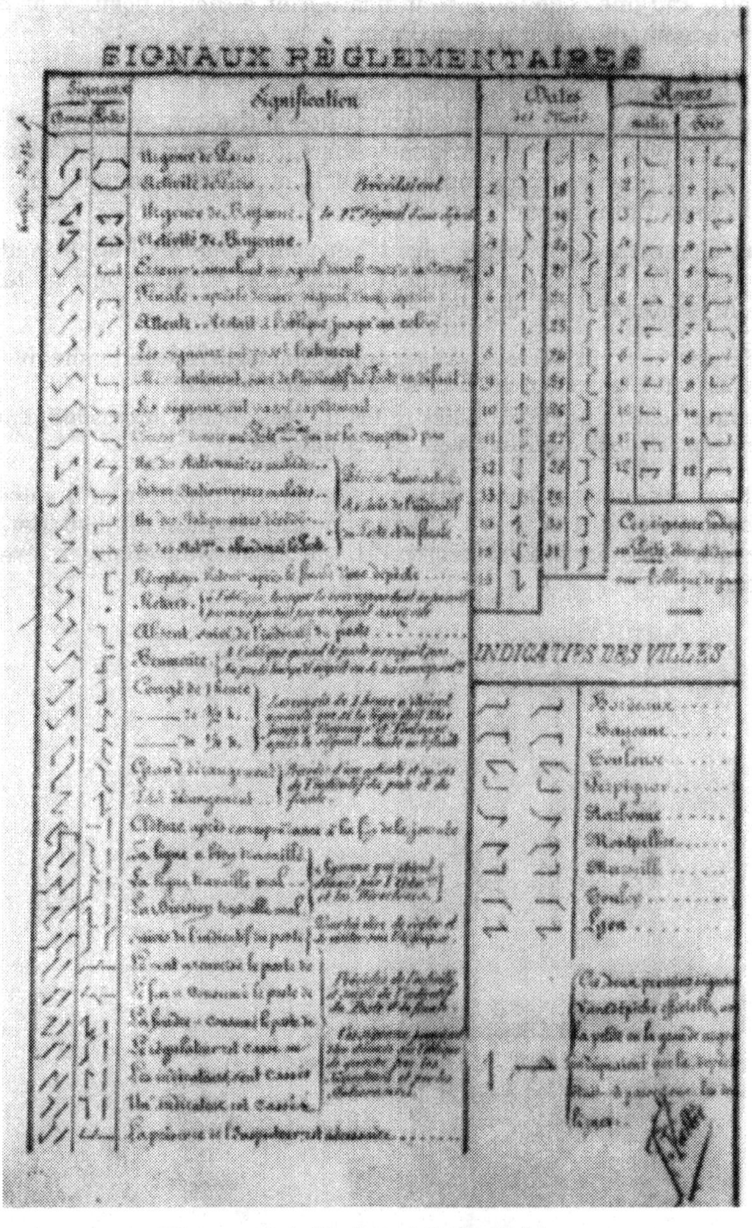

Figure 6.4 Undated Code Table.
(Coll. Musée de la Poste, Paris)

A775, 274, and 555), two variations of negative acknowledgements (A230 and 450), and one code (303) to indicate that either a positive or negative acknowledgement would be sent later.

Hard Problems—Simple Solutions

It is easy to underestimate the importance of the achievements of Chappe and Edelcrantz. Their revolutionary steps in the development of signaling codes are by now so commonplace that it is hard to imagine that at one point it was all unknown.

Johann Bergstrasser, writing about ten years before Chappe made headlines with the beginnings of the world's first working optical telegraph network, summed it up like this:[28]

> Anfänglich scheint öfters etwas schwer, ja unmöglich zu sein; und in der Folge der Zeit wird es uns durch die Gewohnheit fincherleicht.
>
> [At first something often seems difficult, yes, almost impossible, but in due course, mere habit makes it seem like child's play.]

It is the mark of a good scientist to take a hard problem and solve it in a way that makes it look easy. Chappe and Edelcrantz did just that, almost two centuries before we understood the problem well enough to recognize it as hard.

Appendix A
Letters to Gentleman's Magazine

First Letter (September 1794, p. 815)
The telegraphe was originally the invention of William Amontons, a very ingenious philosopher, born in Normandy in the year 1663. Amontons was in the third form of the Latin school at Paris, when, after a considerable illness, he contracted such a deafness as obliged him to renounce all communications with mankind. In this situation he applied himself closely to the study of geometry, made some very accurate observations on the nature of barometers and thermometers, and, in the year 1687, presented a new hygroscope to the Royal Academy of Sciences, which met with general approbation. This philosopher also first pointed out a method to acquaint people at a great distance, and in very little time, with whatever one pleased. This method is as follows: let persons be placed in several stations, at such distances from each other, that, by the help of a telescope, a man in one station may see a signal made by the next before him; he immediately repeats this signal, which is again repeated through all the intermediate stations. This, with considerable improvements, has been adopted by the French, and denominated a Telegraphe; and, from the utility of the invention, we doubt not but it will be soon introduced in this country. *Fas est ab hoste doceri.* [A quote from Ovid, *Met.*, IV. 428, It is right to learn even from an enemy.]

Editorial Response
The following account of this curious instrument is copied from Barrere's report in the sitting of the French Convention of 15 August 1794.

> The new-invented telegraphic language of signals is a contrivance of art to transmit thoughts, in a peculiar language, from one distance to another, by means of machines, which are placed at different distances of between four and five leagues from one another, so that the expression reaches a very distant place in the space of a few minutes. Last year an experiment of this invention was tried in the presence of several commissioners of the Convention. From the favourable report which the latter made of the efficacy of the contrivance,

the Committee of Public Welfare tried every effort to establish, by this means, a correspondence between Paris and the frontier places, beginning with Lille. Almost a whole twelve month has been spent in collecting the necessary instruments for the machines, and to teach the people employed how to use them. At present, the telegraphic language of signals is prepared in such a manner, that a correspondence may be conducted with Lille upon every subject, and that every thing, nay even proper names, may be expressed; an answer may be received, and the correspondence thus be renewed several times a day. The machines are the invention of Citizen Chappe, and were constructed before his own eyes; he directs their establishment at Paris.

They have the advantage of resisting the movements of the atmosphere and the inclemencies of the seasons. The only thing which can interrupt their effect is, if the weather is so very bad and turbid that the objects and signals cannot be distinguished. By this invention the remoteness of distances almost disappear; and all the communications of correspondence are effected with the rapidity of the twinkling of an eye. The operations of Government can be very much facilitated by this contrivance, and the unity of the Republic can be the more consolidated by the speedy communication with all its parts.

The greatest advantage which can be derived from this correspondence is, that, if one chuses, its object shall only be known to certain individuals, or to one individual alone, or two opposite distances, so that the Committee of Public Welfare may now correspond with the Representative of the People at Lille without any other persons getting acquainted with the object of the correspondence. It follows hence that, were Lille even besieged, we should know every thing at Paris that would happen in that place, and could send thither the Decrees of the Convention without the enemy's being able to discover or to prevent it.

Second Letter (November 1794, p. 992)
Explanation of the Machine (Telegraphe) placed on the Mountain of Belleville, near Paris, for the Purpose of communicating Intelligence.

AA is a beam or mast of wood, placed upright upon a rising ground, which is about 15 or 16 feet high. BB is a beam or balance, moving upon the centre of the top AA. This balance-beam may be placed vertically or horizontally, or in an inclined position, by means of strong cords, which are fixed to the wheel D, on the edge of which is a double groove, to receive the two cords. This balance is about 11 or 12 feet long, and 9 inches broad, having at each end a piece of wood C, which likewise turn upon angles by means of four other cords that pass through the axle of the main balance, otherwise the balance would derange the cords; each of the pieces C are about 3 feet long, and may either be placed to the right or left, straight or square with the balance beam. By means of these three the combination of movement is very extensive, remarkably simple, and easy to perform. Below is a small wooden gouge, in which one person is employed to observe the movements of the machine; in the mountain nearest to this, another person is to repeat these movements, and a third to write them down. The time taken to one movement is 20 seconds, of which, moving takes 4 seconds, the other 16 the machine is stationary. The stations of this machine are about 3 or 4 leagues distance; and there is an observatory

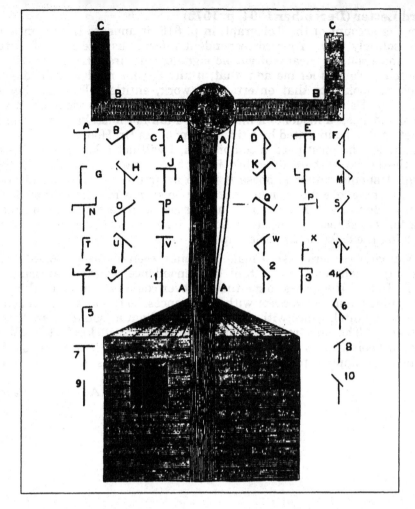

Figure A.1 The French Telegraph.
(Source: Gentleman's Magazine, Nov. 1794, p. 992)

near the Committee of Public Safety, to follow the motions of the last, which is at Belleville. The signs are sometimes made in words, and sometimes in letters; when in words, a small flag is hoisted, and, as the alphabet may be changed at pleasure, it is only the corresponding person who knows the meaning of the signs. In general, news are given every day, about eleven or twelve o'clock; but the people in the wooden gouge observe from time to time, and, as soon as a certain signal is given and answered, they begin, from one end to the other, to move the machine. The machine is painted a dark brown colour.

Third Letter (December 1794, p. 1072)

From the account of the Telegraph in p. 815, it appears the invention is not absolutely new. Your correspondent informs us, the idea of distant communication, by means of visible signals, was first struck by William Amontons. To this let me add, that, if any of your readers will take the trouble to look into that entertaining work, entitled "Rational Recreations" (by Dr. Hooper), they will find, under the article of "visual correspondence," a model of a machine, if I am not mistaken, very similar to that said to be invented by citizen Chappe. As Dr. Hooper's book is confessedly, for the most part, a compilation, I will not take upon me to say that the machine there described is not the same as that of Amontons, though I should rather suppose it to be an improvement upon his rude idea. In the above mentioned work may be seen a machine for auricular correspondence, which, as signals addressed to the eyes are by means of thick fog sometimes rendered inefficient, may be considered as capable of supplying the defect of the Telegraph.

Many of your readers have, I make no doubt, seen different modes of constructing instruments for distant correspondence, whether auricular or visual. Indeed it appears to me that it never could be a difficult thing for an ingenious man, conversant with the sciences, so to construct a machine as to convey intelligence with the swiftness of light or sound to another at a distance. The only reason, I apprehend, why such kind of machines have not been used in sieges, &c. was a persuasion of their circumscribed utility when applied to the ever-varying circumstances and exigencies of war.

A Constant Reader

Regulations for Telegraphic Correspondence (1795)

1. The telegraphic correspondence between Paris and Lille will be temporarily administered by the Telegraph Engineer, under the supervision of the Commission for Public Works.
2. At each terminal station there will be one agent in charge of the transmissions with one assistant. Two inspectors will regularly patrol the line. There will further be two attendants at each station and two reserve attendants at each terminal station.
3. The agents will send and receive the transmissions. They will maintain an exact record of all signals that have been sent and received at their station, and they will forward an exact copy of the above to the Engineer.
4. The agents in Paris may not make any transmission without the written authorization of the Engineer. Those in Lille may not communicate to Paris without having received official instructions, unless the message is related to the administration of the line. Note: This does not apply to the agents in Paris; the Engineer and his two assistants currently perform this duty.
5. The inspectors patrol the line whenever the Engineer deems this necessary. Otherwise, they patrol the line each month to visit the stations; they verify the condition of the machines and of all related instruments, survey the station attendants and give instructions, obtain the record of transmissions at each station and the report to be forwarded to the Engineer each month.
6. They note any repairs that should be made, and they prepare an estimate of the cost of repairs for the Engineer, whose authorization they must obtain. They will immediately have repairs performed that are necessary for the operation of the telegraph.
7. They are charged to make all payments indicated by the Engineer, including the salaries of the station attendants, and those of

repairmen. They will use the funds that will be given to them for this purpose by the Engineer.

8. At the end of each monthly patrol, they forward to the Engineer the record from each station and a report on the condition of each station visited.

9. This report should contain a precise overview of the inspector's activities; in chronological order it should list the time and the day the inspector arrived at and left from each station.

10. He [the inspector] will give a precise account of instruments that were exchanged, of the need for replacement parts at each station, of payments, and of repairs made.

11. The report must give a precise account of the demeanour, the behavior, and the faults made by each station attendant, of the errors, delays, and incorrect signals [of other stations] that were observed [by the attendant], and of the causes for these faults in his [the attendant's] opinion.

12. The inspector will in addition give a detailed account, once every quarter, of the use of the funds he has received, with the supporting documents attached.

13. The station attendants are preferably chosen to be active and intelligent workmen who will be able to perform urgent repairs on their machines.

14. They will be authorized to have repairs performed that they cannot make themselves, but that are necessary for the operation of the machines.

15. The record of expenses for repairs must be submitted to the inspector, who will reimburse them once the urgency of the repairs is confirmed.

16. The station attendants are responsible for the maintenance of the machines and the related instruments.

17. They are also responsible for undue wear of furniture, telescopes, eyepieces, and clocks, if such wear is caused by their negligence.

18. Whenever the inspector notices such negligence, he will assess the damage and will advise the Engineer on the deductions on the salaries that should be made to cover it.

19. To guard the instruments at all times, there must be an attendant on duty at each station also at night and between transmissions in daytime.

20. No attendant may leave his post without permission and without having been replaced first, or he will lose his salary for the entire year.

21. The importance of the functions of a station attendant requires that he will perform them in a scrupulous manner, immediately, without interruption, during each complete correspondence up to the closing signal.

22. Station attendants who do not respond within 4 minutes to an activity signal or to a regular signal during a transmission will lose one quarter of a month's pay; they lose one month's pay if the delay lasts 15 minutes, and they will be dismissed if it lasts a half hour.

23. Those who do not follow a suspension signal with the call signal of the

station within 4 minutes, as is prescribed in the regulations, will lose one month of pay.

24. Any station attendant who prolongs without necessity the fog signal, a suspension signal, or a fault signal, will be dismissed upon receipt of a report from the inspector noticing such a dereliction.

25. When the inspectors approach a station, they must be careful to act in such a manner that they can observe the work of the attendants without their knowledge.

26. It is explicitly forbidden to the attendants, at risk of losing their pay, to allow one of them to watch the signals and operate the telegraph alone, or to allow other than employees of the telegraph to operate the machine.

27. The two attendants who are on duty at each station are each individually responsible for faults covered by articles 20, 22, 23, 24, and 26, except for cases where they could not transmit for reasons beyond their control.

28. They must record precisely, in a journal supplied for this purpose, all signals received and sent; they must also record at the end of each complete correspondence who operated the telegraph and who monitored the signals during each part of the correspondence.

29. A record must be kept of all occasions where one had to transmit suspension or fog signals, and of those that were received. This record must be signed by both attendants for each correspondence in which it occurred.

30. To accurately monitor the operations, the faults made, and the difficulties that were encountered, the Engineer will obtain summaries of the reports submitted to the inspectors. It should contain a record of all correspondence performed at each station, in chronological order, giving the destination of each transmission and the name of the agents on duty, and it should contain a judgment of disagreements between stations about the cause of suspensions.

31. He [the Engineer] may suspend or dismiss the agents who are employed for telegraph correspondence, and who are placed under his direction.

32. He will report to the Commission for Public Works all suspensions and dismissals that he has deemed necessary.

33. The salary of an agent in charge of transmissions will be 4,500 livres, and 4,000 livres for his assistant. For the inspectors it is 5,000 livres, they are further reimbursed for fodder for their horse; they will be provided with horses from the Republic's stables at the same conditions as cavalry officers.

34. The station attendants and reserve attendants receive a fixed income of 1,800 livres, plus a 400 livres bonus per year.

35. The funds obtained by the application of articles 20, 22, 23, and 26 will be divided equally and added to the annual bonus of all attendants.

36. A sum of 3,000 livres will be available for clerical work such as collecting the records of stations, copying letters and reports, and related

administrative duties for the line to Lille. Note, this work requires someone familiar with the meaning of signals and that can be completely trusted. The administrative and postal expenses incurred by them will be reimbursed after the Commission for Public Works has verified their accuracy.

37. The necessary funds for the maintenance of the telegraphic correspondence from Paris to Lille will be obtained from those that are allocated for Public Works; they are allocated by the Commission and payed by order of the Engineer.

38. The salaries set by these regulations will be payed beginning on the first day of last Vendémiaire for those that have been employed since then.[1]

Approved by the Committee for Public Works, 26 Nivôse An III, Lecamus.[2]
For a conforming copy, Chappe, Telegraph Engineer.

Operating Instructions (1809)

There are eighteen control signals. These eighteen signals must be developed with the regulator tilted left. Twelve of these signals may not be given by the intermediate stations, other than to pass them on when they originate at one of the terminal stations. These include the signals for "activity," "priority," "correct reception," "wait," "adjourn", the signals for the "correction" and "repetition" of messages, and the "closing signal." The other six signals, which are for indicating various types of suspensions and operator errors, may be given by the intermediate agents, even when they do not originate at the terminal stations. The only exception is the "delay" (French: *retard*) signal which may originate only at the terminal stations. The control signals are interpreted as message signals when they are developed with the regulator tilted to the right. An exception is the "closing signal," which can only be used as a control signal.

DEVELOPING SIGNALS

All signals, except the simple signals, are developed in three steps. Simple signals are formed in a single step.

1. For message signals, the regulator is tilted to the right; for control signals it is tilted to the left.

2. The indicators are set.

3. The regulator is now set in a horizontal or vertical position, as required; this is called "carrying the signal to completion."

CHANGING SIGNALS AND CORRECTING ERRORS

The most important rule to which the agent must conform with the greatest exactness, is never to carry the signal from an angle to completion, or from a completed signal to an angle, without being certain that the station to which the signal is being passed has duplicated exactly the developed or the completed signal. If that station makes a mistake, either

---

1. The notes to this appendix start at p. 272.

during the development of the signal or for the completed signal, the telegraph should be shaken lightly to indicate that the signal was not reproduced correctly.

If the mistake occurs during the development of the signal at an angle, the operator who makes the mistake can correct it immediately by adjusting his development to match the required signal. If, however, the signal has already been carried to completion, that is to a vertical or horizontal position, the operator who detects the mistake returns to the development position, with the regulator turned at an angle, gives the error signal, and then repeats the complete development of the correct signal.

When the station that has made a mistake does not correct it immediately, in order to avoid a delay, the sending station carries the signal to completion and, as soon as his correspondent has also carried the incorrect signal to completion, follows it with the error signal. The correct signal is repeated when the incorrect signal has been anulled in this manner.[3]

In the same way, when a station that carries an incorrect signal to completion, but does not cancel it immediately, the station that precedes it must send the error signal, and then repeat the correct signal.[4]

SUSPENSIONS

If poor visibility causes communications to be interrupted, the station that can no longer see another must sent the "fog signal" followed by the call-signal of the station that can no longer be seen. The station then returns to the "fog signal," unless the condition has cleared.

If a control signal is send to a station, and the station does not reply within one minute, the "absence signal" is sent, followed by the call-signal of the station that does not reply. The sending station then returns to the "absence signal," if the station still has not replied. "Absence" may not be sent during the transmission of message signals.

When the telegraph fails, the operators of the station send "failure," followed by the call-signal of their post, and then returning to the "failure signal." They can then repair the telegraph. The neighboring stations need not duplicate the signals that are produced while the telegraph is being repaired.[5] In case the failing telegraph cannot produce the failure signal, the operators of the two neighboring stations, upon noticing the problem, should produce the failure signal, followed by the call signal of the station where the failure occurred.

When a telegraph fails and cannot be repaired without the help of the inspector, one sends the corresponding suspension signal, followed by the call signal of the station where the inspectors presence is needed.[6] Then the operators of the neighboring stations take up the function of terminal stations, that is, when required they must send the signals "activity," "correct reception," and "adjourn" (but not for longer than one hour), and they receive all message signals. For the duration of the failure, these stations must announce the failure to the (original) terminal stations from time to time, but at least at the start of each new session. When these stations have received a complete message, they must bring it to the station where the failure occurred, and the operators of that station must have it delivered immediately to the director of the line.

On their part, the operators of the station where the failure occurred must observe the neighboring stations through their telescopes continuously, and record, if possible, all transmissions received by these stations. When they have recorded all the signals of a transmission, they must deliver them to the station that can transmit them to their final destination.

When the communication is interrupted by a suspension, due to "fog," "absence," or "failure," only the terminal stations can resume transmission with the last signal that was sent before the suspension, to check whether the same problem is still present. Then each intermediate station must take up the signal they had before the suspension. To the stations that fail to do so the "absence signal" must be sent.

When a suspension signal is received, all stations must remember their last signal, so that they can repeat it when the suspension ends. The suspension signals must always be followed by a station's call signal, even if the cause of the suspension has disappeared between the transmission of the suspension and the call signal.

When a terminal station wants to know the cause for a delay in signal transmission, it must form on a left oblique the call signal of the second station, the station that it corresponds with. This station must immediately form the call signal of the third station, and this one must signal the fourth, and so on. All these call signals, that are not carried to completion, are also forwarded, one by one, back to the terminal station. When a station does not respond immediately to the call signal by producing the call signal of the station that succeeds it, its correspondent will form the "absence signal," also at an oblique. When this signal, which is also not carried to completion, arrives back at the first terminal station, it indicates that the delay was caused by the station whose call signal appeared last.

A terminal station can take the initiative to determine the cause of a delay, not only after message signals, but also after the "closing signal," the "activity signals," the signals for "correction" and "repetition" of messages, and the "correct reception" signal, whenever they are maintained too long. A "delay" signal is terminated like the other suspension signals.

TERMINATING SUSPENSIONS
When the cause of a suspension disappears, the station that initiated the signal repeats the last signal it had before the suspension, and each operator repeats the last signal set. If an operator arrives at his station and sees a suspension signal at both neighboring stations, he must first accept the signal coming from Paris. The two correspondents terminate the suspension by resuming their last signals (i.e. an activity or call signal), and the operator that caused the suspension selects and duplicates the signal with the higher priority.

CONFLICTING ACTIVITY SIGNALS

When two "activity signals" meet, the signal from Paris takes precedence over that of Brussels. A "priority signal" takes precedence over an "activity signal." When two "priority signals" meet, the signal from Paris has precedence over that of Brussels. When the director of the line in Brussels receives a few signals of a "priority" message from Paris he can interrupt the session by initiating a "priority" message of Brussels. The operators of each station then must accept this priority, and the message signals that follow it.

WAIT SIGNALS

The purpose of this signal is to notify the operators that a signal transmission will start soon, and that they should be attentive.

ADJOURN SIGNALS

These signals are given at the end of a session. They determine the duration of the rest period granted to the operators (one, two or three hours).

CLOSING SIGNALS

This signal is used for two purposes: to indicate the end of a session, and to terminate correspondence at the end of the day.

General Station Regulations (1809)

1. The telegraphists are charged with the operation of the telegraph.
2. They must be able to read and write.
3. They must obey the orders of the telegraph administration, the director, and the inspector.
4. Both telegraphists must be at their post when the telegraph is in use. They alternately keep watch during breaks and at night.
5. Work begins every day one quarter hour before sunrise and it continues until the end of the day.
6. A telegraphist who is absent while the telegraph is in use can be suspended by the director.
7. The two telegraphists are each individually responsible for suspensions caused by absences from their post.
8. A suspension caused by absence is punished by a deduction on the salary of the responsible telegraphists. The deduction is 50 centimes for each minute of absence.
9. An equal share of the 50 centimes is taken from the salaries of both telegraphists on duty.
10. The administration determines if the length of a suspension will be cause for dismissal.
11. Delays in the transmission are subject to the same deductions, but applied only to the telegraphist who operates the telegraph at the time.
12. Delays in the transmission that last longer than 5 minutes will be considered the same as a suspension caused by absence, and both

telegraphists will be held equally responsible.

13. Suspensions caused by failures are considered the same as suspensions caused by absence, and fined accordingly, if they are caused by the negligence of telegraphists to keep their telegraph in good condition.

14. Those who do not give the suspension signal when the instructions call for it will be punished as if they had caused the suspension.

15. To determine the occurrence of suspensions, the director of each division will, on the first of each month, send to the director of the neighboring division, the nature of the suspensions that have been recorded in the journals at the terminal stations of his division in the immediately preceding month. He will record the deductions the inspector shall make in the payments to each station over the month in which the suspensions took place.

16. If any dispute arises between stations over the deductions, the inspector will make a provisionary judgment that is submitted to the director for confirmation.

17. The director collects all deductions, and uses the sum to reward all telegraphists when messages are transmitted expediently.

18. A telegraphist who gives, or prolongs without cause, the "fog signal," will be dismissed and reported to the police, to be punished as if he had attempted to prevent government messages from reaching their destination. This dereliction shall be recorded by the inspector in a written statement.

19. Any telegraphist who operates the telegraph while drunk will be dismissed, and his colleague will be responsible for the mistakes that were made. When a telegraphist has a colleague that is in the habit of getting drunk, he must notify the inspector, or report it to the director.

20. It is forbidden for telegraphists, at risk of dismissal, to allow any stranger to operate the telegraph, even additional telegraphists, without a written order from the inspector or director.

21. The telegraphists may not allow anyone to enter their station while the telegraph is in use.

22. They may have repairs performed that they cannot perform themselves, when such repairs are necessary for the operation of the machine. In this case, they must obtain receipts from the workers they pay, and present these receipts to the inspector when he makes his rounds and they will be reimbursed at that time. All repairs other than those that are absolutely necessary are forbidden.

23. The telegraphists are responsible for the deterioration of the machine, the instruments, and other objects they were given, if this deterioration is caused by their neglect. In this case, the expense of the necessary repairs will be deducted from their pay.

Approved by His Excellency, the Minister of Internal Affairs.

Appendix C
Edelcrantz's Design

General Station Instructions (1808)

1. The telegraphists should be up before sunrise, examine the machine thoroughly, and certify that the strings are not too slack, and also not so tense that the shutters are not straight. They must check that nothing is stuck by making the signal A777 several times, etc. Under strict penalty rules, nothing must be left in disorder, but must be repaired immediately using the tools and spare parts, which according to the inventory are available at each station. Should a more serious defect arise which prevents the use of the machine and which cannot possibly be repaired, this must be indicated by randomly putting up some single shutters. Then help should be sought from the next station towards Stockholm.
2. When your own telegraph is in order, you must verify that the telegraphs of your nearest neighbors are in order. If a neighboring telegraph requires assistance, you must put up the speech signal of that neighbor followed by the signal 222.
3. Soon thereafter, the ready sign A156 is put up, starting from the outmost stations Landsort, Korssö and Örskär and then all the way to Stockholm. No one must put up the ready signal before the station behind has done so. If he is late without reason, it is expedited with 077, for fast.
4. Thereafter you wait until you are called from Stockholm. However, if any of the terminal or intermediate stations has to send an urgent message that cannot be postponed, after A156 or ready has been signaled that station may put up its speech signal, which the subsequent stations must carry forward to Stockholm. Later the attention signal of Stockholm must be transferred backwards.
5. When Stockholm wants to speak, the sign of the station to which the conversation is directed is put up, followed by A000. The intermediate stations repeat these signs, and when they arrive at the right

231

station, that station responds with its attention signal which is transferred back to Stockholm. When Stockholm is calling a station, it is done by putting up the number of the station and thereafter 700. When you are being called, you immediately respond either with A474, or with some other report (without putting up the speech signal or the attention signal).

6. A station's speech signal to Stockholm consists of the station-number followed by A000. The attention signal of Stockholm to the North is 557, to the East 767 and to the South 755. These speech and attention signals must be well known and watched. At all times, except during the hour of leave, one or both of the telegraphists shall sit at the [telescope] tubes so that no delay is caused.

7. When Stockholm grants leave to the North, South or East branch for two, one, or one-half hour, it is done in the following way:

760	North branch leave for	002	Two Hours
761	East branch leave for	001	One Hour
762	South branch leave for	A215	One-half Hour
763	General branch leave		

After the reception of these signs the hour-glass is turned until the leave is over.

8. Only during this time, the stations in this branch can attend to other matters, or speak between each other if they so wish, but no longer. When there are more than three stations on a line, the stations may only speak to their closest neighbors, with the speech signal either 102 or 201 depending on the location of the station in relation to Stockholm, and using the corresponding attention signal.

9. All reports and all conversation should be sent using as few signals as possible. Also during the hour of leave and during private conversation between neighbors, extensiveness should be avoided. While signaling, repeating or intermediate stations must never occupy themselves with investigations of the meaning of the signals in the tables. This must only happen after the end-of-speech signal has been given. All signs should be written down clearly and in the correct order so that later they can be easily translated.

10. There is a list of all speech signals which should be known by heart, and another list of general standing signs which are necessary to know so that you understand what is meant at the first sign of each new signaling.

11. All reports are logged in a diary at each station, on the forms provided. On each report you must enter the date and the hour of signals, all negligence of neighboring stations, everyone who visits the telegraph, and everything else noticeable that occurs.

12. The telegraphists should handle the [telescope] tubes gently, keep dust and moisture from the glasses and carefully look after everything in the inventory of the telegraph.

13. The telegraphists should in general apply themselves to maintain vigilance, attention, and diligence in all matters related to their duty

and the purpose of the establishment. If you do so properly, you will receive a corresponding encouragement or promotion, but otherwise you will be punished in accordance with the War Act or be ordered to other war duty, in order to improve by virtue of a stricter military discipline.

A. N. Edelcrantz   Stockholm, 1 August 1808

Addendum to the Station Instructions (1809)

1. On each telegraph, one of the telegraphists is at the [shutter] control before noon and at the [telescope] tube after noon and vice versa. The person at the tube is responsible for all negligence.
2. The call and the speech signals are made as before using the station sign followed by 700 or by A000 when it is directed towards Stockholm; but when it originates from Stockholm an A is placed in front of the station sign, and it is followed by 700 or A000.
3. When the second station observes that the third station has repeated the call or speech signal, it responds with its station sign to the initiator, when the third station observes that the fourth has repeated, the third sends its station sign, and so on until the last station has sent its station sign. This is always done in the direction of the initiator, whether the conversation comes from Stockholm or from another station.
4. Thereafter A000 or 700 is sent, which goes all the way, without sending station signs back, until it reaches the last station, which either gives the attention signal or responds to the call.
5. The station that receives a [complete] conversation or report always responds without speech or attention signal, using one of the following signals: A227 (understood), A230 (not understood), 274 (yes), 450 (no), A775 (good), A774 (will do), 555 (done), 303 (wait for answer), or with some longer sentence, as long as it can be done immediately and is necessary, and only then is it followed by 700. No conversation can be considered complete before this is done, and no other station is allowed to start a conversation before this.
6. Only the outmost stations are allowed to initiate conversation to Stockholm without being called. The others must await a [polling] call which is always made in order.
7. The outmost stations are in the North Branch: Vaxholm, Köpmansholmen, Söderarm, Arholma, Grisslehamn, Käringö, Örskär, and Gefle.
8. All telegraphists should well remember and be extra-observant of specifically the following equilateral signs: 060, 606, 646; the first two are repeated immediately in the branch involved in the conversation; but 646 is repeated in all branches.
9. When 060 comes, the station where the conversation stopped sends back the sign of the failing station.

10. When 606 comes, either from Stockholm or from one of the outer stations, any ongoing conversation is immediately postponed, 606 is repeated everywhere, and the speech signal of the initiating station is awaited.
11. When 646 comes from Stockholm, it is immediately repeated in all branches, and the outmost station in each branch sends back its normal attention signal. After this, either the next speech signal from Stockholm to the stations in a specific branch is awaited, or a general order to all stations.
12. When the haze is strong, leave is granted from 11:30 A.M. to 2:30 P.M., but otherwise only after an order and notification is issued.
13. Starting at April 15, responsibility and attendance should be taken seriously, and the penal code will be enforced strictly.

A. N. Edelcrantz/C. C. Limnell   Stockholm, 21 April 1809

Penal Code (1809)

1. Any telegraphist who is negligent, careless, or commits an offense, shall be sternly punished according to the circumstances and the penalty shall be either a fine, arrest, prison with bread and water, flogging, or to run the gauntlet. If these offenses are committed frequently, the penalties will be more severe.
2. Any telegraphist who is not immediately aware of calls or messages from the closest stations, shall be fined 8 Sk. on the first offense, and the fine is subtracted from his allowance.
3. Any telegraphist who commits the same fault more often is fined 16 Sk.
4. Any telegraphist who neglects his watch in any manner shall either be fined 16 Sk., arrested, or be given corporal punishment depending on the circumstances.
5. Any telegraphist who has to be waited for several minutes or who repeats messages slowly shall be punished.
6. Any telegraphist who neglects a watch sign shall be punished.
7. Any telegraphist who arrives late or leaves before his hours are done shall be punished.
8. Any telegraphist who is standing by the control panel when his turn is at the telescope or vice versa, shall be punished.
9. Any telegraphist who puts up the signal 431 (cannot see) when the nearest station can be seen, shall be punished by flogging and, if this happens more often, shall be punished more severely.
10. Any telegraphist who sells his supplies or uses them in such a way that they do not last the prescribed amount of time shall be punished.
11. Any telegraphist who mismanages the telegraph's effects and/or his own equipment shall be punished.
12. Any company officer who commits any of the above mentioned offenses shall either be fined twice the amount, punished more

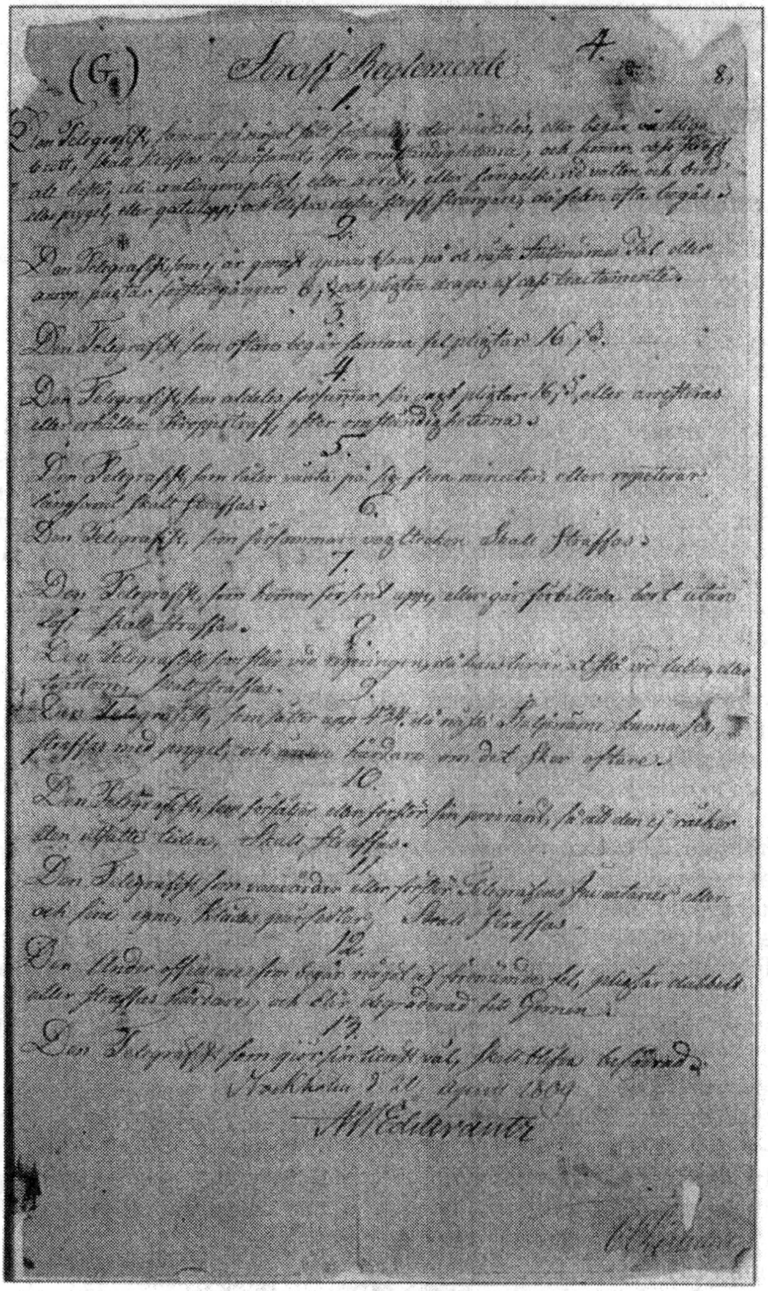

Figure C.1 *Straff Reglemente* (Penal Code).
(Coll. Telemuseum, Stockholm)

severely, or be degraded to the rank of private.

13. Any telegraphist who performs his duties well shall be promoted.

A. N. Edelcrantz/C. C. Limnell   Stockholm, 20 April 1809

Instructions for Telegraph Operators (1837)

1. A telegraph operator is a soldier's equal. He obeys the military law and swears the soldier's oath as far as it can be applied to his duty. He shall, in his way of living, be sober, orderly, and decent, on duty devoted, careful, and observant. Towards his superiors, he shall show obedience, observance, and respect, on duty as well as off duty.
    He shall promptly execute orders and follow rules, and shall learn and exercise the obligations tied to his duty with diligence and endurance. He shall know well all the parts belonging to a telegraph, their composition and usage and shall understand how to maintain them and to keep them in a usable state. He shall be able to swiftly and reliably perceive the telegraph signals, take them down and set them up clearly.
    The reputation and the honor of a telegraph operator rest on his skill and his reliability.

2. Of two telegraph operators at a station, one is always the first officer, and in this capacity is responsible that the rules at a station are carefully observed. The second officer assists the first officer and obeys what assignment he gives him as part of the duty. During signaling they exchange duties in such a way that, one hour each, one looks in the tubes while the other operates the machine.

3. Both should often and carefully examine those parts of the telegraph that are subject to wear, such as the strings, bearings, hinges, etc, and repair those that are defective or replace them with spares, which are always stored at each station. These examinations shall be made before as well as after each transmission and the discovered defects shall be repaired between transmissions. The required spare parts, when missing, shall immediately be ordered by the first officer, according to procedures determined by the officer in charge of each telegraph line.
    A list of all tools and other inventory belonging to a station, signed by the first officer, shall be attached to the wall of the telegraph room. All losses of such items which are not caused by wear or which provably occurred without involvement of the telegraph operators, shall be replaced at the expense of the operators together.

4. When the hour of transmission occurs, this is indicated from the main station, by giving the sign 603, which in table 011 means "the time is" followed by the number signs in the same table indicating the hour and the minutes. This sign is also the call signal and is repeated by all intermediate stations outwards on the lines to the end stations, which respond with the sign 677, "ready," and thereafter whatever

236

there is to be reported. The clocks should be corrected at all stations in agreement with the call sign whereafter both telegraph operators shall go to their tubes or binoculars to carefully watch the neighboring stations.

5. As soon as a telegraph sign becomes visible on either side, the operators calls this out loud and clear and writes it down on his chalkboard. While repeating the sign loud and clear, the other operator then goes to the telegraph control and immediately pushes down the keys corresponding to this sign and sets it up on the telegraph by pushing down the pedal.

   When a new sign meanwhile has become visible, it is written down, called out and responded to in the same way as before, and is taken down on the free keyboard. But the old sign must not be taken down and the new set up until the operator at the tube has observed that the previously set up sign has been repeated by the next station and announced this by saying "let go!" whereafter the sign is immediately changed and new signs are awaited until the sign "end of call" arrives. In this way, it should be possible to perceive 10 signs per minute, including the responses from the following stations, in the absence of poor visibility. If there is a longer intermission between signs, the operation is considered to be slow. But [it is considered to be] fast and commendable if 12 to 15 signs per minute are transmitted.

6. When one station wants to call another, the former, or the caller, sets up the sign of the latter, or receiver. This sign is called "call sign." Then, the caller sets up its own sign, the message and finally 770 or "end of call."

7. If the message is so important that it has to be transmitted before any other message, the sign A is added before the call sign. For all call signs that use this character, any other transmission has to be interrupted and the interrupting call sign followed by the message has to be repeated all the way to the receiving station.

8. If two call signs meet, both without or both with A, the one coming from the outer line towards the main station should go first. The station at which a call sign from the main station meets one from the outer end in this way sets up 772 which means "call signs meet," which is repeated to the main station along with the accompanying message.

   If call signs of the same character arrive at the Trindtorp station from Sandhamn and Dalaro at the same time, the one coming from Sandhamn is transmitted first.

9. If the person to whom the message is addressed does not belong to or does not stay at the station, the sign 277, or "forward to" followed by the name of the addressee is added before the message.

10. If the sender of a message does not belong to the speaking station, the name of the sender is added before the end of call sign.

11. All messages are repeated only by the stations situated between the calling and the receiving stations.

12. A received message shall be answered immediately without call sign,

at least with an answer which indicates whether the message has been understood or not. If an answer cannot be produced immediately, 274 "wait for an answer," or 275 "will be answered as soon as possible" is set up.

A new message cannot be sent until an answer to the previous message has returned, unless it is of great importance, in which case the message must start with 777 "hold everything and repeat immediately the following important message."

13. If a sign has been incorrectly perceived or repeated at the next station, it shall immediately be corrected with 030 "erroneous previous sign." However, both the incorrect sign and the 030 sign should be written down and repeated up to the receiving station as usual.

14. If several stations are addressed simultaneously, which do not have a common sign in the table, this is done by including the sign of all the stations in the call sign followed by A000, or "end of word."

When a message or order is transmitted to all or part of the stations along the line, each addressed station must acknowledge if it has understood the message. This is done as follows: the farthest station responds with 222 "understood" followed by its station-sign and 770, "end of call." Each station repeats this response, adding its own station-sign before the "end of call" sign. The station which has not understood, repeats the rest of the responses but omits its own station-sign. The calling station can in this way renew the message to that or those stations which have not already understood the message.

15. Each intermission occurring during transmission shall immediately be reported to the calling station as soon as the intermission exceeds one minute. The station at which the sign has stopped sets up the one of the signs 771–776 which describes the situation truthfully followed by the station-sign of the station that has caused the stop and "end of call."

When a message is interrupted with one of the signs 773–776 and this sign has been transmitted to the calling station, each one of the stations that has repeated this interrupting sign immediately shall set up the previous sign of the interrupted message and let these signs stand until they are received and retransmitted by the station where the interrupt occurred.

16. If a station observes that a neighboring station has difficulty seeing the signs and the reason can be assumed to be reflections of the sun in the shutters, the declination of the shutters are changed somewhat in order to decrease the inconvenience, if possible, and thus get the signs correctly acknowledged.

When a station, which for the aforementioned reason cannot perceive the signs distinctly, would like the transmitting station to change the inclination of its shutters, it indicates this by changing the declination of its own shutters.

17. If, during transmission, a defect appears which makes the telegraph unusable for the moment but which can be swiftly repaired, the

standing sign is taken down and the telegraph remains idle until the repair is made. The event is reported using 262 "the telegraph is repaired." The previously standing sign is reset and the transmission is continued.

If again the telegraph is so damaged that it cannot be repaired within the transmission time or with the tools available to the operators, this is made known by moving some of the shutters up and down as fast as possible until this is observed by the neighboring stations which then sets up 771 "the telegraph unusable at station," followed by the station-sign of that station.

One of the telegraph operators must remain at the tubes until permission to leave is granted.

It is then up to the calling station to instruct the unusable station, either using sign 270, that the transmission shall continue and as soon as possible be transmitted via telegraph, or using sign 276, that the message should be written down and sent by a messenger. In the latter case such a written message should be made immediately and one of the telegraph operators carry it to the closest usable station, from which it can be transmitted to the receiving station.

If the unusable station is called, it sets up 267 "transmit, we can receive but not repeat." If the telegraph is so badly damaged that this sign cannot be set up, one of the operators must climb up to the lower arm of the telegraph and remain there as long as the transmission lasts and, for each sign acknowledged by the other operator at the tubes, set up one of the shutters of the middle arm and thus respond to each new sign.

When the damage has been evaluated and found impossible to repair by the operators, one of them goes to the closest station manager, who either assists the operators himself, or provides instructions on how to deal with the situation, or notifies the line manager about the situation according to procedures determined for each telegraph line.

When a telegraph is restored into a usable state, this is reported as soon as possible using 262 "the telegraph is repaired," followed by the station-sign which report is repeated to both the main station and to the end stations.

18. For messages between stations, table 001 is used. Such transmissions may only occur when no general transmissions are in question. In all cases, it must immediately be interrupted using the sign "end of call" as soon as a call sign arrives from the main or the end stations.

19. During ongoing transmission, received and transmitted signs should be written down on the chalkboard without decoding. If the message concerns this station, decoding shall be done immediately after the "end of call" sign has arrived, written down on the chalkboard, and the answer transmitted and in the same way written down.

20. At each station, the following items shall be stored:

a. A general telegraph journal in which the messages written down on the chalkboard during operation shall be recorded according to the format given by the columns in the journal.

b. A separate telegraph journal for the station in which orders and reports are recorded with their encoding or decoding.

c. An event journal in which notable events at the station are recorded, such as: something at the telegraph has been damaged and repaired, the use of material and spare parts, the state of the neighboring stations as far as it can be judged from a distance, etc.

At the visits of the telegraph director, these journals shall always be presented for inspection as well as the recording of relevant comments and criticism.

All notes in the journals shall be made after the completion of a transmission and before the next transmission.

Orders and messages arriving through the telegraph which define rules to be followed at the station shall be written down on paper and attached to the wall of the telegraph room, along with the telegraph instructions.

21. During transmission, the telegraph operators must not engage in any conversation or other activity which diverts their concentration from their duty. Neither may, during these periods, any person be admitted to the telegraph room who is not related to the telegraph institution.

22. After a completed transmission hour, the telegraph operators may not leave the station until permission to leave is granted, either from the main station or from the station where the line's director is present at this time.

Carl Akrell/J. F. von Heland[1]   Stockholm, 1 April 1837

---

1. The notes to this appendix start at p. 272.

Illustrations

The origin of each illustration that is reproduced in this book from other sources is given in the corresponding caption. Permission to reproduce those illustrations that carry a copyright is gratefully acknowledged here. In particular we thank the *Musée de la Poste* in Paris, the Telemuseum in Stockholm, the Televerket Archive in Stockholm, and the Rare Books division of the New York Public Library in New York, for their valuable help in our search for illustrations.

Chapter Three, Abraham N. Edelcrantz

Chapter Four, A Treatise on Telegraphs

242

Chapter Five, Other Countries

Chapter Six, About Invention

Appendix A, Letters to Gentleman's Magazine

Appendix C, Edelcrantz's Design

Notes

Preface

1. *[p. vii]* [Miller 1866, p. 6].

2. *[p. vii]* Ibid., p. 7.

3. *[p. viii]* *Gentleman's Magazine* was a monthly magazine published in London. One of the regular contributors was essayist and lexicographer Samuel Johnson (1709–1784), a leading figure in the second half of the eighteenth century.

4. *[p. viii]* The complete text is reproduced in Appendix A, see p. 219.

5. *[p. viii]* As confirmed by a statement in §6 of Edelcrantz's treatise on telegraphs (see p. 139).

6. *[p. viii]* Edelcrantz did know about Chappe's application of the shutter principle in 1796, as witnessed by a reference to it in footnote 33 of his treatise, see p. 261.

7. *[p. viii]* References can also be found in more recent works, such as in the third episode of the Hornblower saga, *Hornblower and the Hotspur* by C. S. Forester (1899–1966), which was written ca. 1940.

8. *[p. ix]* Stendhal was the pen name of the French novelist Marie-Henri Beyle (1783–1842).

9. *[p. ix]* [Dumas 1844, Chapter 34].

10. *[p. ix]* See especially the French *Regulations for Telegraphic Correspondence*, rules 20–26 in Appendix B (see p. 224), and the brutal *Penal Code* for the operators of the Swedish optical telegraph network, reproduced in Appendix C (see p. 234).

Chapter One, Torches and Beacons

1. *[p. 1]* Two people filed for a patent on the telephone on 14 February 1876; one was Elisha Gray, the other was Alexander Graham Bell. By coincidence, Bell filed his claim two hours before Gray and thus obtained the coveted patent. Bell subsequently won all court cases that questioned his priority.

2. *[p. 1]* The modern distance for a marathon of 42.2 km (26 miles) is only loosely based on the distance from Athens to Marathon. It is the distance from Windsor Castle to White City Stadium in London, the course that was run at the 1908 Olympics.

3. *[p. 1]* Herodotus, *The History*, Book VI, 105–106.

4. *[p. 2]* Ibid., 115–116.

5. *[p. 2]* *Grolier's Academic American Encyclopedia* 1992, in the entry for *Postal Services*.

6. *[p. 2]* [Breasted 1906, Vol. 1, pp. 490–497]; quoted in [Dvornik 1974, p. 9].

7. *[p. 2]* [Dvornik 1974, p. 17].

8. *[p. 2]* [Breasted 1906, Vol. 3, pp. 630–635]; quoted in [Dvornik 1974, p. 7].

9. *[p. 3]* [Dvornik 1974, p. 18].

10. *[p. 3]* [Luckenbill 1926, Vol. II, p. 989]; quoted in [Dvornik 1974, p. 19].

11. *[p. 3]* [Dvornik 1974, p. 19], [Fries 1904, p. 117].

12. *[p. 3]* Jeremiah 51:31. King Nebuchadnezzar II reigned from 605 to 562 B.C.

13. *[p. 4]* Xenophon, *Cyropaedia*, Book VIII, 6.17–18; quoted in [Dvornik 1974, p. 28].

14. *[p. 4]* Herodotus, *The History*, Book VIII, 98.

15. *[p. 4]* [Neal 1974].

16. *[p. 4]* Suetonius, *The Twelve Caesars*, Book II, 49, as quoted by [Dvornik 1974, pp. 91–92]. The translation in the Penguin classics edition of the same passage is less elegant.

17. *[p. 5]* [Plaum 1950], [Cherry 1962].

18. *[p. 5]* [Dvornik 1974, pp. 70–71, 94–98, 123].

19. *[p. 5]* Suetonius, *The Twelve Caesars*, Book I, 57.

20. *[p. 5]* Marco Polo, *The description of the World*, pp. 150–151.

21. *[p. 5]* Ibid., pp. 154–155.

22. *[p. 6]* Ibid., pp. 152–153. It reads:

> ... between one post and the next, at a distance of three miles apart, there are stations which may contain as many as forty buildings occupied by unmounted couriers, who also play a part in the Great Khan's postal service. I will tell you how. They wear large belts, set all round with bells, so that when they run they are audible at a great distance. They always run at full speed and never for more than three miles. And the next station three miles away, where the noise they make gives due notice of their approach, another courier is waiting in readiness. As soon as the first man arrives, the new one takes what he is carrying and also a little note given to him by the clerk, and starts to run. After he has run for three miles, the performance is repeated. And I can assure you that by means of this service of unmounted couriers, the Great Khan receives news over a ten day's journey in a day and a night. ... So in ten days they can transmit news over a journey of a hundred days.

23. *[p. 6]* The quote about the delivery of fruit continues:

> At each of these three-mile stations there is appointed a clerk who notes the day and hour of the arrival of every courier and the departure of his successor; and this practice is in force at every station. And there are also inspectors charged with the duty of going round every month and examining all these stations, in order to detect any couriers who have been remiss and punish them. From these couriers, and from the staff at the stations, the Great Khan exacts no tax, and he makes generous provisions for their maintenance.

24. *[p. 6]* [Woods 1965, p. 4].

25. *[p. 7]* [Neal 1974, pp. 121–122].

26. *[p. 7]* [Wilkins 1641, Chapter 16].

27. *[p. 8]* [Woods 1965, p. 63].

28. *[p. 8]* [Woods 1965, pp. 65–66].

29. *[p. 8]* [Bentley 1988, pp 47–48].

30. *[p. 8]* Xenophon, *Hellenica*, Book II, 1.27.

31. *[p. 9]* [Woods 1965, p. 10]. Woods gives no source.

32. *[p. 9]* Suetonius, *The Twelve Caesars*, Book III, LXV, as quoted in [Hennig 1908, p. 15], cf. also [Aschoff 1984].

33. *[p. 9]* Quoted from the Penguin Classics edition of *The Twelve Caesars*, which was published in 1957.

34. *[p. 10]* [Woods 1965, p. 149].

35. *[p. 10]* [Bergstrasser 1785, §244].

36. *[p. 10]* Khevenhiller, *Annales Ferdinandei*, as quoted in [Hennig 1908, pp. 23–24].

37. *[p. 10]* [Woods 1965, pp. 150–153].

38. *[p. 11]* The Morse code itself dates from 1838, see p. 205.

39. *[p. 11]* [Babbage 1851, p. 144].

40. *[p. 11]* Cf. [Woods 1965, p. 151].

41. *[p. 11]* [Babbage 1851, p. 146], [Hyman 1982, pp. 225–226].

42. *[p. 11]* [Woods 1965, p. 155].

43. *[p. 11]* Plutarch, *The Lives of The Noble Grecians and Romans*, p. 253.

44. *[p. 12]* [Dvornik 1974, p. 157].

45. *[p. 12]* [Woods 1965, p. 32].

46. *[p. 12]* [Chappe 1824, p. 90].

47. *[p. 13]* [Woods 1965, pp. 36–37].

48. *[p. 13]* [Lavery 1989, p. 261].

49. *[p. 13]* Chapter Five, p. 195.

50. *[p. 13]* [Keegan 1988, pp. 49–53].

51. *[p. 13]* Ibid., p. 53.

52. *[p. 15]* Since 1836 U.S. patents have been numbered consecutively, but in 1861 patents were sometimes issued two numbers. The (low) number 252 was probably the additional number, used for numbering patents consecutively within a year.

53. *[p. 15]* Longfellow, *Tales of a Wayside Inn*, 1863. "Paul Revere's Ride," St. 2. As reproduced in [Bartlett 1855/1992].

54. *[p. 15]* [Bartlett 1855/1992, 339:4].

55. *[p. 15]* Homer, *Illiad*, Book XVIII, 210–213. Penguin Classics edition, 1950, p. 342.

56. *[p. 16]* Aeschylus, *Agamemnon*, 1–34, as quoted in [Shaffner 1859, pp. 22–24]. See also the translation of Richmond Lattimore in *The Complete Greek Tragedies*, Univ. of Chicago Press, 1959, Vol. 1, pp. 35, 43–44.

57. *[p. 16]* Ibid., 278–316.

58. *[p. 17]* [Hennig 1936, p. 23].

59. *[p. 17]* [Aschoff 1984].

60. *[p. 18]* Aschoff reported that to cover an average of 150 km on a clear night takes a fire with a light output of between 10^4 and 10^5 candela. At

this distance, such a fire produces an image with a brightness of 10^{-6} to 10^{-7} lux, which is near the minimum that can still be seen. He also measured that a large fire produces about 0.2 candela/cm^2, from which the minimum size of the stack can be derived. A candela is a unit for measuring light intensities. Originally it was defined as a the amount of light produced by a single candle. It is now standardized more precisely as 1/60th of the amount of light produced by one cm^2 blackbody (i.e., a perfect radiator) that is heated to the melting temperature of platinum. One lux is the illumination projected on a surface by a light source of one candela at a distance of one meter. For comparison, daylight has a brightness in the order of 10^4 to 10^5 lux. At dusk this reduces to about 10^2 lux.

61. *[p. 18]* Vergil, *The Aeneid*, Book II, 254–259. Penguin Books, 1951, p. 304–305. In the original Latin, the sentence referring to the signal light reads:

> . . . *et iam Argiva phalanx instructis navibus ibat a Tenedo tacitae per amica silentia lunae litora nota petens, flammas cum regia puppis extulerat, fatisque deum defensus iniquis inclusos utero Danaos et pinea furtim laxat claustra Sinon.*

62. *[p. 18]* Isaiah 30:17.

63. *[p. 18]* Jeremiah 6:1.

64. *[p. 18]* Feldman writes in [Feldman 1978, pp. 183–184]:

> When the Court was satisfied that the new moon had actually been seen, the President declared the new moon to be consecrated (Rosh Hashanah, ii. 7 [a reference to the Talmud]) the news was spread to people outside of Jerusalem by means of bonfires, or beacons, on the tops of mountains. When the awaited signal was observed at neighboring mountains, similar fire signals were lit, and thus the information was transmitted to distant places. This method was continued until a deliberate attempt to confuse the Jews was made by the Cuthites, who maliciously lit signals at improper times (ibid, ii. 2). Since then these fire signals were altogether abolished by R. Judah Hanasi (towards the end of the second century) and messengers or couriers, to convey the tidings, were sent out instead (Jer. Rosh Hashanah, ii. 2). As these could not reach the more distant places before the 31st day of the old month, the residents of those places used to celebrate two days for the holidays (pesachim 52a), because they were not sure whether the first of the month was on the 30th or the 31st day.

65. *[p. 18]* Herodotus, *The History*, Book VII, 183.

66. *[p. 19]* Ibid., Book IX, 3.

67. *[p. 19]* Thucydides, *History of The Peloponnesian War*, Book II, 94. Penguin Classics edition, 1954. The Peloponnesian War took place 431–404 B.C..

68. *[p. 19]* Ibid., Book VIII, 102.

69. *[p. 19]* Ibid., Book III, 80.

70. *[p. 19]* Ibid., Book III, 22.

71. *[p. 20]* Aristotle, *Peri Kosmon*, Book 6, as quoted in [Hennig 1908, pp. 6–7]. See also [Dvornik 1974, p. 32], or [Aschoff 1984].

72. *[p. 20]* Herodotus, *The Histories*, Book V, 52–53.

73. *[p. 20]* [Woods 1965, p. 5].

74. *[p. 20]* Xenophon, *Hellenica*, Book II:2.3

75. *[p. 20]* Diodorus Siculus, *Diodorus of Sicily*, Book XIX, 17.7. The passage can also be found in [Aschoff 1984], and in [Hcnnig 1906, p. 13]. The division in provinces (satrapies) was due to Darius II, [Dvornik 1974, p. 24].

76. *[p. 20]* Ibid., Book XIX, 57.

77. *[p. 21]* Julius Caesar, *Bellum Gallicum*, Book VII, 3. Based on the translation in [Hennig 1908, p. 3], which is similar to the one in [Aschoff 1984]. A translation of the same passage in the Penguin Classics edition is more vague.

78. *[p. 21]* Ibid., Book II, 33.

79. *[p. 21]* Plinius the Elder, *Naturalis Historica*, Book XXXV, 48.169. The use of the watch towers for fire signals is mentioned in Book II, 73.181. Similar references can be found in Polybius, *The Histories*, Book I, 19:6–7, and in Livius, *Livy*, Book XXII, 19.6. See also [Aschoff 1984, pp. 33–35].

80. *[p. 22]* Plutarch, *The Lives of The Noble Grecians and Romans*. Random House edition, 1864, p. 687.

81. *[p. 22]* [Woods 1965, p. 2].

82. *[p. 22]* [Shaffner 1859, p. 19], and in [Hennig 1908, p. 12].

83. *[p. 22]* [Aschoff 1984, pp. 59–60].

84. *[p. 22]* Vegetius, *De Re Militari*, Book III, 5.

85. *[p. 22]* E.g., [Bergstrasser 1785], [Bockmann 1794], [Chappe 1824], [Belloc 1888], [Dvornik 1974].

86. *[p. 22]* A plaster copy of Trajan's Column from 1860 is in the Victoria and Albert Museum in London.

87. *[p. 22]* [Dvornik 1974, pp. 117–118].

88. *[p. 24]* Polybius, *The Histories*, Book X, 43.

89. *[p. 24]* Ibid., Book X, 44.

90. *[p. 24]* One cubit is roughly 52 cm (20.5 inches).

91. *[p. 26]* Polyaenus, *Strategematon*, Book VI, 16.2.

92. *[p. 26]* Polybius, *The Histories*, Book X, 45a.

93. *[p. 26]* Ibid., Book X, 45b.

94. *[p. 27]* [Aschoff 1984, pp. 25–27, 52–57].

95. *[p. 27]* Cf. [Shaffner 1859, pp. 19–20], [Hennig 1938], [Herbarth 1978, p. 13], or [Aschoff 1984, pp. 58–59].

96. *[p. 27]* Sextus Julius Africanus does not mention Cleoxenus or Democleitus by name. His description, however, predates Polybius's by at least half a century.

97. *[p. 27]* [Aschoff 1984, pp. 58–59], [Shaffner 1859, p. 19].

98. *[p. 27]* Chapter Four, p. 132.

99. *[p. 28]* According to [Hennig 1908].

100. *[p. 28]* Polybius, *The Histories*, Book X, 46.

101. *[p. 29]* Magnifying telescopes were not built until A.D. 1608, see p. 31.

102. *[p. 29]* Polybius, *The Histories*, Book X, 47a.

103. *[p. 29]* [Aschoff 1984, p. 50].

104. *[p. 29]* Polybius, *The Histories*, Book X, 47b.

105. *[p. 29]* Titus Livius, *Livy*, Book XXVIII, 5.1. See also Book XXII, 19.

106. *[p. 29]* Sextus Julius Africanus, *Kestoi*. See also [Aschoff 1984, p. 59].

107. *[p. 30]* [Dvornik 1974, pp. 142–143]. The original description can be found in Symeon Magister, *De Michaele et Theodory*, p. 681, and is also discussed in [Aschoff 1984, pp. 82–85].

108. *[p. 30]* Berengars I, *Usatges*, as quoted in [Hennig 1936, p. 27], and in [Hennig 1908, p. 17].

109. *[p. 30]* As reproduced in [Woods 1965, p. 149], who refers to William Tegg, *Posts, Telegraphs, and Telephones*, 1878.

110. *[p. 30]* The city archive of Barcelona records that a stone tower was constructed at *Montjuich* in A.D. 1073, to serve as a signaling point. It was, however, most likely used only with beacon fires. In 1534 the introduction of a new signaling code based on discs or spheres suspended from masts is documented for this location, see [Voltesbou 1940, Chapter 7].

111. *[p. 31]* [Ringnalda 1902, pp. 1–11]. See also Figure 1.12, p. 45.

112. *[p. 31]* [Woods 1965, p. 14 and p. 149].

113. *[p. 32]* Chapter Four, p. 133.

114. *[p. 32]* [Kessler 1616, p. 3].

115. *[p. 33]* Ibid., p. 20.

116. *[p. 33]* Ibid., p. 26.

117. *[p. 34]* All are explicitly mentioned. The use of a white piece of cloth is mentioned on p. 26, the use of bells, hammers, or knocking on p. 40.

118. *[p. 34]* Marquis of Worcester, *Century of Inventions*, as quoted in an article on telegraphs in the *Encyclopaedia Britannica*, 1797, pp. 334–337. *Ex re nata* can probably be translated as *by its very nature*.

119. *[p. 34]* Chapter Four, p. 133.

120. *[p. 35]* [Hooke 1726, pp. 142–150]. The text is also quoted in [Appleyard 1930, pp. 282–284], and mentioned by [Aschoff 1984, p. 111].

121. *[p. 38]* See also Chapter Six, p. 210.

122. *[p. 38]* [Wilson 1976, p. 5], mentions that Hooke did perform an experiment with his method. That experiment took place in London, from one side of the Thames river to the other (approx. 800 meters).

123. *[p. 38]* Quoted in [Belloc 1888, pp. 58–59], and in [Hennig 1908, p. 24]. The letter is also mentioned in [Aschoff 1984, p. 112]. According to Aschoff, it was written not in 1690, but on 26 November 1695. Amontons was born in 1663 in the French province of Normandy.

124. *[p. 39]* *Encyclopaedia Britannica*, 1797, pp. 334–337.

125. *[p. 39]* Appendix A, p. 219.

126. *[p. 39]* Chapter Four, p. 133.

127. *[p. 39]* See these notes, p. 260.

128. *[p. 39]* To produce optically perfect images with a single-element lens, the length of the telescope must be proportional to the square of the lens diameter. The image could be made brighter by using a larger than optimal lens, but image quality then suffered.

129. *[p. 40]* In Book 19, Chapter 1 of *Natural magick*, Porta also suggests that the sound can be captured by quickly closing off the ends of the pipe after speaking into it. Porta states that the sound can be replayed later by removing the covers from the pipe again. John Wilkins mentions this in 1641, but discards it as nonsense. Wilkins does mention a wall of 100 miles long, that was built by the Romans in Northern England. The guard-towers of the wall are said to be one mile apart and connected by hollow pipes or trunks through which the guards could exchange warning signals. The wall no longer exists.

130. *[p. 40]* Chapter Four, p. 133.

131. *[p. 40]* [Kahn 1967, pp. 137–143], [Norman 1973, pp. 24–25].

132. *[p. 40]* Porta, *Magia Naturalis*, Book 7, *Proeme*, p. 190. From the English translation published in London in 1658.

133. *[p. 40]* [Fahie 1884, p. 6, and p. 21].

134. *[p. 41]* As it is quoted in [Fahie 1884, pp. 9–11], from a translation that was published in the *Telegraphic Journal*, 15 November 1875.

135. *[p. 41]* Galileo, *Dialogus de Systemate Mundi*, 1632, p. 88, as it was quoted in [Hennig 1908, p. 59]. A slightly different translation appears also in [Fahie 1884, pp. 11–12].

136. *[p. 42]* [Demeulenaere 1993, pp. 28–31].

137. *[p. 42]* According to a popular illustration from [Figuier 1868].

138. *[p. 42]* [Chappe 1824, p. 58].

139. *[p. 42]* [Demeulenaere 1993, p. 30].

140. *[p. 42]* [Herbarth 1978, p. 18]. The method is also described in [Aschoff 1984, pp. 150–152].

141. *[p. 42]* Chapter Four, p. 134.

142. *[p. 42]* Quoted in [Bergstrasser 1796].

143. *[p. 43]* See Huth's device, Chapter Two, p. 90.

144. *[p. 43]* [Hennig 1908, p. 25].

145. *[p. 43]* [Chappe 1824, p. 52].

146. *[p. 44]* Although couriers on horseback are no longer in vogue, messenger services of many kinds still flourish. In New York, for instance, the fastest way to transmit documents or parcels today is a messenger on a race-bike. According to the local newspapers, over 1,500 such bike messengers traverse the city daily. A Dutch newspaper reported in July 1993 that in the Netherlands, outside the normal postal system, ca. 2,500 companies compete with the post office by specializing in courier services of various kinds.

147. *[p. 45]* [Wilkins 1641, Chapters 9 and 17].

148. *[p. 46]* As also noted in [Aschoff 1984, p. 95].

149. *[p. 46]* [Knuth 1981, p. 183].

Chapter Two, Claude Chappe

1. *[p. 47]* The names of the current departments in France date from around 1790. Before 1790, Sarthe was part of a province called Maine.

2. *[p. 48]* Mozart (1756–1791) made a European concert tour from 1762 to 1766, visiting the courts in Salzburg, Versailles, Vienna, and London, among others. He was seven years old when he visited Versailles.

3. *[p. 48]* Ignace Chappe d'Auteroche (1724–1783), caught a severe cold after crossing the Seine on his horse to win a bet. He died of the consequences and was buried in Brûlon. His wife Marie-Renée de Vernay de Vert (b. 1731) was buried beside him in 1803, at least according to the tombstone at Brûlon. Other sources state that Marie-Renée Vernay de Vert lived until 1821, [FNARH 1991, p. 7].

4. *[p. 49]* This was probably the school that is currently known as *Prytanée*

National Militaire, which served as a Christian Royal College from 1776 to 1792. At the time, it was known as the *Collège Royal de la Flèche*. Claude's brother Ignace is said to have attended the same school earlier, see [FNARH 1991, p. 15].

5. *[p. 49]* Cf. [Jacquez 1893, p. 6]. The precise date of Claude's graduation is uncertain. Abraham Chappe, in his preface to the second edition from 1840 of [Chappe 1824, p. xi], states, though, that Claude graduated before his twentieth birthday (i.e., before 1783).

6. *[p. 49]* Claude Chappe joined the *Société Philomatique* in 1792.

7. *[p. 49]* Some of the papers that Claude Chappe wrote on electricity in collaboration with other physicists are [Chappe 1789a, 1789b, 1790, 1791, 1792, 1793]. See also [Jacquez 1893, p. 75].

8. *[p. 49]* [Shaffner 1859, p. 27], cf. [Jacquez 1893, p. 6].

9. *[p. 49]* [Chappe 1824, p. 124].

10. *[p. 50]* In a letter dated 1 February 1805, published in the *Journal de Paris*. The letter is reproduced in [Jacquez 1893, pp. 72–73].

11. *[p. 51]* Ignace Chappe worked at the time as tax collector in Mans, specifically for collecting the taxes on salt, which were abolished in 1789. Pierre-Francois also worked as tax collector in Mans, for stamp-duties. René was *Receveur des Domaines du Roi* in Lassay. Abraham was, like Claude, raised for the church. He graduated in April 1789, and was still looking for his first assignment when the revolution began.

12. *[p. 51]* [Chappe 1824, pp. 54–56], [Belloc 1888, p. 64], [Hennig 1906, pp. 27–28].

13. *[p. 51]* Nelson (1758–1805) became Captain in 1778 and Admiral in 1797.

14. *[p. 51]* [Coudreuse 1991, p. 4].

15. *[p. 51]* [Chappe 1824, pp. 123–124].

16. *[p. 52]* Chapter One, p. 35.

17. *[p. 53]* The oldest source known to us is [Figuier 1868]. It is reproduced without mention of an origin in [Belloc 1888, p. 69].

18. *[p. 53]* [Jacquez 1893, p. 7–8].

19. *[p. 53]* The parental house in Brûlon still exists at No. 1 of what is now called *Rue Claude Chappe*.

20. *[p. 53]* In his letter to *Journal de Paris* from 1805, reproduced in [Jacquez 1893, pp. 72–73]. See also [Fahie 1884, p. 94], and [Appleyard 1930, p. 265]. It had been known for almost fifty years that it was possible to transmit an electrical signal through a wire (cf. p. 204).

21. *[p. 53]* [Chappe 1824, pp. 234–237].

22. *[p. 55]* The speed of a pendulum can be adjusted over a wide range by changing the position of the weights.

23. *[p. 55]* [Chappe 1824], in the revised edition published by Abraham Chappe in 1840, p. xiv.

24. *[p. 56]* Ibid., p. xvi.

25. *[p. 56]* [Jacquez 1893, pp. 14–15]. [Bertho 1981, p. 10], notes that Chappe's speech was given in an evening session of the Legislative Assembly, which was usually devoted to topics of no immediate political urgency.

26. *[p. 57]* The term *tachygraphe* had been used earlier by Henri Linguet, see p. 204.

27. *[p. 57]* [Chappe 1824, p. 125].

28. *[p. 58]* Ibid., p. 166.

29. *[p. 59]* Ibid., p. 125.

30. *[p. 59]* Also known for proposing the abolishment of the Christian calendar on 5 October 1793, and the adoption of a Revolutionary calendar, taking the founding of the French Republic on 22 September 1792 as year zero. Romme fell from favor in 1795 and committed suicide to escape the guillotine. The new calendar was abandoned at the end of 1805.

31. *[p. 59]* [Jacquez 1893, pp. 29–30].

32. *[p. 59]* [Bertho 1981, p. 16].

33. *[p. 59]* The event is also recalled in the *Mémoires* of Miot de Mélito (i.38), which were published posthumously in 1858. Mélito was a count before the french revolution.

34. *[p. 61]* The formal act of the National Convention from this date states that Chappe is accorded the title of *Ingénieur Thélégraphe*. This slip of the pen returns in many subsequent documents.

35. *[p. 61]* The telegraph was originally considered an exclusively military device, and the Telegraph Administration reported to the Ministry of War. Within five years, however, that changed, and the administration was moved to the Ministry of the Interior.

36. *[p. 62]* Others state that it would have been unlikely that Léon Delauney would risk his career by revealing diplomatic codes or cyphering methods. It is known from letters that Léon's brother, Prosper, was a lifelong friend of Claude's. In the correspondence between the brothers Chappe [Contant 1993], in the year preceding the completion of the first line to Lille, there is frequent reference to the design of the new code for the semaphore telegraph. No reference to Delauney's involvement in this project can be found though.

37. *[p. 62]* A number of these letters appears in [Belloc 1888]. A larger set is reproduced in [Contant 1993].

38. *[p. 63]* Parts of this log were reproduced in [Amis 1968, p. 45 and p. 57]. A message from 18 May 1794, for instance, contained the text of a decree of the National Convention, announcing the withdrawal of five-livre banknotes.

39. *[p. 64]* Abraham Chappe started transmitting the message at 5:45 P.M. and completed it at 7:30 P.M., as noted in [FNARH 1993, p. 24]. This message therefore could not have arrived until at least two hours after the recapture had taken place.

40. *[p. 64]* The modern name is Condé-sur-l'Escault. It is about 11 km (7 miles) northeast of Valenciennes. The message was sent at 3 P.M., and had to be terminated, still incomplete, 30 minutes later. Claude Chappe delivered the message without waiting for a retransmission.

41. *[p. 64]* Landau is about 270 km (170 miles) east of Paris.

42. *[p. 66]* See also Chapter Two, p. 71. Claude Chappe long continued to support Monge's design, though. In a letter to *Le Moniteur Universel* of 10 November 1797 he still described the seven-indicator telegraph as the best possible design.

43. *[p. 66]* [Contant 1993, letter A.N. F 90/1427–1428, B 34].

44. *[p. 66]* [Chappe 1824, p. 200].

45. *[p. 66]* As reproduced in [Jacquez 1893, p. 66], and in [Appleyard 1930, p. 271]. "An VI" was the sixth year of the French revolutionary calendar (1798). Ventôse was the sixth month, from 19 February to 20 March, and Prairiàl was the ninth month, from 20 May to 18 June. One of the telegrams is reproduced in Figure 2.8, which is from [Belloc 1888].

46. *[p. 69]* Bréguet and Bétancourt's design used a single semaphore arm that was rotated in 10-degree increments, giving 36 different codes. To distinguish the smaller angles, they used telescopes with the 36 positions engraved into the glass of the eyepiece. To encode messages, Bréguet and Bétancourt assigned a single letter or numeral to each semaphore position, and used a simple spelling method. Clearly, this method was simpler, but also slower than Chappe's. The challenge of Chappe's design lead to a curious exchange of angry letters in the French newspapers between November 1797 and April 1798 by A. M. Eymar, a spokesperson for Bréguet and Bétancourt, and Claude Chappe, which was in part republished as [Chappe 1798]. See also [FNARH 1993, pp. 325–331].

47. *[p. 70]* A newspaper reported that the employees of the Telegraph Administration searched for their missing director for several hours. When his hat was found close to a well in the yard, the well was dredged, and Chappe's body was recovered. It is possible that Chappe had been in the well since the prior evening. Hôtel Villeroy no longer exists. It was located at no. 9, Rue de l'Université in Paris.

48. *[p. 70]* Bulletin of *Les Amis de Paris Central Télégraphe*, No. 20, July 1993, p. 3, wrote that only few newspapers mentioned the existence of this note. The note apparently has not been preserved.

49. *[p. 70]* Quoted in [Belloc 1888, p. 133].

50. *[p. 71]* As reproduced in [Jacquez 1893, pp. 72–73].

51. *[p. 71]* [Chappe 1824, pp. 54–56].

52. *[p. 71]* [Bertho 1981, p. 39 and p. 42].

53. *[p. 72]* *Correspondance de Napoleon I*, XVII, 1808, p. 288. See also Chapter Five, p. 199.

54. *[p. 72]* Ibid., XVIII, p. 416

55. *[p. 72]* [Belloc 1888, p. 140].

56. *[p. 73]* King Louis XVI had been beheaded, and his son Louis XVII had died as a youngster.

57. *[p. 75]* [Massie 1979, pp. 7–8], who also notes that the original transcripts of all telegrams sent on the Paris-Bayonne line between 1823 and 1853 are preserved in the French National Archives under register numbers F90/541–569, and F90/754–776. The data for message traffic after 1847 towards Paris was not included in Massie's study.

58. *[p. 75]* [Bertho 1981, pp. 43–44], [Saint Denis 1979, pp. 2–4], [FNARH 1993, pp. 367–371]. The operators involved in the fraud were tried in 1836, but acquitted on 14 March 1837. Their attorneys successfully argued that their actions had not violated any explicit law.

59. *[p. 77]* The tombstone is formed as a pile of rocks with a replica of the Chappe telegraph on top. The telegraph lost one of its indicators around

1890. The missing indicator was replaced and the tomb restored to its original state in January 1993.

60. *[p. 77]* [FNARH 1991, p. 29].

61. *[p. 78]* In 1990 close to 300 other descendants of the Chappes were alive, as reported in [FNARH 1991, p. 41].

62. *[p. 79]* See also [Field 1994, p. 342], who gives the approximate numbers of people employed by the telegraph administration in 1833.

63. *[p. 79]* [Chappe 1824, p. 199].

64. *[p. 79]* E.g. [Shaffner 1859, p. 34 ff], or [Jacquez 1893, p. 21 ff].

65. *[p. 81]* [Chappe 1824, p. 111].

66. *[p. 81]* [Jacquez 1893, p. 18].

67. *[p. 82]* [Amis 1968, pp. 109–110], also discusses the manuscript and reviews the first codes.

68. *[p. 84]* A system of Dr. J. Guyot was tested around 1840 on a small number of lines, apparently with some success, but it was never extended to the whole network. Guyot's experiment is referred to, among others, in a letter sent by Abraham Chappe to the telegraph administration in 1844.

69. *[p. 85]* The letter is reproduced in [Perardel 1979]. See also [Contant 1993, pp. 12–13], who adds that a second copy of this *vocabulaire* was delivered to Florent Guyot in Lille.

70. *[p. 85]* The original letter is preserved in the Musée de Poste of Nantes.

71. *[p. 86]* A fragment of the first page is reproduced in [Belloc 1888, p. 71].

72. *[p. 88]* [Jacquez 1893, p. 27].

73. *[p. 89]* Chapter Four, p. 266.

74. *[p. 89]* [Macdonald 1819].

75. *[p. 89]* [Amis 1968, pp. 53–54]. According to the logs, during the first experiments in 1794 the time required per signal was often as high as 60 seconds.

76. *[p. 89]* [Belloc 1888, p. 202], [Appleyard 1930, p. 274].

77. *[p. 89]* [Shaffner 1859].

78. *[p. 90]* [Vasseur 1981, p. 4].

79. *[p. 90]* The statistics for all message traffic between Bayonne and Paris from January 1843 until January 1845 can be found in [FNARH 1993, p. 140]. A total of 925 messages was sent in this two year period. Of these, 508 messages, or 55%, arrived on the first day. Another 263 (28%), arrived the second day; 99 (10%) on the third day, and the remaining 55 messages arrived later still. The really long delays were all incurred in winter months.

80. *[p. 90]* [Huth 1796]. See also [Aschoff 1984, p. 209].

81. *[p. 90]* According to [Aschoff 1984], this system was described in a work by Athanasius Kircher, titled *Phonurgia Nova*, which was published by Rudolph Dreher in Kempten in 1673.

82. *[p. 91]* [Herbarth 1978, Fig. 15, p. 25].

83. *[p. 91]* [Bertho 1981, pp. 45–46].

84. *[p. 91]* Ibid., p. 51.

85. *[p. 91]* [Chappe 1824, pp. 12–13].

86. *[p. 92]* [Bertho 1981, pp. 67–68].

87. *[p. 93]* [Belloc 1888, p. 197].

88. *[p. 93]* [Bertho 1981, p. 75]. A copy of the Foy-Bréguet telegraph can be seen in the Historical Collection of the French Telecommunications Museum in Pleumeur Bodou, Bretagne.

Chapter Three, Abraham N. Edelcrantz

1. *[p. 97]* Åbo is located on the west coast of Finland, which was part of Sweden until 1809. The Finnish name of the city is Turku. Finland is officially bilingual.

2. *[p. 98]* This Academy was created by King Gustav III, inspired by the French Academy. It dealt with literature, not the sciences. Edelcrantz would later (1797) also receive an appointment to the Swedish Academy of Sciences.

3. *[p. 98]* "Edel" means "noble." "Crantz" means "wreath."

4. *[p. 98]* The current Opera House stands on the same spot, but dates from 1898. The old Opera House building was demolished in 1892 to make room for the current, larger, one.

5. *[p. 99]* Verdi's opera *A Masked Ball* (1859) is based on this assassination.

6. *[p. 100]* [Ehrenström 1883, Vol. 2, p. 263].

7. *[p. 101]* Chapter Four, p. 141.

8. *[p. 103]* Chapter Four, p. 143.

9. *[p. 107]* King Karl XIII is Gustaf IV Adolph's uncle, and regent, Count Carl, from earlier in the story. Carl's regency ended in 1796. He succeeded Gustaf IV Adolph as king in 1809 when Sweden had lost Filand to Russia. Count Carl then changed his name to King Karl XIII. Gustaf IV Adolph, blamed for the defeat, was exiled that same year.

10. *[p. 108]* Chapter Five, p. 180.

11. *[p. 109]* Chapter Five, p. 188.

12. *[p. 110]* [Edgeworth 1894, pp. 112–113].

13. *[p. 112]* Ibid., p. 114.

14. *[p. 116]* [Risberg 1938, p. 57].

15. *[p. 116]* Ibid., p. 62. See also the penal code from 1809, reproduced in Appendix C, see p. 234.

16. *[p. 116]* Ibid., p. 62.

17. *[p. 117]* It is said that Edelcrantz himself had proposed to use the signal for the letter E in the logo, but did not receive the approval of the king.

18. *[p. 117]* Krigskollegium, *Krigsförvaltningen 1808–09 GIb Huvudboksverifikationer*, Vol. XXXIV–XXXV.

19. *[p. 119]* [Gierow 1964, p. 274].

20. *[p. 120]* Krigskollegium, *Krigsförvaltningen 1808–09 GIb Huvudboksverifikationer*, Vol.XXXIV–XXXV.

21. *[p. 120]* Chapter Five, p. 195.

22. *[p. 120]* Chapter Five, p. 205.

23. *[p. 120]* Chapter Two, p. 94.

24. *[p. 120]* Chapter Five, p. 188.

25. *[p. 126]* The only other country where they remained in service this long in parallel with the electrical systems, was Australia (cf. p. 200). An optical telegraph line in Curacao remained in operation until 1910 (p. 199), but electrical telegraphs had not been installed there before.

26. *[p. 127]* The telegraph house is located at Strindbergsvägen, no. 6.

Chapter Four, A Treatise on Telegraphs

All notes to this chapter are from Edelcrantz's original treatise. As in the main text of this chapter, our annotations are set in a distinct font *[like this]*. Unless otherwise noted, page references within annotations refer to the pages of the book you are holding now.

1. *[p. 132]* Perseus of Macedonia, according to a tale by Polybius *[p. 29]*, is said to have received reports from all his provinces by means of such fires. It is mentioned in the play *Agamemnon*, by Aeschylus *[pp. 16–17]*, that Clytemnestra received the news of the destruction of Troy by means of fires lit on Ida, Lemnos, Athos, Macistus, Messapius, Cythaeron, Aegiplanetus, and Arachnae at Argos. Hannibal, according to a tale by Plinius *[p. 21]*, is said to have arranged for such fires in Africa and Spain at a distance from each other of 67,000 Roman feet, or about two *[Swedish]* miles.

2. *[p. 132]* Torch signals, *phryckti*, are also mentioned by Homer and Pausanius, as being used by Palamedes and Sinon during the Trojan war *[p. 18]*. One can tell how prevalent the Greeks' use of fire signals was, for instance, by the number of words there were to describe fires in the Greek language. The name Φάρος *[Pharos, dating from 285 B.C.]*, for a lighthouse near Alexandria, was a general term for a beacon, πυρσὸς *[pyrsos]* was used for smaller fires, Φρυκτὸς *[phrycktos]* fire used for signals, Φρυκτωρὸς *[phrycktoros]* and πυρσευτὴς *[pyrseutis]* for the person using a fire for sending messages, Φρυκτωρια *[phrycktoria]* for the act of signaling with fires, πυρσηργιον *[pyrsergion]* and Φρυκτώριον *[phrycktorion]* for the location of the fire, Φρυκτωρέω *[phrycktoreo, cf. p. 22]* and πυρσέυω *[pyrseuo]* as verbs, to watch for fire messages or to send them, πυρσεια *[pyrseia]* for the message itself.

3. *[p. 132]* Noteworthy, more for its peculiarity than for its utility, is an invention of Aeneas, a strategist of the old Greeks, which Polybius described in the following way *[p. 24–26]*. Several people are placed at regular distances in the direction in which the messages are to be sent. They each have an equally sized kettle, containing the same amount of water. There is an opening near the bottom of each kettle, identical in size. A slice of cork floats in the water, into which a perpendicular rod is fastened, divided into several equidistant parts. At each division on the rod a slip is fastened containing a previously defined message, report, command, etc. All people also have a torch and when the first person raises his torch he also removes the plug from his kettle; the second person does the same and so on down the line. When the water in the first kettle has sunk so far that the division on the rod reaches the intended message, the first person lowers his torch and replaces the plug; all people down the line follow suit and can thus determine which message the first person wanted to communicate.

4. *[p. 132]* The Greek war signals were divided into *simbola* and *semeia*; the former were further divided into *phonica*, sounding signals, and *orata* visible signals; audible signals, which included watchwords and passwords, were also called *synthemata*; and visible signals, gestures of hands, weapons, and so on, were called *parasynthemata*. *Semeia* is said to have consisted of flags, banners, etc. See Halle, *Fortges. Magie*, Vol. 7, p. 338.

5. *[p. 132]* Telegraph comes from the word τελε *[tele, cf. p. x]*, distant, and γραφω *[grapho]*, writer. The combination is new, but it does not quite convey the idea, since the usefulness of this invention is more in its speed than in the distance covered. I do not know who used the word first in this sense; unless it was Paulian whose *Dictionaire de Physique* includes a description of the term *Telegraph*.

6. *[p. 133]* Therefore, according to the Greek alphabet, which contained 24 letters, one torch on either side, for instance, indicated α, and five torches on one side and four on the other indicated the letter ω.

7. *[p. 133]* The only description of this method is *Epist. ad Arnold Bostium* by Trithemius, which is part of *Thaumaturgus Physicus*, Lib. I, by V. Schottus. See also Vallin *Disput. de arte Thrithemiana scribendi per ignem. [According to Wilkins (1641), Ch. XV, Trithemius's book was branded "diabolical magic" by the church, and burned.]*

8. *[p. 133]* Some even older experiments are mentioned in *Delic. Mathem. P. VI quaest. 15* by Dan. Scheventerius *[published in Nürnberg, in 1636]* and in *Magia Natur.*, Vol. XVII, Cap 1, by J. B. Porta *[1545–1615]*, but in such a summary and unclear manner that they cannot be considered. See *Magia Univers. Pars I, Vol. VIII, prooem* by C. Schottus *[published in Herbipoli, in 1657; cf. p. 40]*.

9. *[p. 133]* In his *Ars magna lucis & umbrae*, where this art is called *Cryptologia Catoprica*.

10. *[p. 133]* *Mag. Natur.*, Vol. XVII, Cap. 17.

11. *[p. 133]* *Philos. Occulta*, Vol. I, See Porta I.c.

12. *[p. 133]* *Technica Curiosa*, Vol. VII, Cap. 6.

13. *[p. 133]* In a dissertation titled *Verborgene, Geheime Künste*, by Kessler *[Hidden, Secret Arts, published in Oppenheim, in 1616]*.

14. *[p. 133]* See *Gentleman's Magazine [p. 219]* and *Journal für Fabrik, Manufactur und Handlung [Journal for Production, Manufacturing and Trade]*, Dec. 1794.

15. *[p. 134]* See his *Experiences sur la propagation du son dans des tuyaux prolongés [Experiments on the propagation of sound through long tubes]*.

16. *[p. 134]* Diodorus Siculus mentioned that even the Persians transmitted messages by shouting over a distance that corresponded to a thirty-day journey *[p. 20]*.

17. *[p. 134]* In *Recreations Physics et Mathematiques*, see *Fortgesetzte Magie [Advanced Magic]*, Vol. 7, p. 435, by Halle. I have not been able to find the place in the German translation. The newspapers report that similar experiments were made in England using transparent letters, which were illuminated by lights, using reflection and telescopes, in the same way as described by Argand.

18. *[p. 134]* In the author's opinion, only 200 signals could be produced in this way. However, if we suppose that each individual section and the distance between them can be properly distinguished, the possible number of signals increases. Because, if all possible variations of a series of objects can be expressed by $a, b, c, ...$, the total number of possible variations of these objects is equal to the product of these numbers $a.b.c$, and consequently if $a = b = c = \ldots$ and the number of objects is n, the number of variations becomes a^n and thus in this case, where $a = 2$ and $n = 10$, the number of signals is $2^{10} = 1{,}024$. On the other hand, in order to avoid the similarity of several signals, if one supposes that one row, for instance the uppermost, must always be visible so that the location of the others can be determined, the number will be at least 512.

19. *[p. 134]* Prof. Bockmann *[often spelled Boeckmann, cf. p. 205]* from Carlsruhe suggests that Mr. Chappe has borrowed his entire invention from Linguet and gives two reasons for this. First, according to a secret description (it is not known where or how Mr. Bockmann found it) Linguet's invention looked like a measuring rod and was similar to the French telegraph. Second, since Linguet was arrested at the end of 1793 and went to the guillotine in June 1794, while the first announcement of Mr. Chappe's telegraph was made in August of that same year. Apart from the moral issue, the decision if this could be true must be left to the reader. Those who are familiar with Linguet's writing, however, have noted his scanty knowledge of the subject matter, evidenced by several of his writings, such as his *Canaux Navigables*. It is also improbable that he would not have claimed the honor of his invention publicly during the time after his first arrest.

20. *[p. 134]* I have not had a chance to see this work, but Mr. Bockmann described it in his *Telegraphy*. According to him, with this method 8,000 cannon-shots or as many rockets are needed to send 22 words over a distance of 50 *[German]* miles.

21. *[p. 135]* The Greek method required at least ten torches.

22. *[p. 135]* See *Journal der Manufactur und Handlung* Dec. 1794. It is said that Mr. Burja tried another telegraphic device and found it fairly useful, when two persons known to each other happened to be arrested at the same time, and also happened to be placed in adjacent rooms. It consists of their alternatively scratching and knocking on the wall dividing their cells, thereby devising an alphabet which gave them the possibility of communicating with each other. See *Fortgesetzte Magie*, Vol. 7, p. 322, by Halle, where I found this anecdote.

23. *[p. 135]* See the previously mentioned *Journal der Manufactur* and the *Berlinska Tidningen [Berlin News]* of 3 March 1795, according to which experiments were conducted with a transportable field telegraph of Mr. Achard's design [cf. p. 184] between Spandau and Berlin, roughly one German mile apart. This machine could be dismantled by eight carpenters in 17 minutes, and placed in a wagon in three more minutes. The wagon could be pulled by two horses. According to the second newspaper, messages could be encoded not just with three but also with five signal elements, whereby not only the alphabet but also 23,750 words, phrases, and sentences could be produced. I wish that a more detailed description of this invention were published, since it is one of the few that has been tested on a larger scale and which combined a method for encoding messages with a mechanical means of transmitting them. The latter is the most difficult part to realize, since more signals are needed than for a normal alphabet.

24. *[p. 135]* See Figure 2. Such a board is divided into two parts, painted in different colors which are easily distinguished from each other. By rotating a board we obtain four clearly distinct positions, and six boards suffice to make the 24 signals of the alphabet. If necessary, by using more boards, arbitrarily many signals can be represented.

25. *[p. 135]* See Figure 3. These boards are either white with red figures or red with white figures. The number of combinations is the same as before.

26. *[p. 135]* If the field in Figure 4 is assumed to be black, and the figure cut out or transparent, it is easy to understand this method as a variation of the ones above.

27. *[p. 135]* Cutout dark letters, as used by Hooke, or other dark figures whose profiles are visible against the sky or a light, as shown in Figure 5.

28. *[p. 135]* The *Hamburg. Polit. Journal* reports on a method devised by Mr. Pfeninger to signal messages with drums and flags, and Bernouilli's *Kleine Reisen [Small Journeys]*, Vol. 8, mentions a method using five bells. They don't seem to contain anything new though. In general, the use of all audible signals creates many problems, since no instrument has been invented that enhances our ability to hear like the telescope enhances our ability to see. Mr. Von Moulines is said to have published a thesis on telegraphy, but its contents seem to be mostly historical. The newspapers reported that Mr. Wolke in Petersburg *[p. 180]* conducted experiments with a telegraph invented by him, and that similar ones have been conducted in Denmark *[p. 180]*, but no detailed description of these experiments has been published.

29. *[p. 136]* Apart from Linguet, one usually credits the invention to both Amontons and to Hooke *[pp. 34–39,52]*, but there is no real evidence to support this. See *Journal für Fabrik, Manufactur und Handlung* Dec. 1794, p. 487.
It often happens, with regard to new inventions, that one part of the general public finds them useless and another part considers them to be impossible. When it becomes clear that the possibility and the usefulness can no longer be denied, most agree that the whole thing was fairly easy to discover and that they knew about it all along. I have not collected the above historical information with that same purpose in mind. On the contrary, I want to prove that nothing of what was done before diminishes the importance of Mr. Chappe's invention.

30. *[p. 137]* The telegraph in Paris is placed on the Louvre and is shown in Figure 7. According to reports from travelers it is painted in the three French national colors. Below it there is kind of an observatory with windows, or rather walls of glass, all around.

31. *[p. 138]* It is easy to see that the characters in Figure 8 are only a few of the possible positions of this telegraph, also shown in Figure 7. The meaning of these signals can be established as needed and can also be adapted by changing the code. The particular version of the code given in a report on the Paris telegraph, published in Leipzig in 1794, which listed the coding table shown here, is not particularly well-chosen, and probably quite different from the one that is used by Mr. Chappe *[pp. 86, 223]*. It is unlikely that upper and lower-case letters are encoded separately or that all punctuation marks of ordinary writing are encoded in the same way. An example of a report about the conquest of Condé, written in telegraphic style, is shown in Figure 9, taken from Halle's *Advanced Magic*, Vol. 7, Tab. VII.

32. *[p. 138]* According to footnote 18, the number of signals in this case is $4 \times 8 \times 8 = 256$. If the arms are moved in 30 degree instead of 45 degree increments the number would be $6 \times 12 \times 12 = 864$. Therefore, it would be easy to increase the number of signals by reducing the increments when needed, if this didn't reduce the visibility of the signals.

33. *[p. 138]* The conference report given by Mr. Lakanal, as deputy for the Committee of Public Education, in which a telegraph is described as consisting of three frames that resemble Venetian blinds with which one hundred signals could be formed *[p. 57]*, differs considerably from the later reports about this machine, although it may have been similar to Mr. Chappe's first device, before it was improved. Mr. Buschendorff in Leipzig published a fairly detailed description of a telegraph that looks and functions similarly to the French system, under the title *Der Telegraph für Deutschland [The telegraph for Germany]*, in the *Journal der Fabrik und Manuf.* of Dec. 1794. The mechanical design, however, the setting and encoding of signals, he says he could not find out from France, and are his own invention.

34. *[p. 139]* The first important message transmitted to Paris by the French telegraph concerned the conquest of the fortress Condé, situated four French miles from Lille. The telegraph in Lille, 47 *[French]* miles from Paris, transmitted the following dispatch in 20 minutes: "Condé is in the hands of the Republic and its troops have been made prisoners of war" *[p. 64]*. The Convention responded with the following decree: "The fortress will no longer be called Condé, but Nord Libre, and the Northern Army well-deserves praise by its country." This decree was sent by telegraph and within 75 minutes, during the same session, the Convention received the reply that "The decree has arrived and has been sent by special courier to Nord Libre." A messenger from the army, confirming the report of the conquest of the fortress, did not arrive until 20 hours later.

35. *[p. 140]* As early as November 1794, the invention of a telegraph with 1,024 signals was announced, described in §7. See *Inrikes Tidn.* 5 November 1794. See also *Hamburger Correspond.* for November and *Journal der Manufactur und Handlung* for December of the same year. However, I thought I should postpone a report to the general public of my own efforts, in order to offer not only possibilities but also the results of actual large scale experiments.

36. *[p. 142]* See §9.

37. *[p. 144]* This weight consists of a box made from wire or metal which is filled to a greater or lesser degree with stones in proportion to what the action of the wind on the shutters might require.

38. *[p. 144]* This wire runs across a small pulley, attached to the end of *l p* in Figure 16.

39. *[p. 144]* Apart from the fact that the number of signals offered by ten shutters is more than sufficient, I restricted the telegraph to this number for the reason that the combinations and movements of the fingers alone are sufficient to produce all the signals on smaller machines.

40. *[p. 146]* According to what was mentioned earlier, the number of the positions for each shutter is two, with the number of shutters n, the number of combinations is 2^n for all machines of this type. In this case $n = 10$, and therefore $2^n = 1,024$. Were the telegraph to consist of four columns with four shutters each, the number of signals would be $2^{16} = 65,536$. One can see from this that if all the shutters were placed in a single row, the number of signals would not change. It is only for the ease of construction and especially for the ease of expressing the signals by numbers that they have been divided into several columns.

41. *[p. 146]* It becomes apparent that this way of counting would be just as easy with horizontal rows, and similarly, that the counting could begin at any of the other three corners of the grid, and that, as a result, each signal could be expressed by numbers in eight ways according to this principle. For instance, the signal in Figure 19 could be read:

Vertically	Horizontally
170	322
071	622
074	223
470	226

The way of counting that I chose seemed to me the most natural and especially the easiest for the operation of the machine.

42. *[p. 147]* Therefore, to say: *Fienden är slagen [The enemy has been defeated]* one sends 137, 734, 561, 003, 166. And the message 547, 460, 372, 144, 621, 222 means: *Shlicka ob mere folk til hjelp [Send more troops to help]*.

43. *[p. 147]* If one wanted to put together ordinary numbers using all possible permutations of the ten single digits, the number of signals, according to the law of permutation, would be $1 \times 2 + 1 \times 2 \times 3 + 1 \times 2 \times 3 \times 4 + \ldots 1 \times 2 \times 3 \times 4 \times 5 \times 6 \times 7 \times 8 \times 9 \times 10 = 4,037,912$. All such signals, however, would become subject to much uncertainty, since it would then be necessary to observe not only which shutters are visible, but also in which order they were displayed.

44. *[p. 148]* Thus the number 900,000 is encoded as 400, 236, 631.

45. *[p. 148]* There are certain common words in every category. War on land, war at sea, ministerial letters, business and private correspondence of all kinds have their own jargon, which will be studied when such a table is constructed.

46. *[p. 148]* For the same reason, everything transmitted by the telegraph should be written as briefly as possible and all abbreviations which can be understood should be used.

47. *[p. 150]* If this number is not equal to one square, the next lower suitable number should be used. I use the code table here as an example for the telegraph described in §6, whose signals number 16.

48. *[p. 151]* Thus, if the key is *Svensk*, the code signal 112, 456 means that the edge e should be at the top and the word *Svensk* be placed over 456. The code signal 325, 670 means that the edge l on the reverse should be at the top and the key corresponds to 670, and so on.

49. *[p. 152]* Some of the words and syllables, however, may be similar.

50. *[p. 154]* When the visibility is good, repetition between two adjacent stations can be eliminated, increasing the speed somewhat. However, the assurance of an accurate reception of the signals is lost.

51. *[p. 155]* Their meaning can be understood without much explanation. If a correspondent transmits too quickly or too slowly, the former is corrected with 770, and the latter with 077 *[a rate and flow control method]*. If you want to ask him to wait, for some reason, 525 is used; to repeat 707. If his telegraph is not working, 222 is used to advise him. A change in code is indicated with 727. When fog or darkness or anything else impedes vision, 757 is transmitted, etc.

52. *[p. 155]* One of sixteen pages, eight encoded with shutter A, and eight without.

53. *[p. 158]* For distances larger than 18–20,000 feet.

54. *[p. 164]* I experienced this several times at Grisslehamn where, close to sea level, I could not see the telegraph at Signilsskär at all, or could hardly see it, while those who were at the observatory in Grisslehamn, which is about 300 feet above sea level, could see it perfectly well.

55. *[p. 164]* The effect of these phenomena, which generally occur close to large lakes, has been described by Mr. Wetterling, Swedish Academy of Sciences, *Nya Handlingar [New Proceedings]*, 1788, p. 3.

56. *[p. 164]* It is probably a physical truth that the increased impression of greater brightness makes an object more visible, but when it comes to several objects that need to be separated from each other and to a clear view of several parts of a compound object, that is generally not the case. That is when (without regard to the various colors) contrast, or the negative impressions of light, compared to the positive, contribute most to clarity. If all bodies in nature were white, and equally illuminated, on a clear day one would not be able to see a thing.

57. *[p. 164]* Lambert studied several colors in order to determine their specific brightness. The following table shows the results when the amount of perpendicular light equals 1.

Regal paper painted white	0.4230
A book of the whitest paper	0.4102
A single sheet on a black background	0.1538
Paper painted with red lead	0.2932
Paper painted with juice from bacc. rhamni	0.2620
Paper painted with Spanish green	0.1149

58. *[p. 164]* Although white paint reflects most light, and this is correct on optical principles, it happens sometimes that other colors, such as red, reddish yellow, etc., make a stronger impression on the eye, and as a result under certain circumstances they are more quickly discerned among several objects, even though they are less bright than white. The limits of this treatise do not permit explaining the reason for this experience, nor the instrument which measures the relative effect of colors, which is not constant for all persons or all occasions.

59. *[p. 165]* If the sun at an angle of 60 degrees illuminates a piece of paper painted with lead white, placed perpendicular to its rays, the average of the brightness of the air compared to that of the paper is 1:2.538 or 2:5. Lambert, *Photometr.*, §915.

60. *[p. 165]* The amount of light that hits an object is reduced by its angle of incidence, but the brightness of an object, or the amount of the light that is reflected is reduced even more. Bouguer's experiments have shown that the brightness of white paper at 45 degrees inclination to the light is half, and at 30 degrees only one third of the brightness at 90 degrees. *Traité d'Optique*, p. 165. In these cases the brightness is almost the same ratio as the angle, but this law does not hold for all inclinations.

61. *[p. 165]* Lambert, *Photometr.*, §930.

62. *[p. 165]* The most suitable method for this purpose would be to cover them with fabric or to give them a surface similar to the cloth wallpaper that used to be in vogue.

63. *[p. 165]* More about this can be found in Jurin's essay on distinct and indistinct vision. We must add, to Jurin's efforts to determine the necessary distance between two black objects on a white field in order to make them clearly distinguishable, that the distance between white objects on a dark field must be greater, since it is generally the lighter of two surfaces that expands its edge at the expense of the darker.

64. *[p. 166]* This must seem strange when you know that the diameter of the shutter is eight to ten times greater than that of the grid, but one has to take into consideration, and experience shows, that to the same degree that objects near the limit of where their size, expressed by the visual angle, cannot clearly be discerned by the eye, their proportions become equally difficult to compare. This applies both to very small and to very large objects. The relation between the lengths of 1, 2, and 4 ells is easy for the eye to discern, while the relation between 1, 2, and 4 tenths of a line at the same distance is difficult to determine, even though the objects are still visible. In addition, the movement of the air can increase the diameter of a smaller object and reduce that of a larger object being compared to it.

65. *[p. 166]* *Hist. de l'Academie de Paris*, p. 200. Jurin did see a fine silver thread and a piece of silk on a white paper, the first at an angle of 3½ and the second at an angle of 2½ sec. It seems that the first would be visible at a greater distance on a black background.

66. *[p. 166]* There are doubts about the smallest possible visual angle at which opaque objects become visible and the differences in opinion in this matter have sometimes been based on incorrect or at least inexact ideas. First of all, it does not seem right to measure the absolute size of an object's surface with a visual angle that does not express more than the diameter or one of the dimensions of the surface. The size should rather be based on the visible area, which must be determined from several dimensions or several different visual angles, except for circular objects. Second, for the same reason it is not right to say absolutely that an object becomes visible if the visual angle is increased sufficiently, because if its one dimension is fairly small, no matter how much the visual angle to its length is increased, if the visual angle to its width is not increased the object will remain invisible. Thirdly, neither is the absolute size, nor the visible area sufficient by themselves to make an object visible, since a certain light intensity is also required. Therefore, even though opaque objects are not visible at a visual angle of less than 30 seconds, one can see stars whose visual angle is less than one second.

The impression on the optic nerves, the strength of which makes an object visible, might perhaps be more correctly measured by the product of the amount of light with the visible area of the surface.

As far as the apparent size of an object is concerned, it must, except for the actual visible area as expressed by the dimensions of the visual angles, depend on so many other circumstances, such as the condition of the eye and its nerves, habit, prejudice, and so on, some of which cannot be calculated mathematically, that its determination is difficult.

67. *[p. 167]* The clarity in seeing the telegraph depends, as mentioned earlier, on the difference in brightness between the shutters and the background. Since a greater magnification cannot make the former noticeably darker, but can make the latter much less clear, the clarity will be reduced although the visual angle is increased.

68. *[p. 167]* A larger magnification than 60 to 70× would be necessary here, but 30 to 40× is sufficient most of the time, since clarity and light are generally more important than a greater magnification.

69. *[p. 167] Encyclopaedia Britannica* Opt. 278.

70. *[p. 168]* Although according to Jurin's experiments this increase in clarity does not amount to more than 1/13, it should not be disparaged, since according to Lambert's calculations a 1/50 to 1/60 difference in the brightness of opaque bodies is noticeable to the eye.

71. *[p. 168]* According to several articles in the papers, those who are employed at the French telegraphs are said to have needed more than a year before acquiring the necessary skills for understanding and operating the movements of this machine.

72. *[p. 169]* The particular advantages of this device are: the speed of movement, one's memory does not need to be burdened with the meaning of each signal, and the signals are never ambiguous during the operation of the machine because they are separated by 000.

73. *[p. 169]* The curvature of the earth at a distance of 6000 ells or 41/2 *[Swedish]* miles is considered to be 33 feet or about 16 ells. Since this increases with the square of the distance, it would be 1031/8 ells at about 11 *[Swedish]* miles. According to Lambert's table on the effects of refraction in his *Proprietés remarquables de la route de la lumière par les airs*, p. 87, horizontal objects should show 15 ells higher at a distance of 15,110 fathoms (about 21/2 *[Swedish]* miles). If one subtracts this quantity from 1031/8 ells, 881/8 remains for the actual curvature. The difference between this and the height of the telegraph, 100 ells or 117/8, is sufficient for making the grid visible at the horizon from the ground at a distance of 21/2 *[Swedish]* miles. Thus, if another telegraph is erected at the same distance and of the same height at the other side, they should be able to see each other at a distance of 5 *[Swedish]* miles.

74. *[p. 169]* The color of the air itself contributes somewhat to obscuring opaque objects that are being viewed through it, but this effect is insignificant at the distances in question. The mountain Chimborazu in Peru is said to be visible to the naked eye through the gigantic mass of air from a distance of 45 French miles. Bouguer, *Traite d'Optique*, p. 363.

75. *[p. 169]* According to articles in recent papers, in London, where the air is almost always filled with coal smoke, less than 25 days a year are clear enough for this purpose, but it seems that the telegraphs there, as well as the French, are not visible against the sky, without which great difficulties with their use must arise.

76. *[p. 169]* Even this distance must be reduced by one-half or one-third in the vicinity of large rivers, which are always surrounded by smoke and vapors. In general the French stations are supposed to be situated 2 to 2 1/2 French miles apart, but the first one outside Paris at Montmartre is no further than 1/2 French mile from that city.

77. *[p. 169]* In my opinion it is not suitable to allow this room to be almost completely surrounded by windows as in Paris.

78. *[p. 170]* This time could be reduced if greater certainty in the reading and composition were not more important than a speed increase of a few seconds.

79. *[p. 170]* Therefore, if another telegraphic device were, for instance, to use an average of one station per message, each signal expressing only one letter and each signal needing 20 seconds, its speed would relate to the speed of the device described here as $(1 \times 1)/2 : (2 \times 2)/1$ or as $1 : 8$.

The speed of the telegraph in relationship to the distance is generally so great that the speed of composing the signals would seem to be insignificant, but it is also quite valuable, especially at distant intermediate stations, where changes in the air often interfere with the operation of the machine and sometimes only 30 minutes can be used at a time.

80. *[p. 170]* If there were 50 stations between Stockholm and Petersburg and 25 between Stockholm and Helsingborg, a message consisting of 50 signals would arrive at the former in 16 2/3 minutes and at the latter in 12 1/2 minutes *[p. 88]*. The accounts of the speed of the French telegraph vary. According to the initial reports 20 seconds are required for each signal. Some papers state that a dispatch between Lille and Paris requires 30 minutes, while others say several hours. The difference is probably mostly due to the varying lengths of the dispatches, but circumstances at the stations might cause a dispatch to be stopped somewhere on the way, until the weather or other factors allow it to be send on.

81. *[p. 170]* This vibration is always present in the eye. This is demonstrated by the following experiment by Jurin, which can hardly be explained in any other way. A narrow white line between two black ones on a white field disappears or combines with them to one black wide line, while such a line alone on a black field is clearly visible.

82. *[p. 170]* See §24.

83. *[p. 170]* It has long been known that on sunny days one cannot see clearly in a mine at a depth of 60 fathoms, while on overcast days one can read a book fairly well at a depth of 100 fathoms. See Swedish Academy of Sciences, Doc. for 1741, p. 114.

84. *[p. 170]* A hygrometer clearly demonstrates that the vapors which float in the air and reduce its transparency, such as haze, etc., are not always caused by humidity. Saussure found this fact proven both by his own experience and by affidavits from the inhabitants of the Alps. See his *Voyages aux Alpes* and his *Hygrometrie*, §355. When the air cleared for a while during several days of continuous rain, I have several times clearly seen the telegraph across the Åland Sea from Signilsskär. I experienced the same thing this past summer, which was fairly rainy, in other places as well. The reasons for the special modification of the humidity in the air which causes actual fog and which at other times invisibly resolves itself into rain, do not seem to be discovered as yet.

85. *[p. 170]* Thus, if you form 425, Figure 32, in the normal manner, where *l–l* shows the lights and *m–m* the shutters that are pulled up to form the signal, it is easily noticed that the signal cannot be read as 425, since the shutters are not visible, but it is read as another signal 352, which is formed by the lights. But the signal 352, found in the nighttime column, will give the required syllable just as easily. Furthermore, 425 will be found on the other side as it was formed by the controls and the shutters.

86. *[p. 171]* The major problem is the difficulty of signaling in several directions, since the movements of the shutters do not change anything behind the lights.

87. *[p. 172]* The limits of this treatise do not permit the description of the various experiments with the applications of light for the use of telegraphs at night and their relation to telescopes. To extend this idea to include daytime use I will describe them to the public in the future. I want to mention briefly that during experiments across the Åland Sea the use of light signals was found to be advantageous and certain at a distance of three *[Swedish]* miles, when the size of the flames was one inch, the distance between them seven feet, and the telescope magnified 60×.

88. *[p. 172]* These obstacles and the interruptions that follow occur less frequently than people think, especially at stations located at normal distances. Except for rain or snow and for the warmest part of the summer, it is unusual that a whole day passes without the telegraph being visible, when it is raised above the horizon. Quite the opposite, it has often been in use for weeks on end, and during the experiments performed recently on both sides of the Åland Sea the telegraphs corresponded at a distance of three Swedish miles for nine consecutive days without interruption, except for a few hours of rain. Besides, during three of those days a storm was raging.

89. *[p. 172]* If you suppose the shortest distance to be 1/2 Swedish mile and the greatest to be three Swedish miles, the cost of telegraphs with iron shutters would be approximately 10 to 75 *Riksdaler* and could be constructed in just one day. The cost for the stand and elevating it above the horizon, which will be more in some places than in others, is not included in this calculation. The cost for the necessary telescopes should be small at all stations, since length and image reversal are of no consequence. To see the telegraphs across the Åland Sea I have found 10-foot telescopes with simple lenses to be completely sufficient. These can be bought in Stockholm for 9–10 *Riksdaler*. The installation of the French telegraph to Lille cost 6,000 French *livres* or 1,000 *Riksdaler* per station, and for all 16 of them 96,000 *livres* or 16,000 *Riksdaler*.

90. *[p. 173]* In times of war, when it is often necessary to have rapid communications between several armies or divisions of the same army in several different directions, stations should first of all be planned between these locations. They should be situated on mountains, church towers, or in tall trees, in case there are woods in the direction that would be difficult to penetrate. When the stations are constructed, they should be arranged in such a manner that a telegraph is both easily installed and dismantled as the need arises. For these reasons the latter must be portable and specially designed in several pieces that can be put together or taken apart. Such a machine could then easily be transported by one horse or carried by two to three people charged with operating and running the station. In this respect, an army should necessarily have a special small corps or a few people at each regiment trained in this kind of service. When portable machines are used, the distance between the stations should be reduced and should not exceed one *[Swedish]* mile.

91. *[p. 173]* Although storms were mentioned in §35 as a problem in the use of a telegraph, one should not think that they completely prevent it. On the contrary, they are sometimes useful in some respects, since they often interfere with the shimmering of the air, without harming the transparency necessary for the observations.

92. *[p. 173]* It would be especially useful from and between ships that are at anchor. The movement and turns of the ship under sail might cause problems in the installation, control, and observation of the machine.

93. *[p. 173]* Private correspondence could be carried out in the following manner. Two people agree on certain modifications to the code table, known only to them. The letter is written and addressed according to the common code table and is delivered to the post office which communicates with the nearest telegraph station, from which it can be sent openly through all the telegraphs without anyone knowing the contents.

94. *[p. 173]* For this purpose, and where there is no question of several intermediate stations, there is less need for elevating the telegraph above the horizon. The shutters could be white against a black roof, or black against a white wall. The size of the machine would be decided by the distance and the power of the telescope being used.

95. *[p. 173]* The anemometer, attached for that purpose to a telegraph, could also indicate how much weight should be added to or removed from the shutters in order to make them equal to the force of the wind.

96. *[p. 173] Essai sur l'Hygrometrie*, §371.

97. *[p. 173]* See the description of this instrument in *Observations sur la Physique et sur l'Hist. Natur.*, by Rozier, 1791, p. 199.

98. *[p. 174]* Such a communications instrument, which could be fairly portable, should include a code table or dictionary explaining the signals in all languages.

99. *[p. 174]* See *Inrikes Tidningen* and *Hamb. Correspond.* for the year

1794, and *Journal der Manufact. und Handlung* for December of the same year. On 1 November 1794, which was the king's birthday, the telegraph transmitted the following quatrain:

This greeting from the Swedish nation
That loves and honors their King
Today to His Heart will bring
A blessing to this new creation

100. *[p. 174]* Several foreigners, among them Englishmen *[pp. 169, 191]*, have also witnessed these experiments.

101. *[p. 174]* During all these experiments I have been supported with both friendship and expertise by Mr. Öfverbom, first engineer at the Royal Office of Surveys.

102. *[p. 174]* The distance from Stockholm to Drottningholm is 1 *[Swedish]* mile; to Fredricsborg, with an intermediate station which can often be omitted, 21/2 *[Swedish]* miles; to Carlberg 1/4 *[Swedish]* miles; to Vaxholm from Fredricsborg 1/2 *[Swedish]* miles.

103. *[p. 174]* This station is probably the furthest that has been tried anywhere. 31/4 Swedish miles or 117,000 feet is 42/3 German, 81/8 French and 23 English miles. *[The distance is really 114,000 feet, 4.56 German, 8.14 French, or 21.58 English miles.]*

104. *[p. 174]* The distance between Stockholm and Grisslehamn is 111/8 *[Swedish]* miles and from there to Åbo another 303/4 *[Swedish]* miles, a total of 417/8 *[Swedish]* miles. This route could be shortened by the telegraphs, although because of the location of the hills, they would not always be placed in a straight line. In a study ordered by the king, Mr. Öfverbom found that the stations between Fredricsborg and Grisslehamn would be most suitably placed at

Nyboda Islet	at	11/4	*[Swedish]* miles
Furusund		23/4	miles
Arholma Beacon		21/2	miles, from where the distance to
Grisslehamn	is	23/4	miles.

105. *[p. 175]* See §6 and §42.

106. *[p. 177]* As an example of the many ways one can use abbreviations, I only want to mention that instead of the date at the beginning of a letter, only one signal can be used, where 000 to 036 indicate the days in January, 040 to 074 the days in February, 100 to 136 the month of March, etc. Thus 571 at the beginning of a letter indicates December 26, etc.

107. *[p. 177]* There are soldiers at regiments stationed in Stockholm, who are specially chosen and trained for this purpose, and who constitute a kind of separate telegraphic company.

108. *[p. 177]* One remark, which in its proper place was passed over, must be added here. Frequently when entering a telegraphic observatory from the outside, especially on a bright day, it is difficult to see through the telescopes. This improves after a couple of minutes, however. The reason is not always that the air has become clearer, but that the eye has adapted and become more adjusted to receiving impressions from less light. Therefore, one should not be too hasty in judging the possibilities of seeing or not seeing the movements of the telegraph.

Chapter Five, Other Countries

1. *[p. 179]* Chapter Four, footnote 29, p. 260.
2. *[p. 179]* Appendix A, p. 219
3. *[p. 180]* Chapter Five, p. 185, p. 196, and p. 201, respectively.
4. *[p. 180]* [Ellefsen 1994].
5. *[p. 181]* [Poulsen 1994].
6. *[p. 182]* [Elo 1994].
7. *[p. 182]* [Bergstrasser 1785].
8. *[p. 182]* See also Chapter One, p. 42.
9. *[p. 184]* E.g., [Bockmann 1794], [Edelcrantz 1796], and [Chappe 1824].
10. *[p. 185]* [Herbarth 1978, pp. 41–42].
11. *[p. 185]* Chapter Five, p. 196.
12. *[p. 186]* Two of the stations still exist, and can be visited today. They are located in Köln-Flittard and in Söven.
13. *[p. 186]* In France the private operation of a telegraph line had been forbidden by the state in 1837, see Chapter Two, p. 91.
14. *[p. 188]* O'Etzel had studied and experimented with electro-magnetic telegraphy since 1837.
15. *[p. 188]* See also Chapter Three, p. 109.
16. *[p. 189]* [Holmes 1983, p. 30].
17. *[p. 189]* The letter was reprinted in London in 1797, and included in the *Transactions of the Royal Irish Academy*, published in Dublin that year.
18. *[p. 189]* [Woods 1965, p. 15].
19. *[p. 190]* He did not, however, mention Edelcrantz's earlier work.
20. *[p. 191]* See Chapter Four §43–44, and footnote 100, p. 269.
21. *[p. 192]* [Macdonald 1819].
22. *[p. 193]* Chapter One, p. 13.
23. *[p. 193]* Quoted in [Appleyard 1930, pp. 313–314].
24. *[p. 194]* Quoted in [Holmes 1983].
25. *[p. 196]* Chapter Five, p. 185.
26. *[p. 196]* Chapter Four, footnote 75, p. 266.
27. *[p. 197]* As reproduced in [Appleyard 1930, p. 297].
28. *[p. 197]* [Romburgh 1991, pp. 149–160], [Brink and Schell 1954, pp. 1–15].
29. *[p. 199]* [Ringnalda 1902, pp. 1–11], [Staring 1890, pp. 279–234].
30. *[p. 199]* The find is documented in [Haviser 1994].
31. *[p. 199]* [Wilson 1976].
32. *[p. 200]* [Masters 1949,1973].
33. *[p. 201]* Chapter One, p. 11.
34. *[p. 201]* Chapter One, p. 15.
35. *[p. 201]* [Michaelis 1965, p. 14], and [Wilson 1976, p. 210]. See also [Morrison 1921, p. 163 and p. 229].
36. *[p. 201]* [Field 1994, p. 345], [Wilson 1976, p. 211].
37. *[p. 201]* [Wilson 1976, pp. 210, 216–217].
38. *[p. 201]* [Field 1994, pp. 345, 319].
39. *[p. 202]* Chapter Five, p. 196.
40. *[p. 202]* Chapter Five, p. 185.

41. *[p. 202]* [Lewis 1970, 1990, p. 27]. Alexander Field also notes that a line was installed along this route by Christopher Colles, [Field 1994, p. 345].

42. *[p. 202]* [Field 1994, p. 345–346].

43. *[p. 202]* *Scots' Magazine*, Vol. XV, p. 73,

44. *[p. 203]* The Leyden jar dates from 1746.

45. *[p. 203]* [Fahie 1884, pp. 73–77].

46. *[p. 203]* [Hennig 1906, pp. 68–69]. [Fahie 1884, p. 541].

47. *[p. 203]* [Fahie 1884, pp. 61–62].

48. *[p. 204]* [Chappe 1824, pp. 47–48].

49. *[p. 204]* Quoted in [Fahie 1884, pp. 85–86].

50. *[p. 204]* Chapter One, p. 43.

51. *[p. 204]* Chapter One, p. 12.

52. *[p. 204]* Chapter Two, p. 59.

53. *[p. 204]* See also [Belloc 1888, p. 60].

54. *[p. 204]* [Bockmann 1794].

55. *[p. 205]* [Chappe 1824].

56. *[p. 205]* U.S. House of Representatives, *Telegraphs for the United States: Letter from the Secretary of the Treasury Transmitting a Report upon the Subject of a System of Telegraphs for the United States*, 25th Cong., Second Session, 1837, H. Doc. 15. Alexander Field, in [Field 1994, p. 319], notes that the primary proposal being considered was for an optical telegraph system based on Chappe's design. Samuel Morse was one of those opposing this plan, by suggesting the use of electrical telegraphs. See also [Bertho 1981, p. 67].

57. *[p. 206]* In early 1994 the company also changed its name from the acronym A.T.&T., short for American Telephone and Telegraph Company, to *AT&T Corporation*, where the first part no longer signifies an acronym, and is to be written without dots. On 19 June 1994, columnist William Safire wrote a short eulogy on this event in the *New York Times Magazine*, commemorating the disappearance of the word *telegraph* from our vocabulary after a lifespan of 200 years.

Chapter Six, About Invention

1. *[p. 207]* Motto on the title page of [Bockmann 1794].

2. *[p. 207]* *Grolier's Academic American Encyclopedia*, 1992.

3. *[p. 208]* Chapter One, p. 24.

4. *[p. 208]* Chapter One, p. 35.

5. *[p. 208]* In the first article on the optical telegraph, pp. 334–337.

6. *[p. 208]* Polybius, *The Histories*, Book X, 47b.

7. *[p. 208]* [Kessler 1616, p. 3].

8. *[p. 208]* Quoted in [Fahie 1884, p. 14].

9. *[p. 209]* Chapter One, p. 40.

10. *[p. 210]* Chapter One, p. 26.

11. *[p. 210]* Chapter One, p. 27.

12. *[p. 211]* Chapter One, p. 12.

13. *[p. 211]* [Chappe 1824].

14. *[p. 211]* Chapter One, p. 27.

15. *[p. 211]* Chapter One, p. 35.

16. *[p. 211]* Chapter One, p. 38.

17. *[p. 211]* See p. 223, and p. 231, respectively.

18. *[p. 211]* Chapter One, p. 40

19. *[p. 211]* Chapter Four, §11–14.

20. *[p. 211]* Chapter Four, §8.

21. *[p. 213]* The term *monitif* is no longer used in modern French. *Monitio, monitionis* in Latin, however, means the act of warning, advising, admonition. Signal 7H8 was used a preparatory signal for 7H1. Signal 7H1 itself was used to periodically synchronize the clocks on all the telegraph stations, similar to the clock message on the later Berlin-Koblenz line (Chapter Five, p. 188).

22. *[p. 213]* Specifically, in Chapter Four, §15–17.

23. *[p. 213]* Reproduced in Appendix B, p. 223.

24. *[p. 214]* E.g., [Holzmann 1991].

25. *[p. 215]* Chapter Four, footnote 51, p. 263.

26. *[p. 216]* The strategy was first suggested by Stenning in 1976. [Holzmann 1991, p. 90].

27. *[p. 216]* Reproduced in Appendix C, p. 231.

28. *[p. 218]* [Bergstrasser 1784, p. 172]. See also Chapter Five, p. 179.

Appendix B, Chappe's Design

1. *[p. 226]* Vendémiaire (vintage) was the first month of the French revolutionary calendar. It corresponds to 22 September to 21 October on the Gregorian calendar. The reference is to 22 September 1794.

2. *[p. 226]* Nivôse (snow), was the fourth month of the revolutionary calendar, from 21 December to 19 January. 26 Nivôse An III corresponds to 15 January 1795.

3. *[p. 227]* The error signal seems to work as a single backspace.

4. *[p. 227]* The sender and the receiver can make independent mistakes. Clearly, if the sender makes a mistake, the receiver will duplicate it. The sender can then correct it with an error signal. If the sender sees that the receiver makes an independent mistake in passing the signal further down the line, however, it must also correct the receiver, and send the error signal.

5. *[p. 227]* A curious problem remains. How should it be determined by the neighboring stations that the telegraph has been fixed and the signals are to be trusted again?

6. *[p. 227]* There were two types of failure signals; one for failures that did not require the presence of an inspector, and one that did.

Appendix C, Edelcrantz's Design

1. *[p. 240]* From 1838 to 1856, the Swedish Telegraph Institution was part of the Topographical Corps of the military, which was headed by Carl Fredrik Akrell (1779–1868). In 1856 the administration of the optical telegraph was combined with that of the new Electrical Telegraph Institution, which was also headed by Akrell. Akrell was later succeeded as head of that body by J. F. Von Heland.

Bibliography

Amis de l'Histoire des PTT d'Alsace. *Le Télégraphe Aérien en Alsace—de la Révolution au Second Empire* [The optical telegraph in the Elsas, from the revolution to the second empire]. [A collection of articles by various French authors, issued at the opening of the reconstructed optical telegraph in Haut-Barr in France]. Strasbourg, 1968.

Appleyard, Rollo. *Pioneers of Electrical Communication*. London: MacMillan, 1930.

Aschoff, Volker. *Geschichte der Nachrichtentechnik: Beitrage zur Geschichte der Nachrichtentechnik von ihren Anfangen bis zum Ende des 18. Jahrhunderts* [History of communication techniques: a contribution to the history of communication techniques from their start until the end of the eighteenth century]. Berlin and New York: Springer Verlag, 1984.

Babbage, Charles. *Charles Babbage and his Calculating Engines: Selected Writings by Charles Babbage and Others*. Ed. Philip Morrison and Emily Morrison. New York: Dover, reprinted 1961. Orig. 1851.

Bacon, Francis. *De Dignitate et Augmentis Scientiarum* [On the Dignity and Growth of Sciences]. London, 1623.

Bartlett, John. *Bartlett's Familiar Quotations*. Boston: Little Brown and Company, 16th edition 1992. Orig. 1855.

Belloc, Alexis. *La Télégraphie Historique, depuis les temps le plus reculés jusqu'à nos jours* [History of Telegraphy, from the most ancient times until our days]. Paris: Libraire de Firmin-Didot, 1888.

Bentley, Jon L. *More Programming Pearls, Confessions of a Coder*. Reading, Mass.: Addison-Wesley, 1988.

Bergstrasser, J. A. B. *Über sein am 21 Dezember 1784 angekündigtes Problem einer Korrespondenz in ab- und unabsehbaren Weiten der Kriegsvorfälle oder über Synthematographik* [On his on 21 December 1784 announced problem on communication within and beyond the viewing distance of a scene of war, or about synthematography]. 5 Vol. [A copy of the first volume presented by Bergstrasser to

273

King George of England on 12 November 1785 is in the British Museum Library in London.] Hanau, 1785–1788.

Bergstrasser, J. A. B. *Über Signal-, Order und Zielschreiberei in die Ferne mit neuen Angaben und dreizehn Kupfertafeln, oder über Synthematographe und Telegraphe in der Vergleichung, etc.* [On signal, command, and directed writing in the distance, with new additions and thirteen copper imprintings, or on the comparison of synthematographs and telegraphs, etc.]. Frankfurt, 1796.

Bertho, Catherine. *Télégraphs and Téléphones—de Valmy au micro-processeur* [Telegraphs and telephones, from Valmy to the microprocessor]. Paris: Brodard et Taupin, 1981.

Bockmann, J. L. *Versuch über Telegraphie und Telegraphen, nebst der Beschreibung und Vereinfachung des Franzosischen Telegraphen und der Anzeige Einiger von ihm vorgeschlagenen neuen Methoden* [Treatise on telegraphy and telegraphs, with a description and simplification of the French telegraph and the proposal of some of his own new methods]. Carlsruhe, 1794.

Breasted, J. H. *Ancient Records of Egypt, Historical Documents from the earliest times to the Persian conquest.* 4 Vol. Chicago: University of Chicago Press, 1906–1907. London: Histories and Mysteries of Man, reprint 1988.

Brevost, M.; d'Amont, R. (Eds.), Biography of Claude Chappe. In: *Dictionnaire de Biographie Francaise.* Vol. 18, pp. 431–434. Paris, 1959.

Ten Brink, E. A. B. J.; Schell, C. W. L. *Geschiedenis van de Rijkstelegraaf 1852–1925* [History of the Dutch State Telegraph 1852–1925]. The Hague, Netherlands: PTT, 1954.

Caesar, Julius. *Bellum Gallicum, The Conquest of Gaul.* Transl. S. A. Handford. London: Penguin Classics, 1951. Orig. 52 B.C..

Chappe, Claude. "Lettre à M. de la Métherie sur une appareil propre à distinguer les deux espèces d'électrisation" [Letter to Mr. de la Métherie on an apparatus for distinguishing the two types of electricity]. *Journal de Physique*, T. 34, 1789.

Chappe, Claude. "Lettre à M. de la Métherie sur un électromètre" [Letter to Mr. de la Métherie on an electrometer]. *Journal de Physique*, T. 34, 1789.

Chappe, Claude; Sylvestre. "Lettre de Sylvestre et Claude Chappe à M. de Fourcroy. Description d'un appareil pour la décomposition de l'eau par l'électricité' [Letter of Sylvestre and Claude Chappe to Mr. de Fourcroy. Description of an apparatus for the decomposition of water by electricity]. *Annales de Chimie*, T. 6, 1790.

Chappe, Claude. "Découverte d'un tissu transparante composé uniquement de la matière soyeuse du ver-à-soie" [Discovery of a transparent tissue, composed uniquely of silk from silk-worms]. *Annales de Chimie*, T. 11, 1791.

Chappe, Claude. "Exposition des principes d'ou d'écoule la propriété qu'ont les points pour recevoir et émettre à de grandes distances la matière électrique" [Explanation of the principles on which is based the property of points for receiving and emitting electrical matter over great distances]. *Journal de Physique*, T. 40, 1792.

Chappe, Claude; Robbilard; Sylvestre. "Répétition des experiences de Galvani et de Volta" [A repetition of the experiments of Galvani and Volta]. *Bulletin des Sciences de la Société Philomathique*, Paris, March 1793.

Chappe, Claude. *Lettres sur le nouveau télégraphe* [Letters on the new telegraph]. [A collection of three letters, two by A. M. Eymar advancing a new telegraph design by Breguet and Bétancourt, and one response by Claude Chappe. The letters originally appeared in several journals, including *Le Moniteur* and *Republicain*.] Paris, 1798.

Chappe, Ignace; Chappe, Abraham. *Histoire de la télégraphie* [History of telegraphy]. Paris: L'Imprimerie de Crapelet (first edition, 1824). Mans: C. Richelet (second edition, 1840, with a new preface by Abraham Chappe).

Cherry, Colin. "On Communication before the days of radio." *Proc. of the IRE*, Vol. 50, pp. 1143–1145, May 1962.

Contant, Gérard. "Claude Chappe et le Télégraphe Optique" [Claude Chappe and the Optical Telegraph]. In: *Claude Chappe et Ménilmontant, Les débuts du télégraphe optique* [Claude Chappe and Ménilmontant, the beginnings of the optical telegraph]. Association d'Histoire et d'Archéologie du XXe Arrt., pp 5–20. Paris, Oct. 1993.

Contant, Gérard. *Correspondance des Frères Chappe, 1792–1798*. Paris: France Telecom, 1993.

Coudreuse, Claude. "La première liaison Chappe entre Brûlon et Parcé" [The first Chappe connection between Brûlon and Parcé]. Proc. Seventh Bi-annual Colloquium on the Optical Telegraph. Brûlon and Le Mans: F.N.A.R.H, 1991.

Cyrus, Allan. *Den Optiska Krigstelegrafien* [Optical telegraphy during the war]. Stockholm: P. A. Norstedt and Sons, 1912.

Demeulenare–Douyère, Christiane. "Un Autre Procédé de Communication à Distance: le Projet de 'Télégraphe Pneumatique' de Dom Gauthey en 1782" [Another method for communicating at a distance: the pneumatic telegraph of Dom Gauthey from 1782]. In: *Claude Chappe et Ménilmontant, Les débuts du télégraphe optique*, pp. 28–31. Paris: Association d'Histoire et d'Archéologie du XXe Arrt., Oct. 1993.

Diodorus Siculus. *Diodorus of Sicily*. Transl. Russel M. Geer. London: W. Heinemann. New York: G. P. Putnam's Sons, 1933–1967. Orig. 1st Cent. B.C.

Dumas, Alexander. *The Count of Monte Christo*. Transl. Lowell Bair. Paris: Bantam Classic, 1956. Orig. 1844.

Dvornik, Francis. *Origins of Intelligence Services: the ancient Near East, Persia, Greece, Rome, Byzantium, the Arab Muslim Empires, the Mongol Empire, China, Muscovy*. New Brunswick, New Jersey: Rutgers University Press, 1974.

Edelcrantz, Abraham N. *Avhandling om Telegrapher, och Försök Til en ny Inrättning däraf* [Treatise on Telegraphs, and experiments with a new construction thereof]. Stockholm: Johan Pehr Lindh, 1796.

Edgeworth, Maria. *The life and letters of Maria Edgeworth*. 2 Vol. Ed. Augustus J. C. Hare. Cambridge: The University Press, 1895.

Edgeworth, Richard L. *A letter to the Right Hon. The Earl of Charlemont on the Tellograph, and on the Defence of Ireland*. Dublin and London, 1797.

Ehrenström, Johan A. *Statsr det Johan Albert Ehrenström's efterlemndae historiska antecknigar* [Historical notes left by Councilman Johan Albert Ehrenström]. Stockholm: S. J. Boëthius, 1883.

Ellefsen, Terje. "To the Memory of Captain Ole Olsen." *Symposium on The*

Optical Telegraph, Stockholm: Telemuseum, 1994.

Encyclopaedia Britannica. First article on the Telegraph. London, Vol. XVIII, pp. 334–337, 1797.

Elo, Maija. "The Finnish Optical Telegraph." *Symposium on The Optical Telegraph*. Stockholm: Telemuseum, 1994.

Fabre, Maurice. *A history of communications*. [Translated from the original French edition.] New York: Hawthorne Books, 1963.

Fahie, John J. *A history of electric telegraphy to the year 1837*. London: E. & F. N. Spon (first edition 1884). New York: Arno Press (reprint 1974).

F.N.A.R.H. *Fédération Nationale des Associations de Personnel des Postes et Télécommunications pour la Recherche Historique* [National Federation of Organizations of PTT Personel for Historical Research]. *La Famille Chappe*. [Special edition issued at the 1991 bicentennial celebration of the first experiment of Chappe in Brûlon]. Nancy, France: F.N.A.R.H., 1991.

F.N.A.R.H. *La Télégraphie Chappe*. [A collection of papers on the Chappe system by twelve French authors]. Nancy, France: Editions de l'Est, 1993.

Feldman, William M. *Rabbinical Mathematics and Astronomy*. New York: Hermon Press, third edition 1978.

Field, Alexander J. *French Optical Telegraphy, 1793-1855: Hardware, Software, Administration*. In: Technology and Culture, April 1994, Vol. 35, No. 2, pp. 315–347, 1994.

Figuier, Louis. Le Télégraphe Aérien, *Les Merveilles de la Science, ou description populaire des inventions modernes* [The marvels of science, or a popular description of modern inventions]. Eds. Frune, Jouvet & Co. Paris, approx. 1868.

Fries, C. *Zur Babylonischen Feuerpost* [On the Babylonian Fire Post]. Klio, Vol. 4, 1904.

Galfano, Georges. *Histoire des Télégraphes et Téléphones dans l'Aude*. Narbonne, France: ARHISCOM [Association de Recherche Historique sur les Techniques de Communications], 1990.

Gerspach, M. Edouard. *Histoire Administrative de la Télégraphie Aérienne en France*. Paris, 1861.

Gierow, K. R. *Abraham Niclas Clewberg–Edelcrantz*, Stockholm: Norstedts, 1964.

Haviser, Jay B. "An archeological investigation at optical telegraph sites on Curacao." *Symposium on The Optical Telegraph*. Stockholm: Telemuseum, 1994.

Hennig, Richard. "Die Alteste Entwickelung der Telegraphie und Telephonie" [The oldest developments of telegraphy and telephony]. *Wissen und Können*, Vol. VIII, band 2. Ed. B. Weinstein. Leipzig: Verlag Johann Ambrosius Barth, 1908.

Hennig, Richard. *Verkehrsgeschwindigkeiten — in ihrer Entwicklung bis zur Gegenwart* [The speed of traffic — in its development until today]. Stuttgart: Ferdinand Enke Verlag, 1936.

Herbarth, Dieter. *Die Entwicklung der Optischen Telegrafie in Preussen* [The development of optical telegraphy in Prussia]. Arbeitsheft 15, Landeskonservator Rheinland, Cologne, Germany: Rheinland–Verlag, 1978.

Herodotus. *The History*. Transl. David Grene. Chicago: University of Chicago Press, 1987. Orig. ca. 440 B.C.

Hodge, F. W. *Handbook of American Indians North of Mexico*. Part 2, Bureau of Ethnology, Bulletin 30. Washington: Smithsonian Institution, 1910.

Holmes, Thomas W. *The semaphore: the story of the Admiralty-to-Portsmouth shutter telegraph and semaphore lines, 1796 to 1847*. Ilfracombe, Devon: Stockwell, 1983.

Holzmann, Gerard J. *Design and validation of computer protocols*. Englewood Cliffs, New Jersey: Prentice Hall, 1991.

Holzmann, Gerard J.; Pehrson, Björn. "The First Data Networks." *Scientific American*. pp. 124–129, Jan. 1994.

Homer. *The Iliad*. Transl. by E. V. Rieu. London: Penguin Classics, 1950. Orig. ca. 700 B.C.

Hooke, Robert. *Philosophical Experiments and Observations of the late Eminent Dr. Robert Hooke*. pp. 142–150. London: Royal Society, 1726. Orig. 1684.

Hubbard, G. *Cooke and Wheatstone and the Invention of the Electric Telegraph*. London: Routledge & Kegan Paul, 1965.

Huth, Johann S. G. *A treatise concerning some acoustic instruments and the use of the speaking tube in telegraphy*. [Also containing a translation into German of J. H. Lambert's book *Sur quelques instrument acoustiques* from 1763.] Berlin, 1796.

Hyman, Anthony. *Charles Babbage, Pioneer of the computer*. Princeton, New Jersey: Princeton University Press, 1982.

Jacquez, Ernest. *Claude Chappe, Notice Biographique*. Paris: Alphonse Picard et Fils, 1893.

Kahn, David. *Codebreakers, the Story of Secret Writing*. New York: Macmillan, 1967.

Keegan, John. *The Price of Admiralty, The Evolution of Naval Warfare*. London: Penguin books, 1988.

Kermabon, A. *Atlas des lignes télégraphiques aériennes construites en France de 1793 à 1852* [Atlas of optical telegraph lines constructed in France between 1793 and 1852]. Ed. M. Jaquez. Paris, 1892.

Kessler, Franz. Conterfeter von Wetzlar, *Unterschiedliche bisshero mehrern Theils Secreta oder Verborgene Geheime Kunste etc.* [Various until now mostly secret and hidden arts etc.]. Oppenheim: Hieronnimo Gallern, 1616.

Knuth, Donald. *The Art of Computer Programming*. Vol. II, Second Edition. Reading, Mass.: Addison-Wesley, 1981.

Koenig, Duane. "Telegraphs and Telegrams in Revolutionary France." *The Scientific Monthly*, pp. 431–437, 1944.

Lavery, Brian. *Nelson's Navy, The Ships, Men and Organisation 1793–1815*. Annapolis, Maryland: Naval Institute Press, 1989.

Lewis, Emanuel R. *Seacoast fortifications of the United States: An introductory history*. Missoula, Montana: Pictorial Histories, reprint 1990. Orig. 1970.

Livius, Titus. *Livy*. 14 Vol. English translation by B. O. Foster, et al. Cambridge,

Harvard University Press, 1982–1988. London: W. Heinemann, 1919–1967. Orig. ca. 10 B.C.

Luckenbill, Daniel D. *Ancient records of Assyria and Babylonia*. New York: Greenwood Press, 1968.

Macdonald, John. *A treatise on Telegraphic Communication, with some considerations on the present state of the Marine code, and of naval signals*. London: T. Egerton, 1808.

Macdonald, John. *A circumstantial and explanatory account of experiments, etc. to which is subjoined an Appendix being an exposé of the present state of telegraphic communication in this country, etc.*. London, 1819.

Mallery, J. "Sign Language among North American Indians." *Bureau of Ethnology Annual Report*, Vol. 1. Washington: GPO, 1879.

Malmgren, E. "Den optiska telegrafen i Furusund" [The optical telegraph in Furusund]. *Daedalus*, [annual]. Stockholm: Swedish National Museum of Science and Technology, 1964.

Marland, E. A. *Early Electrical Communication*. New York: Abelard-Schuman, 1964.

Massie, Jean-Francois. "Le Télégraphe Chappe a Bayonne (1823–1853)" [The Chappe Telegraph at Bayonne (1823–1853)]. Proc. First Bi-annual Colloquium on the Optical Telegraph. Blois, France: F.N.A.R.H., 1979

Masters, W. E. *The semaphore telegraph system of Van Diemen's Land*. Hobart, Australia: Cat & Fiddle Press, reprint 1973. Orig. 1949.

Michaelis, A. R. *From Semaphore to Satellite*. Geneva, Sw.: International Telecommunication Union, 1965.

Miller, James. *Miller's Stranger's Guide-book to the Cities of New York, Brooklyn and adjacent places*. New York: Miller, 1866.

Morrison, Samuel E. *Maritime History of Massachusetts 1783–1860*. Boston: Houghton Mifflin, 1921. NorthEastern University Press, reprint 1979.

Myer, Albert J. *A manual of signals, etc.* New York: D. Van Nostrand, 1868.

Neal, Harry E. *Communication from stone age to space age*. New York: J. Messner, 1974.

Norman, Bruce. *Secret Warfare, The battle of codes and ciphers*. New York: Dorset Press, reprint 1987. Orig. 1973.

Olbricht, P. "Das Postwesen in China unter der Mongolenherrschaft im 13. und 14. Jahrhundert" [The Postal System in China under Mongol Rule in the 13th and 14th Century]. *Göttinger Asiatische Forschungen*. Vol. I. Wiesbaden, Germany, 1954.

Parker, John R. *A treatise upon Telegraphic Science, with some remarks upon the utility of telegraphs, etc.* Boston, Mass., 1835.

Parker, John R. *A treatise upon Telegraphs, embracing observations upon the semaphoric system, with a few remarks upon the utility of the marine telegraph flags*. Boston, Mass., 1842.

Paulian, Aimé Henri. *Dictionnaire de Physique Portatif, contenant les découvertes les plus intéressantes de Descartes & de Newton & les traités de mathématiques nécessaires a ceux qui veulent étudier avec succès la physique moderne* [Portable dictionary of physics, containing the most interesting discoveries of Descartes and Newton, and the mathematics required for those who want to study modern physics]. Several editions. Paris, 1761–1787.

Pausanius. *Description of Greece.* Transl. Arthur R. Shilleto. London: George Bell and Sons, 1886. Transl. W. H. S. Jones. Cambridge, Mass.: Harvard University Press, 1918–1935. Orig. ca. 150 B.C.

Perardel, Claude. "La Télégraphie Aerienne dans le Nord de la France" [The optical telegraph in the north of France]. Proc. First Bi-annual Colloquium on the Optical Telegraph. Blois, France: F.N.A.R.H., 1979.

Plaum, H. G. *Essai sur la Cursus Publicus sous le Haut-Empire Romaine* [Study of the cursus-publicus in the high Roman empire]. Paris: Imprimerie Nationale, 1950.

Plinius the Elder. *Naturalis Historica* [Natural History]. Cambridge, Mass.: Harvard University Press, 1938–1962. Orig. ca. A.D. 77.

Plutarch. *The Lives of The Noble Grecians and Romans.* Transl. John Dryden, 1864. Ed. Arthur Clough. New York: Random House, Modern Library. Orig. ca. A.D. 100.

Polo, Marco. *The description of the World.* 2 Vol. Transl. A. C. Moule and P. Pelliot. London, 1938. Also published as: *The Travels.* Transl. Ronald Latham. London: Penguin Classics, 1958. Orig. ca. A.D. 1298.

Polybius. *The Histories.* Transl. by W. R. Patton. Cambridge, Mass.: Harvard University Press, 1925. Orig. ca. 150 B.C.

Poppe, Adolph. *Die Telegraphie von ihrem Ursprunge bis zur neuesten Zeit mit besonderer Berücksichtigung der ausgeführten telegraphischen Systeme* [Telegraphy from its origin to the most recent times, with special attention of the telegraphic systems that were built]. Frankfurt a.M., 1848.

Poppe, Adolph. *Die Bedeutung und das Wesen der antiken Telegraphie* [The meaning and nature of ancient telegraphy]. Frankfurt a.M., 1867.

Porta, Giambattista della. *Natural magick.* New York: Basic Books, transl. 1658, reprint 1957. Orig. A.D. 1553.

Poulsen, Peder B. "The Danish Optical Telegraph." *Symposium on The Optical Telegraph.* Stockholm: Telemuseum, 1994.

Prescott, G. B. *Electricity and the Electric Telegraph.* New York, 1877.

Reid, J. D. *Telegraph in America.* New York: John Polhemus, 1886.

Ringnalda, W. *De Rijkstelegraaf in Nederland, Hare opkomst en ontwikkeling* [The State Telegraph in the Netherlands, creation and development]. Amsterdam: Scheltema and Holkema, 1902.

Romburgh, C. P. P. van. *De Hollandse Kustbeseining 1794–1813* [Dutch Coast-Signaling 1794–1813]. Master's Thesis. Leiden, Netherlands: University of Leiden, 1989.

Romburgh, C. P. P. van. "Seinmeester Theodorus Pansier en de Hollandse Kustbeseining, 1803–1814" [Signalmaster Theodorus Pansier and Dutch Coast-

Signaling, 1803–1814]. *Tijdschrift voor Zeegeschiedenis*, [Journal for Naval History], Vol. 10, Nr. 2, pp. 149–160, 1991.

Risberg, N. J. A. *Svenska Telegrafverket* [Swedish Telegraphy]. Göteborg: Elanders Bocktryckeri, 1938.

Saint Denis, G. De. Autour de la Loi du 2 Mai 1837 [About the law of 2 May 1837]. Proc. First Bi-annual Colloquium on the Optical Telegraph. Blois, France: F.N.A.R.H., 1979.

Shaffner, Tal. P. *The Telegraph Manual*. New York: Van Nostrand, 1859.

Sider, Sandra. *Maps, Charts, Globes: Five Centuries of Exploration*. Exhibition catalogue. New York: Hispanic Society of America, 1992.

Staring, W. C. A. "De Optische Telegrafen in Nederland" [The optical telegraphs in the Netherlands]. *Tijschrift Koninklijk Instituut van Ingenieurs*, pp. 279–234. The Hague, Netherlands: KIVI, Sept. 1890.

Still, A. *Communication through the ages, from Sign Language to Television*. New York: Murray Hill Books, 1946.

Suetonius. *The Twelve Caesars*. Transl. Robert Graves, 1957. London: Penguin Classics, reprint 1989. Orig. ca. A.D. 121.

Thucydides. *History of The Peloponnesian war*. Transl. Rex Warner, 1954. London: Penguin Classics, reprint 1972. Orig. ca. 431 B.C.

Vasseur, M. "La Télégraphie Optique et le Climat" [The optical Telegraph and the Climate]. Proc. Second Bi-annual Colloquium on the Optical Telegraph. Nancy, France: F.N.A.R.H., 1981.

Vegetius, Flavius Renatus. *De Re Militari* [On the Military Art]. Transl. John Clark, 1944. Ed. Thomas R. Phillips. Harrisburg, Penn.: The Telegraph Press. Greenwood Press, reprint 1985. Orig. ca. A.D. 375.

Tahvanainen, K. V. *Ord I Sikte, Den optiska telegrafen i Sverige 1794–1881* [Words made visible, The optical telegraph in Sweden 1794–1881]. Teleböckerna No. 7. Stockholm: Telemuseum, 1994.

Vergil. *The Aeneid*. Transl. John Conington. Ed. Basil Davenport. Viking Portable Library. London: Penguin Books, 1951. Orig. ca. 20 B.C.

Voltesbou, Pedro. *Historia de Montjuich y su Castillo* [History of Montjuich and its Castle]. Barcelona, 1940.

Wilkins, John. "Mercury, or the secret and swift messenger, showing how a Man may with Privacy and Speed communicate his Thoughts to a Friend." *Foundations in Semiotics*, Vol. 6. Ed. A. Eschbach. Amsterdam, Philadelphia: John Benjamins, 1984. Orig. 1641. First publ. 1707.

Wilson, George. *The old telegraphs*. Chichester, England: Phillimore, 1976.

Woods, David L. *A history of tactical communication techniques*. New York: Arno Press, reprint 1974. Orig. 1965.

Xenophon. *Cyropaedia*. Transl. William Barker, 1567. Ed. James Tatum. New York: Garland, reprint 1987. Orig. fourth century B.C.

Xenophon. *Hellenica or A History of My Times*. Transl. Rex Warner. London: Penguin Classics, 1978. Orig. fourth century B.C.

Index

282

Colophon

How this Book was Made

This book was designed and typeset in New Century Schoolbook on a computer running the Unix® operating system. The camera-ready copy was produced with *troff −ms*, and standard preprocessing filters such as *grap, pic, tbl,* and *eqn.*

The index was computer-generated from the *troff* output and a list of keyword/ index-term pairs. The table of contents and all internal page-references were also computer-generated and inserted into the text automatically. Page balancing on the *troff* output was done with special postprocessing software, which, like the indexing and page referencing software, was specifically written for this book by the first author.

All illustrations that appear in this book, with the exception of line drawings, are reproduced from originals that were digitized at 300 dots per inch, used in digital form throughout the design process, and finally (re)printed from the digital versions for reproduction in this book.

About the Authors

Gerard J. Holzmann is a distinguished member of technical staff in the Computing Science Research Center at Bell Laboratories in Murray Hill, New Jersey. He received a Ph.D. in Technical Sciences from the Delft University of Technology in the Netherlands in 1979. He has been with Bell Laboratories since 1980.

Björn Pehrson chairs the department of Teleinformatics at the Royal Institute of Technology in Stockholm, Sweden, and is board member of the Swedish Institute of Computer Science. He received his Ph.D. from Uppsala University in 1975.

Holzmann and Pehrson had studied the history of telecommunications methods independently for many years when they discovered their common interest in 1989. This book is the product of their collaboration since then.

IEEE Computer Society
http://www.computer.org

Purpose

The IEEE Computer Society Press advances the theory and practice of computer science and engineering, promotes the exchange of technical information among 100,000 members worldwide, and provides a wide range of services to members and nonmembers.

Membership

All members receive the monthly magazine *Computer*, discounts, and opportunities to serve (all activities are led by volunteer members). Membership is open to all IEEE members, affiliate society members, and others seriously interested in the computer field.

Publications

Books: For guidelines on preparing Computer Society Press books please write the managing editor at the publications office (email csbooks@computer.org).

Periodicals: The society publishes six magazines and five research transactions. For more details refer to our membership application or request information as noted above.

Computer **magazine:** In-depth articles on topics across the computer field, as well as news, conference reports, book reviews, calendars, calls for papers, interviews, and new products.

Conference proceedings, tutorials, and standards documents: the IEEE Computer Society Press publishes more than one hundred titles every year.

Activities

Standards working groups: Over one hundred working groups produce IEEE standards that are used throughout the industrial world.

Technical committees: Over thirty technical committees publish newsletters, provide interaction with peers in specialty areas, and directly influence standards, conferences, and education.

Conferences and Education: The society holds about one hundred conferences each year and sponsors many educational activities, including computing science accreditation.

Chapters: Regular and student chapters worldwide provide the opportunity to interact with colleagues, hear technical experts, and serve the local professional community.

Membership and general information: (714) 821-8380
Phone orders: (800) 272-6657 Fax: (714) 761-1784
Email orders: csbooks@computer.org
Web site for additional information: http://www.computer.org